Learning without limits

Learning without limits

Susan Hart, Annabelle Dixon
Mary Jane Drummond, Donald McIntyre

with Narinder Brach, Claire Conway, Nicola Madigan,
Julie Marshall, Alison Peacock, Anne Reay,
Yahi Tahibet, Non Worrall, Patrick Yarker

Open University Press

Open University Press
McGraw-Hill Education
McGraw-Hill House
Shoppenhangers Road
Maidenhead, Berkshire
England SL6 2QL

email: enquiries@openup.co.uk
world wide web: www.openup.co.uk

and Two Penn Plaza, New York, NY 1012–2289
USA

First Published 2004

A catalogue record of this book is available from the British Library

ISBN 0 335 21259 X (pb)   0 335 21260 3 (hb)

Library of Congress Cataloging-in-Publication Data
CIP data has been applied for

Typeset by BookEns Ltd, Royston, Herts.
Printed and bound in Great Britain by MPG Books Ltd, Bodmin, Cornwall

This book is dedicated to
Brian Simon 1915–2002

His work has been deeply influential
in our thinking and we acknowledge
our debt to him.

Contents

Foreword

It is highly appropriate that this ground-breaking book should be dedicated to the late Brian Simon, surely one of the greatest educationalists of the twentieth century. He rejected totally the concept of fixed ability or potential, and this led him to spend most of his working life campaigning for both the abandonment of streaming practices in the primary school and the adoption of genuine comprehensive education at the secondary level.

I know that Brian would have been heartened by the essential message and optimistic tone of this book, summed up in its apt title, taken from the research project that forms the basis for its analysis.

The *Learning without Limits* project was, we are told, set up at the University of Cambridge School of Education in 1999. The key idea was to bring together a group of classroom teachers who had rejected ideas of fixed ability and to study their practice in order to try to identify the chief concepts and methods that are distinctive of teaching free from determinist assumptions about ability. Of those teachers who applied to participate in the project, nine were chosen to comprise the final team – representing infant, primary and secondary (comprehensive) schools in a range of social contexts. It is the exciting individual accounts of these nine teachers' thinking and practice that constitute the core of the book.

As a classroom teacher myself, I was always profoundly influenced by Brian's guiding principle that the key to human development is not *heredity* but *education*. Only by starting out with an unshakeable belief in everybody's capacity to learn can schools successfully educate all young people. What binds these nine accounts together, as the authors show, is not just a determination to reject the template of 'fixed ability' at the level of thinking and practice. The teachers have developed a pedagogy based on a different mind-set entirely, one that emphasizes the power of education to transform learning capacity, one that accepts that everybody's learning is important and that everybody can contribute to the learning environment.

Clyde Chitty
Goldsmiths College

Acknowledgements

We would like to thank the Wallenberg Research Centre for the Improvement of Education for the generous grant that funded the first 18 months of the project, as part of a broader programme of research under the umbrella title *Beyond Conventional Classrooms*.

Continuing funding was received from the Faculty of Education Research and Development Fund, for which we are very grateful. This grant enabled us to continue working with the teachers to develop the model of pedagogy that we present in this book.

We would like to thank the staff and students at the nine schools where we carried out the research. They made us feel very welcome and we were privileged to be included in their staff group over the period of the project.

We would also like to thank the many colleagues who contributed to our thinking at conferences, seminars and in informal discussion.

The project has been expertly managed by members of the administrative staff at the University of Cambridge Faculty of Education: Christine Zwierzanski, Suzanne Fletcher and, most recently, Alison Craig. All made valuable contributions. We are particularly grateful to Alison Craig for her meticulous work in preparing the manuscript for publication.

Note: The teacher members of the project team are referred to by their real names, but all the young people who contributed to the study have been given pseudonyms.

PART 1
Beyond ability-based teaching and learning

1 Ability, educability and the current improvement agenda

This book is about two very different kinds of learning: one that is widespread, and one that is, at present, much less commonplace. The first is the learning that starts in the very earliest days of schooling, as young people begin to hear and understand the judgements that their teachers make about them and everything they do. They learn very quickly about their standing in comparison with their peers, particularly in relation to their supposed 'ability'. The words 'more able', 'average' and 'less able' may not be spoken in their hearing, but young people soon learn the category they belong to, and where their friends fit into this hierarchy of ability. Even when neutral labels are used for the groups to which children are assigned, or for the tables at which they sit, the messages are easy to read. Formal reports, marks, grades, levels and comments on written work: these are all sources of information about young people's supposed ability. This kind of learning is reinforced daily, through many different kinds of experiences: it is not difficult to learn one's place, though it can be extremely damaging, as we will argue throughout this book.

There is an alternative, a second kind of learning, which in this book we are calling 'learning without limits'. This is learning that is free from the needless constraints imposed by ability-focused practices, free from the indignity of being labelled top, middle or bottom, fast or slow, free from the wounding consciousness of being treated as someone who can aspire at best to only limited achievements. Learning without limits becomes possible when young people's school experiences are not organized and structured on the basis of judgements of ability.

Commitment to reconstructing the curriculum and organization of schools to foster this second kind of learning is by no means new. For some advocates of comprehensive education, this idea was at the heart of the original campaign for comprehensive reform. Since comprehensive reorganization, many teachers committed to comprehensive ideals have indeed attempted to develop, in their own classrooms, learning free from the constraints imposed by judgements of ability. However, the public task of developing a convincing and practical alternative to ability-based teaching and learning has, until now, not been seen as a priority. In this book we explain why we believe this task is such an urgent one. Drawing on a recent research study with a small group of teachers, we describe what they have taught us about classrooms that foster this second kind of learning, about the principles that guide their teaching and about their own role in creating learning without limits.

Ability and identity

When young people's learning is dominated by judgements of ability, their sense of identity may be profoundly affected, not just while they are at school, but beyond, into adulthood. Readers of this book will no doubt be able to bring to mind people they know whose lives have been affected by being written off as incapable of serious academic achievement at crucial points in their education. Narinder, one of the teachers whose work is featured in this book, describes how she was told, as a pupil, 'not to bother staying on at school as this would be a waste of my time and the school's. This was the message to a devastated youngster in the 1960s.' She duly left school and went to work in a factory. Later, with encouragement from a supportive family, she went back into education. She trained as a teacher and in time became the head of a large, multicultural primary school in the Midlands. Nevertheless, she says, 'this message has always stayed with me; and although I constantly guard against other youngsters suffering the same fate, I am even more acutely aware of injustice, particularly with the dawn of school targets, where only the level 4s are seen as an asset to the school.'

For Mark, a much sought-after house painter and decorator of our acquaintance, the decisive moment in his education came much sooner, when he failed the 11 plus. The 11 plus was a public examination, a combination of intelligence and attainment tests, which, until the 1960s, was taken by nearly all pupils in English state schools, in order to allocate them to different kinds of secondary schools, with very different levels of status and prestige. The practice persists in a few local education authorities. Mark says that, having received the message that he was 'thick', he went on to 'muck about' at secondary school. His family were supportive of him personally but were not worried about success at school as long as he got a job – which he did, with his uncle who worked in the timber trade. Despite now having his own successful business, Mark still thinks that the world probably sees him as thick because he failed the 11 plus and because he is not (in his words) a 'fast reader'. He feels that the failure was largely his fault, but the experience has made him a strong supporter of the comprehensive system for his own children. He thinks that comprehensive education 'gives kids a second chance' and they're 'not written off' as they used to be.

Anne, another of the teachers whose work is featured in this book, reports that for years she was placed in the bottom set and not expected to achieve academically because of difficulties with reading. Luckily, she had supportive parents and in time encountered some more open-minded teachers. She too went on to teacher training college and later gained a degree in mathematics and statistics. Some years later, when she noticed that her daughter was experiencing similar difficulties with her reading, she was able to take action to help to prevent her daughter's learning being held back in the way that her own had been.

Narinder, Mark and Anne feel strongly that what happened to them should not have happened, and should not be allowed to happen to future generations of children. Yet the ideas about ability and potential that informed and were used to justify the judgements made about earlier generations continue to have currency in schools. Indeed, in recent years, these ideas have gained renewed strength and legitimacy as part of government-sponsored initiatives to raise standards and improve practice in schools.

As we explain in more detail in Chapter 2, in this book we take a critical view of ability thinking in all its guises. We argue that basing teaching on perceived differences of ability undermines teachers' efforts to provide a fair, enabling and fulfilling education for all young people, and their determination to give everyone the best possible start in life. We believe that many teachers will be familiar with our arguments and already share our concerns about ability-led practices. However, we also recognize the considerable pressures that teachers are under in the current context, where discourses of good practice insistently promote differentiation by ability as an essential feature of good teaching. We recognize, too, that when teachers use the concept of ability to categorize pupils, they bring to these practices their own values and find their own ways of making them work to fulfil their professional purposes. In order to present our critique of the concept of ability and the practice of ability labelling in a way that is respectful of these intentions, we must first examine some of the ways in which they can be construed as both helpful and necessary to educators in carrying out their professional work.

What do we mean by ability?

In a useful overview of the development of the notion of ability, Jill Bourne and Bob Moon (1995: 26) describe ability as a 'common-sense' concept that, in the United Kingdom, in the twentieth century, came to be seen as 'a natural way of talking about children'. Yet, they note, the fact that we have words such as 'intelligence' and 'ability' does not mean that they exist, any more than the unicorn does. The concept of ability is culturally and historically specific: 'not so long ago, children and their achievements were looked at very differently, as they are in other places of the world today' (*ibid.*). But, because talking about ability seems a natural way of talking, people do not normally stop, in conversation, to rush to the dictionary or to question each other's meanings. When we do take time to look more closely, we realize that there is considerable scope for confusion. When young people are identified as 'more able' or 'less able' than others, are we saying something about innate intelligence or inherent capacity to learn? Are we implying a fixed or stable difference in degree between those deemed more able and those deemed less able? Or are we simply saying something about differences in their current ability to perform certain tasks, their observable ability to do certain things – like reading or mathematical calculations – according to agreed criteria? Although the distinctions between various meanings of 'ability' easily become blurred, there are significant differences between them that warrant closer examination.

The view of ability as 'inborn intelligence' has been deeply influential in education in England over the past century. According to this view, ability is seen as a genetic inheritance, a given amount of innate, general, cognitive power distributed according to the normal patterns of variation of all naturally occurring phenomena. This general cognitive ability is assumed to drive learning, so when young people of different abilities put maximum effort into learning, differences of attainment will inevitably result. According to this view, then, ability labels not only *explain* differences in attainment but also *predict* future events. Because learning is thought of as determined by ability, and the amount of any individual's ability is given, it seems, on the surface, a reasonable assumption that people assessed as 'more able' or 'less able' will always remain so; someone who is judged less able today cannot become more able tomorrow unless the original judgement turns out to have been mistaken. According to this view, it is important for teachers to know each individual's ability and potential in order to adapt their teaching accordingly. Judgements about ability are the points of reference against which teachers formulate expectations, make decisions about appropriate learning opportunities, decide how to interact with pupils and evaluate their progress.

This view of ability has its origins in theories of intelligence and the practice of intelligence testing, which claimed to offer objective means for reliably measuring inherent ability and potential. This practice promised to serve as an instrument for achieving greater justice and equality in education, by distributing opportunity on the basis of measured intelligence rather than social circumstance. However, over the years since IQ testing was first introduced, many of the old claims and certainties that gave credence to ideas of fixed, inherent ability have long been abandoned. Since the 1920s, psychometricians have themselves continually revised their theories about what precisely intelligence tests measure. While they continue to use the measurement of IQ to compare individuals and make predictions of various kinds, most no longer hold to the view that IQ is fixed, since their own studies have clearly demonstrated that this is not the case. Equally, they have abandoned the idea that what IQ tests measure is raw intelligence, undistorted by differences in environment and opportunity. While debate continues over what constitutes intelligent behaviour, there is now broad agreement among psychometricians that IQ tests do not measure raw intelligence; what such tests measure can only ever be what has been learned (Sternberg 1998).

The idea that differences of attainment reflect fixed or stable differences of ability is not, however, necessarily incompatible with the recognition that all abilities are learned. There is a second view of ability, which places great emphasis upon the influence of environmental factors in the development of intelligence, especially during the crucial formative years up to the age of 5. This view is informed and supported by the knowledge that measured intelligence (in terms of rank order) tends generally to be fairly stable, that it is quite a good predictor, from the age of 5, of people's likely success within the educational system and that it is a very good predictor when people are tested at the age of 11. This psychometric evidence provides reassurance that there is a scientific basis for ability labelling. The problem with this view, as we show in detail in Chapter 2, is that it dis-regards the impact of the school upon differential attainment. Without a state education system, it certainly seems probable that the relative educational achievements of most people would be largely determined by their families' relative social and economic advantages during their childhood. But, with a highly developed educational system, are we prepared to accept that the influence of schooling is so slight that the success of students within it is largely determined not by their learning experiences at school, but by what happens to them before they start school at the age of 4 or 5? We view that as an unnecessarily pessimistic and determinist position. We believe that not only we, but also all our readers, have sufficient experience of individuals who have, at school or later, achieved high levels of educational success for none of us to be at all persuaded by the counsel of despair.

An educator who makes use of ability labels may not, however, be subscribing to the idea of ability as a fixed or inherent attribute. Ability labels can be used simply to refer to differences in young people's current abilities to *do* certain things. According to this third view, 'more able' and 'less able' pupils are those who are demonstrably better or worse than others at, say, reading, or maths calculations, or historical analysis, or literary criticism, according to agreed criteria. Ability labels are used simply to compare attainments or performances on a range of measures. Their purpose is to assist in the process of differentiation, enabling the teacher to match the range of tasks provided to the range of current abilities represented in the class. Thinking of differences within a class on the basis of three broad categories (more able, average, less able) also helps to make the teacher's task manageable. It seems safe to assume that the pupils in each category can be treated in the same way: they have reached similar levels of ability, and therefore can be assumed to have similar learning needs, in the sense of the next steps that they are poised to take in their learning. According to this 'performance' view of ability, comparative judgements do not purport to explain differences of performance. Nor do they necessarily claim to predict potential; although there is often an underlying assumption that this might be the case, it is also perfectly possible for the ranking order of ability of young people to change. In theory, the less able readers of today could become the more able readers of tomorrow.

A teacher may therefore feel comfortable in using ability labels in this comparative sense, while consciously rejecting the idea that potential is permanently fixed. This purely 'performance' view allows for a much more complex view of individual abilities. Any particular individual might, in theory, be among the most able in science, mathematics or art, and among the least able in reading. In practice, though, it often seems that the same people come to be seen as 'more able' and 'less able' in most areas of the curriculum, or at least in the high-status academic subjects. In the absence of an alternative explanation, the temptation is to infer from these recurring patterns that differences of attainment do indeed reflect differences in underlying general cognitive ability. Indeed, as we saw in Anne's story above, differences of attainment in key curriculum areas, such as reading, can be – and are – frequently assumed to be reliable indicators of differences in overall academic ability and potential. This assumption is especially dangerous when applied to reading attainment, since we have expectations, in the UK, that success and achievement in reading should start (and therefore failure can be identified) at a much earlier age than is considered appropriate or desirable in continental Europe.

Ability in the current context

The conviction that it is helpful, indeed essential, for teachers to compare, categorize and group young people by ability in order to provide appropriate and challenging teaching for all has been reinforced again and again in reports by Her Majesty's Inspectorate (HMI) since the late 1970s. It has also been given strong endorsement by government-sponsored initiatives to raise standards since the Education Reform Act of 1988. OFSTED inspectors are briefed (and trained) to check that teaching is differentiated for 'more able', 'average' and 'less able' pupils. Teachers are expected to make explicit in their schemes of work how this differentiation is to be achieved.

Government policy specifically recommends ability grouping as the basis for effective teaching in secondary schools (DfEE 1997); the National Literacy and Numeracy Strategies both firmly endorse ability-based grouping.

In these various developments, what exactly is meant by 'ability' is not made explicit, so there is scope for teachers to interpret what is being recommended in ways that fit their own beliefs and values. However, the new emphasis on target setting and value-added measures of achievement have made it increasingly difficult for teachers who reject the fixed view of measurable ability to hold on to their principles, since they are continually being required to act as if they subscribe to it. The practice of measuring children's attainments, and predicting future achievement, starts early, in the last year of the Foundation Stage, if not even earlier in the nursery or pre-school, for which many local authorities are now developing an 'entry profile'. The Foundation Stage Profile, introduced as a statutory requirement in the academic year 2002–2003, requires educators to use 13 different scales, each of nine levels, to record children's achievements during the year in which they turned 5. They are formally assessed again, in Year 2, when at least one-third of them have not yet turned 7, and yet once more in Year 6, at a time when one-third of them will not yet have turned 11. At both Year 2 and Year 6, targets are set for each school and each local authority, specifying the percentages of children who are to achieve particular levels. The Year 6 targets are set with reference to the Year 2 results, and the Year 2 targets will in future be set with reference to the Foundation Stage Profiles. Early years educators who do not conceptualize their young children's learning in terms of scores, levels and targets are, nevertheless, required to carry out these procedures.

Secondary teachers, too, are compelled to comply with practices that may conflict with their espoused values and beliefs: for example, they are required to sort their students into sets geared to tiered examinations. Just at a time when adolescents perhaps need most encouragement and stimulus to commit their best efforts into study at school, they have to be sorted into groups that they and their teacher know impose preset ceilings on possible future performance. This constant requirement to predict future levels of achievement, and to reach prespecified targets, makes sense and can be justified only if it is assumed that current differences between young people in terms of their test results will persist in future tests and examinations. It presupposes that current patterns of achievement reflect stable differences in young people's potential.

However, the view of ability that underpins the current improvement agenda is not quite the same as the first view of ability discussed in this chapter. While it shares with the first view the idea that differences of attainment reflect inherent differences of ability and potential that cannot be changed, it assumes that overall attainment can be improved. This 'improvement' view of ability challenges expectations about what young people at particular points on the ability range are capable of achieving. Ability measurement helps in drawing attention to the scope for raising achievement. The claim is that there is scope for everyone's achievements to be raised, because ceilings of achievement, as currently predicted for young people of different abilities, are set too low. The task for improvement efforts is to raise expectations of potential – predicted ceilings of achievement – for everyone, and devise measures that will enable schools to realize this newly recognized untapped ability or potential.

We trace the roots of this fourth view of ability back to a particular analysis and critique of what was happening – and what was thought to be going wrong – in schools in the decades prior to the Education Reform Act of 1988. According to this analysis, a major cause of the so-called crisis of standards in schools was failure on the part of teachers to differentiate their teaching adequately to cater for the needs of pupils at different points on the ability range. The point was reiterated again and again in HMI reports in secondary and primary schools, particularly in relation to teaching in 'mixed ability' classes (Hart 1996a). This explains why a major focus of reform initiatives has been to endorse differentiation by ability as an essential feature of good practice, and to fund development initiatives designed to support educators in refining their skills in differentiating teaching.

On the surface, this fourth view of ability has considerable appeal, raising everyone's sights about what individuals can achieve, and going some way to reinstate the notion of entitlement, emphasized in the 1988 Act, but since then largely neglected, and dropped from the national agenda. However, there is mounting evidence that, in practice, it is serving not as much to extend opportunity and enhance achievement for all, as to ration opportunity and resources and justify anew writing off some young people as incapable of significant improvement. For example, in a deeply alarming study, Gillborn and Youdell (2000) explore the impact of government initiatives, including league tables and target setting. They studied two secondary schools with very different traditions, ethos, grouping practices and patterns of student achievement. Their analysis shows that the idea of fixed ability is being used, in association with the push for 'improvement', to justify, morally and educationally, the selection and concentration of resources and effort needed to maximize success in examinations – what Gillborn and Youdell call the A–C economy. Judgements of fixed potential now sanction the practice of dividing pupils into three categories: 'safe' ones (who would perform well anyway without extra input), the 'without hope' group (who would not achieve five A–C passes even if extra resources were to be put in) and the 'underachievers', where it is worth placing extra effort, and offering extra support and additional resources (*ibid.*: 134). Predictably, Gillborn and Youdell found that boys, students receiving free school meals and Black students were overrepresented in the 'without hope' groups.

Similar processes can be seen at work in primary schools, where extra resources are allocated to children who are thought likely to move up a crucial level in their SAT results at Key Stage 2, boosting scores so that their schools make a good showing in the league tables and meet the targets set for them by both the LEA and central government. It is important to acknowledge that these are by no means just unfortunate and unintended effects of the pressures created by externally imposed targets and league tables. Schools have been provided with extensive 'booster' programmes specifically designed to raise levels of achievement for particular pupils thought capable of reaching crucial grade thresholds with extra support. The constant pressure to improve young people's attainments in a context where, at the very same time, ideas of fixed ability are being strengthened, emphasized and officially endorsed places educators without question in an intolerable professional double bind. They are held accountable for meeting development targets and for improving performance, while those who set the targets, and to whom they are accountable, resolutely promote a view of fixed ability that places the principal determinants of achievement outside the educators' control.

We believe that the current improvement agenda is based on erroneous assumptions and is profoundly misconceived. Its proponents have failed to appreciate that many teachers had already embarked on their own, self-inspired reform agenda and, in line with comprehensive ideals, were trying to construct an education system based on a more optimistic view of human educability. We have a very different interpretation of 'what went wrong' during the decades prior to 1988. Our argument is that, during the early years of the development of comprehensive education, too little priority was given, for a variety of reasons, to the crucial pedagogical task of developing and elaborating approaches to teaching free from the constraints imposed by ability labelling. Since this interpretation provided the stimulus for the research that forms the basis for this book, we explain our argument in detail in the next section.

Ability and the development of comprehensive education

As we noted above, rejecting the idea of fixed ability was, for some educators at least, at the heart of the campaign for comprehensive reform. Clyde Chitty, a longstanding campaigner and advocate of the comprehensive ideal, recalls his own beliefs and aspirations at the time as follows:

> We believed that the comprehensive reform has no meaning unless
> it challenges the fallacy of fixed ability or potential in education. It
> should aim to dismantle all the structures rooted in that fallacy that
> act as barriers to effective learning while, at the same time, it should
> facilitate practices that enable everyone to enjoy a full education.
>
> (Chitty 2001a: 20)

Rejecting 'the fallacy of fixed ability' opened the way for an education system
to be built on a more optimistic view of human educability, one responsive
to the natural propensity of human beings not just to learn but to *change*
over time. The reconstruction of education that the advocates of comprehensive education called for involved not just structural changes but also
the transformation of forms of internal organization and teaching
approaches. Teachers committed to this vision of the future of education
approached their work in a spirit of enquiry and adventure, aware that
modes of teaching appropriate in the new, non-selective environment had
still to be invented.

Much important pioneering work was certainly carried out in both
primary schools and secondary schools, in the 1960s and 1970s, to explore
new approaches to pedagogy capable of enabling 'all young people to
succeed' (Chitty 2001a: 22). But energy was diverted from this task into
fierce debates surrounding the relative merits of ability and mixed ability
grouping. Resisting forms of grouping that would reconstruct the selective
system *within* a comprehensive framework seemed to be the most urgent
priority. As Brian Simon, a leading critic of intelligence testing and campaigner for comprehensive reform, notes in his autobiography: 'If the new
schools were to be rigidly streamed and the children divided into a set of
hierarchical teaching groups, the whole purpose of making the change to
comprehensive education might be subverted' (Simon 1998: 106).

Debates about the best forms of grouping were rehearsed again and
again, but never finally resolved. It is perhaps not surprising, then, given
the duration and intensity of these debates, that somewhere along the way
comprehensive ideals started to be equated (by supporters, in some cases, as
well as critics) with the struggle to defend mixed-ability grouping and
teaching. While a great many teachers were certainly engaged in the
crucial pedagogical task of developing teaching approaches free from the
limits imposed by any ability labelling, the public tasks of articulating in
generalized terms what they were doing and helping them to develop and
refine their practices slipped off the agenda. Yet, as the terminology of the
debate all too clearly reveals, a commitment to mixed-ability grouping and
teaching does not necessarily imply a radical break with ideas of fixed ability.
It is possible to defend mixed-ability approaches as more just and educationally sound than ability-based grouping, while still holding fast to ideas

of fixed ability. Indeed, ideas of fixed ability, which had clearly survived the abolition of selection, emerged alive and well at the heart of these debates.

Researchers who might have been helping to articulate and develop the new pedagogies were side-tracked into trying to help to resolve these organizational issues, but repeatedly failed to produce conclusive results, at least with respect to measures of academic achievement. These outcomes were widely reported as a failure to prove the case for mixed-ability grouping. However, they could also be interpreted as a striking failure on the part of advocates of ability-based grouping to demonstrate its superiority over mixed-ability teaching. This was despite teachers' inevitable lack of experience in managing mixed-ability classes and the lack, as yet, of any clearly defined models of pedagogy to support them in developing teaching approaches to fit the new situation. When researchers failed to substantiate claims that mixed ability would produce better achievement, as well as better attitudes and behaviour, their findings tended to reinforce fears and presuppositions that commitment to mixed-ability teaching was ideologically, rather than educationally, driven. For those who are convinced that the ability range is a natural and unalterable fact of life, it seems pointlessly impractical to insist that children of self-evidently different abilities should be taught together.

Meanwhile, in the primary sector, with the abolition of 11 plus selection, non-streamed or mixed-ability classes had rapidly become the norm. Just as in the secondary sector, primary teachers had to adjust their thinking and practice to respond to the new situation. John Coe, a head teacher, writing in the journal *Forum* in 1966, acknowledged that 'bringing down the selective barriers is not enough. This is only the first step that gives us freedom. Now our concern must be to devise ways of using that freedom so that we might bring a greater good to all our children' (Coe 1966: 79). In the primary sector, however, issues of organization and grouping often seemed to take priority, in research and literature, over issues of pedagogy (e.g. Galton *et al.* 1980). Within-class ability grouping became a widely used organizational strategy. There was widespread use of graded schemes, particularly in language and mathematics, to cater for different levels of attainment.

We now believe that it was the failure to move on from preoccupations with grouping to concentrate on the elaboration of effective pedagogies that caused the all-through comprehensive project to falter. When the backlash came – directed particularly against mixed-ability grouping and teaching – teachers committed to the radical reconstruction of education as the necessary consequence of the rejection of fixed ability thinking were not ready to defend their cause. We (for we count ourselves amongst them) had neither a convincing theoretical rationale nor the empirical evidence capable of persuading policy-makers and fellow practitioners of the feasibility and desirability of our alternative agenda. Commentators on the educational scene succeeded in recasting the problems of underachievement, originally seen as the product of a selective system (and so justifying comprehensive reform), as the failure of the comprehensive project.

Our alternative interpretation of 'what went wrong' leads us to very different conclusions. Like Clyde Chitty, we are convinced that 'one of the great tragedies of the last hundred years has been our failure as a nation to take on the essential concept of human educability and thereby challenge the idea that children are born with a given quota of "intelligence" which remains constant both during childhood and adult life' (Chitty 2001b: 115). 'What went wrong' is that we failed to press forward with the task of reconceptualizing pedagogy to reflect this more optimistic view. The lesson we must learn from that period is that, if we are to take forward the vision of a system of schooling that 'allows everybody to enjoy a full education' (Chitty 2001a: 2), the pressing task, for practitioners and researchers, is to develop convincing and clearly articulated models of teaching as alternatives to ability-based pedagogy.

The Learning without Limits project

This is the task we set ourselves in the research project that forms the basis for this book. The *Learning without Limits* project was set up in 1999 at the University of Cambridge School of Education. The name of the project was inspired by a powerful passage in Stephen Jay Gould's *The Mismeasure of Man*, which seemed to capture our central concerns. He writes:

> We pass through this world but once. Few tragedies can be more extensive than the stunting of life, few injustices deeper than the denial of an opportunity to strive or even to hope by a limit imposed from without but falsely identified as lying within.
>
> (Gould 1981: 29)

Our research strategy (as we describe in detail in Chapter 3) was to bring together a group of teachers who had rejected ideas of fixed ability and to study their practice, in order to explore and try to identify what was distinctive about teaching free from ability labelling. The response to our advertisement in the national press reinforced our conviction that there were many other educators who shared our concerns. We held 17 interviews, and a team of nine teachers (four primary and five secondary) from a range of very different teaching contexts was eventually established.

Over the following year, members of the university team spent many hours in the teachers' classrooms, observing and interviewing both teachers and pupils. We also met together to share our thinking and develop the research collectively. In constant collaboration with the teachers, we gradually built up individual accounts of the key constructs at the heart of each teacher's thinking, and an understanding of how these constructs worked together to create their distinctive pedagogy. These detailed individual accounts form the core of the book and can be found in Part 2. We hope that teachers reading them will find, as well as inspiration, elements that relate directly to their own work.

We then summarized the key ideas in each account and collectively looked across all nine accounts for common themes and differences, in order to try to identify the key concepts and practices that might be distinctive of teaching free from determinist ideas about ability. In Part 3 of the book we explore the central ideas of an alternative pedagogy that emerged from the research, and the purposes and principles through which the teachers translated them into practice.

Common concerns

Although it could seem naive to think that there is a chance of halting the juggernaut of reform as currently conceived, our grounds for hope lie in our awareness that there is actually a degree of overlap between the values of our project and some of the values underpinning the current standards agenda. For instance, there is a common concern that the talents and capabilities of many young people remain untapped throughout their formal education. There is a common wish to challenge assumptions that not much can be expected of young people from disadvantaged social backgrounds, and (according to a report in the *Times Educational Supplement* of 4 January 2002) a common commitment to concerted action to reduce class-based discrepancies in achievement. The current programme of reforms rightly recognizes the power that schools and teachers have to influence young people's development. It is just possible, then, as results reach a plateau and evidence accumulates of the undesirable and dysfunctional effects of many of the externally imposed reforms, that there might come a compelling opportunity to present a more powerful, promising and equitable improvement agenda built around a critique of theories of intelligence, the use of intelligence testing and the practices of ability labelling. When that moment comes, we need to be in a position to exploit it to the full. The purpose of the research described here was to prepare ourselves and the wider professional community to seize that opportunity.

2 What's wrong with ability labelling?

In this chapter, we explain the basis for our conviction that ability labelling damages young people's learning, and prevents teachers from fulfilling their professional commitment to making a positive difference to young people's lives. In developing our critique of ability labelling, we draw upon a substantial body of research and literature developed over many decades. This work will help us to explore and illustrate what is known about how ability labelling affects young people, how it affects teachers and how it affects the school curriculum. It will also help us to explain why we believe that it is so important, in the interests of justice and entitlement, to develop approaches to teaching free from the limits imposed by ability labelling. Indeed, we are convinced that there is scope for learning to be liberated on a scale previously unimaginable, if successful and workable alternative approaches to teaching, free from ability labelling, can be articulated in a public and generalized way and come to be used widely in schools.

Fixed ability: the educator's paradox

As we saw in Chapter 1, the view of fixed ability that originates from early psychometric theories of IQ and intelligence testing includes these assumptions:

- that young people are born with a given amount of intellectual power;
- that some young people have considerably more intellectual power than others;
- that the amount of power is measurable through the use of appropriate tests;
- that this in-born power is the principal determinant of learning in school.

These points were succinctly summarized in the Spens Report (Board of Education 1938) as follows:

> *Intellectual development during childhood appears to progress as if it were governed by a single central factor, usually known as 'general intelligence' which may be broadly described as innate, all-round intellectual ability. It appears to enter into everything which the child attempts to think, to say, or do, and seems on the whole to be the most important factor determining his work in the classroom* ... Our psychological witnesses assured us that it can be measured approximately by means of intelligence tests.
>
> (Spens Report 1938: 123, italics in original)

We believe that this view of ability has had, and continues to have, considerable currency in schools because it offers what has come to be thought of as the obvious explanation for the vast differences in young people's learning, achievements and responses to classroom activities that confront teachers every day of their professional lives. Some young people undeniably do seem to grasp ideas much more rapidly than others; they retain what they learn more readily, seem more curious and probing in their thinking, show more imagination in their ideas, and appear more articulate in expressing their thinking than others. It is undeniable, too, that some young people seem to be more easily confused, fearful or simply uninterested in learning; they appear to have difficulty in keeping their mind on anything for any length of time, need things explained continuously, and often forget what they have learned from one day to the next. Both informal observations and formal measures of attainment reveal vast differences in the knowledge, understanding and skills of young people of the same age; there seems to be a tendency, too, for differences to increase as young people move through the school, and for patterns of attainment to persist, no matter what strategies teachers employ. How are we to make sense of these patterns, if not as a reflection of natural differences in young people's ability to learn, in their academic potential?

The argument that we present in this chapter is that explaining differences in terms of inherent ability is not only unjust and untenable, but also deprives teachers of the chance to base and develop their practice upon a more complex, multifaceted and infinitely more empowering understanding of teaching and learning processes, and of the influences, internal and external to the school, that impinge on learning and achievement. The inherent ability explanation traps teachers in the uncomfortable paradox that, while their professional responsibility and commitment is to promote learning, the most important determinant of learning (inherent ability) is identified as something over which they have no control. According to this view, whatever teachers do, however lively and inspirational their teaching, however positive their relationships, however illuminating their explanations, they are powerless to do anything to change inherent intellectual limits. Susan Isaacs vividly captured the sense of powerlessness induced in the mind of an educator using the idea of inherent ability to make sense of differences when she wrote:

> Of all the differences between one child and another, inborn intelligence turns out to be the most stable and permanent. It is the most significant for success in school and career. The best teaching in the world may prove barren if it falls on the stony ground of an inherently dull and lifeless mind.
>
> (Isaacs 1932: 28)

It is testimony to the power and pervasiveness of this view of ability – and this explanation for differences – to see it reflected even in the early writings of an educator much admired as one of the most insightful pioneers of primary education in England in the twentieth century. No doubt there are few educators today who would express their expectations of some young people's learning in such fatalistic terms. Yet as long as young people continue to be categorized by ability, inferred from perceived differences in attainment, the same paradox remains: the most important determinant of learning is something that teachers can do nothing about. The most teachers can hope to do is to influence the uses to which fixed ability is put, for example, through the quality of their teaching, through the quality of their relationships with young people, through the range and quality of learning opportunities they provide. But they cannot change what is given. Teachers can make a difference, but only a limited difference, by influencing how young people choose to use their ability and by helping them to fulfil (what is presumed to be) their maximum potential.

The essence of our argument is that the idea of fixed, inherent ability does not represent an immutable law of human nature, a world where, self-evidently, some people are brighter than others. It is a particular template that we place on our experience to make sense of perceived differences; once it is in place it shapes and directs our thinking in such a way that it becomes impossible to make sense of differences in different, and potentially more empowering, ways. This particular template emerged, as we noted in Chapter 1, in a specific historical and cultural context; it seems far less natural and self-evident as soon as we examine it from a historical and cross-cultural perspective. As Bourne and Moon (1995) point out, when mass schooling was first introduced in England, in the nineteenth century, differentiation was based not upon supposed inherent mental characteristics but upon young people's place in the social hierarchy. The content and goals of education differed on the basis of social class. It was not until the twentieth century, under the influence of psychometric theories of intelligence, that intellectual 'ability' or 'intelligence' became naturalized as a biological construct.

Elsewhere in the world, educators' thinking about differential achievements is informed by very different ideas and traditions. For example, Stevenson and Stigler (in Alexander 2000) contrast the Confucian belief in human perfectibility with Anglo-American ideas about fixed and innate ability. They explain the emphasis on effort that characterizes Chinese and Japanese education in terms of Confucian beliefs, and contrast this with the fatalism and tolerance of low levels of effort that, in their view, characterize American education. Similarly, in a study of Russian education in the last years of the Soviet regime, Muckle (also in Alexander 2000) notes the very different meanings that Russian educators associate with the notion of 'potential'. 'The weak child', he writes, 'has greater, not less, potential than the bright one, because the zone of next development is larger. An English teacher might well say that such a child "has little potential", neatly illustrating that the meanings of that word and the Russian *potensial* are opposites rather than synonyms.'

Throughout the twentieth century, and particularly from the 1950s onwards, the claims of intelligence testing to measure and predict overall academic ability and potential were challenged and progressively discredited (e.g. Simon 1953, 1955; Heim 1954; Floud 1963; Rose and Rose 1979). Psychologists moved on to formulate new theories of intelligence, recognizing the part that experience and culture play in the formation of intelligence; psychometricians acknowledged that intelligence tests, as noted above, can only measure learned abilities. Yet the idea of inherent ability continued to exert a strong influence in education, despite this critique. What was most lastingly discredited, it seems, was the reliability of the mechanisms of testing used to identify differences of potential, not the underlying idea about the nature of differential ability itself.

During this period and as part of this critique, new templates were emerging for making sense of differences that focused upon the differential impact of environmental influences on learning rather than the impact of inherent intellectual ability. A particular focus of sociological interest over many years was documenting, and probing the reasons for, the strong relationship identified between social class and school achievement. New templates stressing 'disadvantage' and cultural/linguistic 'deprivation' were elaborated to explain persistent patterns of relative underachievement on the part of young people from working-class backgrounds, and the government responded in the late 1960s by funnelling extra resources into localities designated as Educational Priority Areas.

Initially, these new templates inspired a sense of optimism that strenuous efforts to compensate for supposed 'deprivation' could empower and enable young people from 'disadvantaged' backgrounds to succeed in school. When patterns persisted, despite these efforts, the impact of these templates of 'disadvantage' and 'deprivation' was to introduce a new layer of determinism into teachers' and policy-makers' understanding of differential achievement. Whether differences were explained with reference to inherent cognitive factors, social background factors or a combination of the two, both types of template located the most important determinants of learning outside teachers' control.

What the new templates did do, however, by drawing attention to the relationship between background factors and achievement, was to make visible the flaws and injustices inherent in the use of the template of ability. To infer differences in ability and potential from differences in present attainment is clearly unfair if these judgements do not take account of differences in young people's prior experiences and opportunities to learn; and since educators never can be in a position where they can safely assume that the young people whose attainments they are comparing have had similar opportunities to learn, such inferences of ability can never be justified. This was the endemic problem of IQ testing, as Valencia and Solorzano (1997) note; it was one of the reasons why, in the end, IQ theorists gave up claiming that tests were capable of measuring raw intelligence undistorted by experience and opportunity. We believe that this irremediable flaw necessarily invalidates any attempt to infer differences in underlying ability from differences in attainment.

The effect of these new templates, then, was, if anything, to increase the sense of powerlessness on the part of teachers. It seemed that there was little teachers could do, in the face of such all-powerfully determining social forces, to alter existing patterns of achievement and make a positive difference to young people's future lives. One influential study carried out in the USA, having surveyed the evidence, concluded that 'schools bring little influence to bear on a child's achievement that is independent of his background and general social context' (Coleman 1966). This pessimism about the power of education to compensate for society was further reinforced by evidence that the strong relationship identified between background and academic performance actually increases as young people progress through school. A later study concluded that the 'characteristics of a school's output depends largely on a single input, namely the characteristics of the entering child. Everything else, the school budget, its policies, the characteristics of the teacher – is either secondary or completely irrelevant' (Jencks *et al.* 1972).

The research studies that supported explanations focused on social background factors were usually large-scale statistical analyses concerned with establishing patterns of correlation. These researchers did not see the need to examine what was actually going on in schools; they interpreted evidence of recurring, strong correlations between social background and achievement as showing that the social processes underlying these patterns were independent of what was occurring in schools. However, alongside studies of this kind, a new tradition of research in education was beginning to develop. Researchers started to examine what was happening inside schools (for example, Jackson 1964; Hargreaves 1967; Lacey 1970; Nash 1973; Ball 1981). Their studies began to provide insight into the dynamics that were actually producing these persistent patterns. Some exciting and empowering new theories began to take shape, explaining how features of schooling (and consequently what teachers do) are themselves implicated in creating and maintaining persistent patterns of differential achievement.

From this accumulating body of research, it gradually emerged that the idea of fixed ability is not just a deeply flawed and unjust way of explaining differences in learning and achievement; it also exerts an active, powerful force within school and classroom processes, helping to create the very disparities of achievement that it purports to explain. It does this in subtle and unintended ways through the effects it has on teachers' thinking and practices, through the impact it has on young people's self-perceptions, hopes and aspirations for their own learning and through its narrowing effects upon the curriculum and the methods of assessment used to recognize and evaluate achievement.

In the remainder of this chapter, we draw selectively on this research to explain and illustrate the many subtle ways in which ability labelling operates to curtail opportunity and achievement for all young people, including and especially those who find themselves located at the lower end of the so-called ability range. Although we have space to refer to a limited number of studies only, it is important to emphasize that the literature in this area is vast and well worth exploring in greater detail. From the studies reviewed, we will demonstrate that patterns of learning and achievement in schools are profoundly affected by processes internal to the school over which teachers do have considerable control.

We believe that all experienced teachers have a rich fund of knowledge about the forces that shape and limit achievement, and will recognize the validity of the account of them presented here. The problem is that when this knowledge is used in conjunction with the template of fixed ability, its potential power and impact are greatly reduced. We will explain how and why we believe that such knowledge and understanding can play a central, not peripheral, role in enhancing achievement, and specifically how we believe it would benefit everyone, teachers and learners, if we were to build a new agenda for school improvement around the development of effective pedagogies that are free from ability labelling.

Effects on pupils

As we consider, first, the impact of ability labelling on pupils, it is important to reiterate that what we are looking at throughout this discussion are the unintended effects of judgements of ability and ability-based practices. We take for granted that teachers' conscious intentions are always to do the best they possibly can for their pupils. Decades of research have shown, however, that what young people experience and learn in school is often very different from what teachers intend. There is a hidden curriculum of schooling, operating independently of teachers' intentions, the impact of which on pupils' attitudes, motivation and attainment can undermine everything that teachers are consciously working to achieve through their classroom teaching.

Since Rosenthal and Jacobson (1968) published their famous study *Pygmalion in the Classroom*, the notion of the self-fulfilling prophecy has become part of the folklore of teaching. Teachers know that, to an extent, their pupils live up to or down to what they think is expected of them. How pupils think they are perceived by their teachers, and their response to that perception, become, in themselves, significant determinants of learning. In a study of the relationship between teachers' perceptions and pupils' performance, for example, Roy Nash (1973) explored some of the hidden curriculum processes and interactions that help to construct self-fulfilling prophecies. He commented: 'Whatever else children learn or fail to learn in school, they learn to measure themselves against their classmates ... Schools teach hierarchical levels of personal worth more successfully than anything else' (Nash 1973: 16). In the primary and secondary schools he studied, Nash found that pupils' perceptions of how they and their classmates were perceived by their teachers were remarkably accurate. He also found noticeable differences in academic and other behaviour depending on whether pupils thought that their teacher liked them or not. Pupils not only knew where they were in the teacher's rank order of ability, they also tended to choose friends who were similarly perceived. There was a kind of safety and solidarity in each group's sense of identity, and Nash found that its members actively worked to maintain their distinct status and separateness. In this way, he argues, young people's perceptions of themselves and others worked to maintain existing achievement hierarchies.

Nash's study shows that young people's perceptions of how teachers perceive them become important factors in their learning, with continuing and cumulative effects upon their achievements. If a teacher's thinking is shaped by the template of ability, he or she will approach a class of diverse pupils expecting to find three levels of ability (bright–average–weak), normally distributed across the group (Ball 1986). So, in such a classroom, all but those pupils identified as the top 25 per cent will pick up from the teacher negative messages about their ability, at least in comparison with those judged most able. Moreover, ability labels 'carry rich connotations of pupils' moral worth', as David Hargreaves asserts.

> Those who are designated 'bright' know that by that very fact they are being complimented and credited with a valuable attribute. The 'less able' understand that they lack the very quality on which the school sets most store; a sense of failure tends to permeate the whole personality, leaving a residue of powerlessness and hope-lessness.
>
> (Hargreaves 1982: 62)

Hargreaves argues that ability labelling, along with other aspects of traditional secondary schooling, leads to 'a destruction of dignity so massive and pervasive that few subsequently recover from it'. Ability labelling, he says, strips young people of their sense of being worthy, competent, creative, inventive, critical human beings, and encourages them to find other ways of achieving dignity, often through oppositional means. Hargreaves acknowledges that this diagnosis of how young people feel about being labelled by ability is often belied by appearances. Most young people do not give the impression of lacking dignity; teacher–pupil relationships are often warm, friendly and encouraging; most pupils accept what happens to them at school without overt complaint. 'But there is a distinct minority', Hargreaves continues, 'which reacts with overt bitterness and hostility, and the issue at stake is how we interpret that reaction' (Hargreaves 1982: 19).

Hargreaves's insights into young people's feelings about and reactions to ability labelling derive in part from a series of related studies, which examined how young people responded to streaming and other forms of ability-based grouping (Hargreaves 1967; Lacey 1970; Willis 1977; Ball 1981). His own classic study of streaming in a secondary modern school explored how the stream to which pupils were allocated affected their attitudes and expectations. Gradually a polarizing effect occurred, with pupils allocated to the lower streams becoming increasingly oppositional and resistant, while those allocated to the top streams remained closely identified with the aims and values of the school. Hargreaves argues that the behaviour of the oppositional students needs to be understood 'as an attempt to remove and negate the indignities meted out to them by the hidden curriculum' (Hargreaves 1982: 19). When school destroys their dignity, Hargreaves explains, the pupils set up an alternative means of achieving status and respect by turning the school's value system upside down.

Since these reactions are unintended consequences of ability labelling, and since they happen despite teachers' best efforts to counteract them through praise and encouragement, it seems likely that such reactions will continue to be a feature of schooling as long as ability labelling, and grouping by ability, continue to be practised by teachers in what they believe to be the best interests of their own teaching and pupils' learning. It is interesting to note that Colin Lacey (1970) found similar processes of polarization happening in a grammar school. Hightown Grammar, the school Lacey famously studied, accepted the top 15 per cent of the age cohort at age 11, and streamed them after the first year into an express group, plus A, B and C streams. By the end of the second year, he found that the 'climates' in the different classes were quite distinct; 2C were regarded by their peers and their teachers as bullies and 'tough eggs'. One teacher commented, 'There's not one boy in the class who has any sort of academic ability. In fact most of them shouldn't be in the school at all' (*ibid*.: 67).

Stephen Ball (1986) compared the findings of these two studies with his own study of a comprehensive school moving from a system of banding to mixed-ability grouping. He noted that, while all the pupils in Hightown Grammar were ostensibly 'band 1', the attitudes and aspirations of the 'band 1' class at the comprehensive school resembled most closely those of the grammar school express stream. These were the 'best' pupils in the school and they reflected best pupil attitudes and behaviour back at teachers. The implication that Ball draws from this is that, where grouping systems are in operation,

> the identity of these pupils is to a great extent an artifact of the grouping system employed. The status system of bands, the pupils' self image and the teachers' attitudes and behaviour towards them combine in a powerful process of definition and reaction. The very opposite effect is achieved by the same process at work in reverse with the lower bands.
>
> (Ball 1986: 87)

Ball's study of what happened after the shift from banding to mixed-ability grouping also makes interesting reading. While, in the earlier part of the study, he established that young people's attitudes and behaviour reflected the status of the group in which they found themselves, he also found similar processes operating in mixed-ability classes. Although teaching mixed-ability classes meant that teachers had to 'make' rather than 'take' evaluations of pupils based on the ability group they were in, Ball found that teachers would still 'approach their mixed-ability classes with strong expectations of finding a three-fold categorisation of ability, bright–average–weak, normally distributed in each group'. Contrary to what might be expected, he found that mixed ability classes appeared to create 'a situation of heightened awareness about relative levels of achievement. The teachers became very concerned about identifying the "ability" of individuals as quickly as possible' (*ibid.*: 97). Indeed, Ball felt that, ironically, the criteria used to evaluate or categorize pupils were narrowed rather than broadened by the introduction of mixed-ability teaching.

This part of Ball's research enabled him to refine his understanding of the processes he was studying, leading him to conclude that young people are reacting to the judgements of ability that they perceive teachers to be making about them, rather than to the status of the group that they find themselves in. So a shift to mixed-ability grouping does not necessarily improve things and, indeed, may even exacerbate the impact of those judgements if teachers employ strategies to cope with differences that render them more overt and visible. The destruction of dignity and the processes of progressive polarization and alienation associated with it, can and do happen in mixed-ability and unstreamed classes, if teaching continues to be informed by the ability template, with differences responded to accordingly.

There is, considerable consensus among this group of re-searchers that ability labelling deprives many young people of a sense of competence, dignity and personal efficacy, and that they frequently respond to this deprivation in ways that are inimical to learning and achievement in school. It is hardly surprising, Hargreaves (1982: 64) argues, that young people who find themselves perceived as 'less able' cease even to try. By refusing to try, they save themselves from possible failure, and so are able to 'retain the last vestiges of a crumbling dignity'.

Loss of dignity combined with an internalized sense of inadequacy creates psychological conditions that impair the capacity to learn. Attribution theory (for example, Dweck 2000) has elucidated the impact of children's belief systems about their abilities on their learning. An important idea in attribution theory is the 'locus of control': whether young people see their behaviour and learning as being caused by something internal or external, something within their power to influence or beyond it. If they attribute success or failure to something within themselves that they can control, they will be motivated to work to improve their learning and achievements. If, on the other hand, they attribute success and failure to something, internal or external, beyond their control, they will lose faith in their power to influence their own learning. The effects of ability labelling are potentially detrimental to young people's sense of power and control, and consequently to the learning of all learners, whatever the category of ability in which they find themselves.

A series of studies by Robert Hartley (1985) provides an interesting illustration of the limiting power of young people's self-perceptions. In his account of this work, intriguingly entitled 'Imagine you're clever', Hartley describes how he set out to explore the hypothesis that young people would be able to demonstrate more powerful problem-solving abilities if, when carrying out the tasks, they acted the part of someone other than themselves, someone who was clever. Hartley found that when young people were acting as 'someone who was clever', they demonstrated quite different learning characteristics from when they were doing similar tasks as themselves. 'Children who had persistently displayed impulsive or inaccurate modes of responding ... performed in a fluent, composed and highly efficient way' when acting as someone who was clever, 'approaching the task in a reflective manner with an apparent ease. This contrasted with the more scanty, less composed and error prone nature of prior performance' (*ibid.*: 393). Another interesting finding was that one young person disavowed the flawless performance she had achieved when being someone clever. She insisted that it could not have been her who completed the task; someone else must have done it. Hartley's interpretation of this response concurs with Nash's findings discussed above. He argues that because people desire self-consistency, a person who holds low expectations of success will prefer to 'undo' such experiences rather than change his or her expectations to correspond with the disconfirming feedback.

Given that self-perceptions are so critically important in young people's learning, it is important to be aware that the negotiation of identity, including ability identity, is a part of the agenda of all classroom interactions. In a book summarizing more than two decades of research into factors contributing to the successful education of bilingual students, Jim Cummins (2000: 6) contends that 'interactions between educators and students represent the direct determinant of bilingual students' success and failure'. In classroom interactions, important messages are communicated about what is accepted, respected and seen as normal in the classroom community. Interactions between students and teachers, and between students themselves, are 'more central to student success,' Cummins argues, 'than any method for teaching literacy, or science or math ... When students' developing sense of self is affirmed and extended through their interactions with teachers, they are more likely to apply themselves to academic effort and participate actively in instruction' (Cummins 1996: 2).

For Cummins, then, the most important determinant of achievement is not something inside pupils' heads but something very subtle and intangible happening at the level of classroom interaction. Far from being powerless in their interactions with students, teachers play a determining role – for good or ill – in the dynamics of achievement. However, Cummins is careful not to disconnect his analysis of the importance of interactions at classroom level from wider social forces. He recognizes that 'the ways in which identities are negotiated in these interactions can be understood only in relation to patterns of historical and current power relations in broader society' (Cummins 2000: 7). It is a reflection of these power relations, he argues, that issues of cultural and linguistic diversity have been ignored or treated as an after-thought in teacher training, with the result that the 'generic student' whom trainee teachers are prepared to educate is 'white, middle-class, monolingual and monocultural'. It is not surprising, then, if teachers find it difficult to manage successfully the subtle process of affirmation of identity through their interactions with students whose backgrounds, social class and life experience differ markedly from their own.

Classroom environments are also, by their very nature, places where individual affirmation is not all that easily come by. As Philip Jackson (1968) has described so vividly, pupils have to learn to live as part of a crowd, subject to constant evaluation by their teachers and peers. There is an endemic risk that where the classroom climate is permeated by messages of greater and lesser worth associated with ability labels, some children will be made to feel incompetent, unsafe, unfavourably perceived by their teachers. Such a negative sense of self leaves them ill-placed to engage successfully with curriculum experiences, to take risks or independent initiatives that might further their learning. The hidden curriculum of fear, of which John Holt (1990) has written so persuasively, is deeply bound up with ability labelling. Pupils invent a whole range of coping strategies that can directly inhibit their learning in order to avoid looking stupid in front of their teachers and peers. They become dependent upon teachers' support, they constantly search for right answers and construct their role as essentially one of pleasing the teacher, rather than expanding their understanding of the world.

Some styles of classroom discourse may unwittingly reinforce such responses, as Mary Willes (1983) has demonstrated. Although teachers may be firmly committed to encouraging young people to become active, independent learners, prepared to question ideas and think things out for themselves, the messages that young people pick up about what is, in fact, required of a 'good pupil' may be very different in nature. Willes showed that traditional styles of classroom discourse tend to encourage brevity and passivity on the part of pupils, especially in the first years at school, when they learn to stop using in school the kinds of language they had learned before coming to school. According to Willes, we would be wrong to assume that because only a minority of children achieve freedom, independence and self-motivation in their learning, most lack the intelligence or the ability to do so; the implication of her analysis is, instead, that some styles of classroom discourse encourage a view of what is required of a pupil that actively militates against the maintenance and development of such qualities and dispositions.

In particular, young children are swiftly socialized into the role of valuing and competing for teacher approval. Willes describes one 5-year-old pupil, Chatinder, who does not grasp this simple, early lesson:

> Chatinder seemed ... quite unresponsive to the idea that most children seemed already to understand that there was competition in the classroom for approval and success, into which everyone entered. Chatinder seemed by contrast uncomprehending of that part of the role of the pupil, or unwilling to undertake it ... within a day or two of arrival, he was identified as a problem.
>
> (Willes 1983: 140)

The fact that Chatinder's first language was not English was not, apparently, recognized by the teacher as a significant factor in the 'conflict of wills' that Willes observed being played out between teacher and pupil. In the teacher's terms, Chatinder was simply not behaving like a pupil: 'finding out what the teacher wants and doing it constitutes the primary duty of a pupil' (*ibid*.: 138).

Willes's work illustrates how it can happen that limits on learning constructed through the dynamics of classroom interaction are perpetuated because they are assumed to reflect pupils' own inherent characteristics and limitations. Indeed, using the template of fixed ability to make sense of differences in young people's learning and achievements actively encourages such false attributions. This template not only helps to create the differences in achievement that it purports to explain, through its effects on young people's identities, their sense of personal efficacy and expectations for their learning; by focusing attention on differences, and what appears to account for differences, it also diverts attention from the effects of classroom processes that may be limiting learning for everyone.

Effects on teachers' thinking and practice

In the discussion so far, we have tried to maintain a specific focus on how ability labelling affects young people's thinking and learning, but it has been difficult to do so without also making reference to its effects on teachers' thinking and practice. We argued above that the template of fixed ability, as a way of understanding differences in attainment, creates a sense of pessimism on the part of teachers about how much scope they have to influence learning. In this part of the chapter, we try to penetrate further below the surface of teachers' thinking in order to explore how using the template of ability can affect teachers' attitudes and their responses to the differences in young people's learning and achievements that they encounter every day in schools.

One important way in which the fixed ability template affects teachers' thinking is that it creates a disposition to accept as normal, indeed inevitable, the limited achievement of a significant proportion of the school population. If we think that differences in learning reflect the so-called ability range, and that the ability range is a natural, normal and inevitable fact of life, then we will expect to find young people who make only very slow progress and find learning a continual struggle. When they appear in our classrooms, we are not surprised. Nor are we surprised if they do not show significant progress, despite receiving extra encouragement and support. As long as this template shapes our thinking, it blocks off from our view alternative explanations for, or ways of construing, the difficulties that we perceive to be occurring. The ability template discourages us from asking important, penetrating questions about how our own practices may unwittingly contribute to the difficulties we observe; so it denies us creative opportunities continually to learn from experience, to reconstruct our practice to support and encourage learning more successfully (Simon 1953; Dixon 1989; Drummond 1993; Hart 1996b, 2000). In a seminal critique of selection based on intelligence testing, Brian Simon expressed his interpretation of how the notion of fixed ability acts as a constraint on teachers' thinking and creativity as follows:

> If, led astray by theories of mental testing, [the teacher] believes the child's achievement is predetermined by the nature of his inborn 'abilities', then all he can aim to do is to make their in-born abilities actual. He does not conceive that a child can rise above his inheritance. From the start, therefore, he does not set out to educate in a creative way. If, on the other hand, the teacher believes that the development of a child's abilities depends primarily on the careful control of his activity in school, that is on the nature and character of his own teaching, then his attitude will be entirely different. In that case, he holds that it is possible to *educate* the child in the fullest sense of the term, and he will exert his skill and his art precisely to assist him constantly to rise above himself, to make ever new achievements, to overcome all obstacles in his path.
>
> (Simon 1953: 105)

There is evidence, too, that the act of categorizing young people by ability reifies differences and hardens hierarchies, so that we start to think of those in the different categories as different *kinds* of learners with different *kinds* of minds, different characteristics and very different needs. The category to which we ascribe them becomes the principal source of our knowledge about learners and their needs. It shapes our interpretations of classroom interactions in such a way that our perceptions tend to become self-reinforcing, as George Kelly argued with respect to judgements of high and low IQ:

> A child who is nailed to the IQ continuum has just that much less chance of changing his teacher's opinion about him. If he is 'low', his unorthodox constructive ventures will never be given a thoughtful hearing; if he is 'high' his stupidities will be indulged as the eccentricities of genius.
>
> (Kelly 1955: 454)

Moreover, ability categories incline us to believe that we cannot effectively teach young people of different abilities together. Of course, when we use categories of differential ability to describe and explain differences, our assumption is that we are simply representing learners as they are. However, the long tradition of research into the effects of ability-based grouping suggests that, on the contrary, we *create* different types of learners by believing that there *are* different types, and by teaching them accordingly. Brian Jackson's classic study, *Streaming: An Education System in Miniature* (1964), was one of the first in this tradition of research, and the findings of his study were endorsed by many subsequent studies. Jackson's own experience as a teacher led him to question the part that school practices and influences might be playing in children's learning and achievement. In particular, he was interested in the impact of streaming in primary schools and 'the values that create streaming' (*ibid.*: 13). The study involved a survey of 660 primary schools, followed by a closer study of patterns of learning within and between 21 streamed and unstreamed primary schools. Jackson found that most of the teachers surveyed took the view that academic talent or ability was extremely scarce, and that there were distinct 'kinds' of children who needed different kinds of education. These beliefs justified the widespread practice of sorting children into A stream, B stream and C stream classes. These selections were most frequently made on the basis of teacher assessment or report; ability was inferred from patterns of achievement.

Examining patterns of achievement in reading as they evolved up to age 11, Jackson found that the groups moved, year by year, as three distinct blocks. The Bs never caught up with the As, or the Cs with the Bs; indeed, the gaps between them widened. Rates of progress appeared to be linked to stream placement, and although transfer between streams remained a theoretical possibility, it rarely occurred in practice. For most, the original placement (usually around the age of 7) was final. Jackson also noted that the organization of different classrooms, and the evidence of pupils' work, displayed all around the room, implied that a very different ethos, coupled with different opportunities and different forms of encouragement to learn, was in operation, depending upon which stream the pupils found themselves in.

Jackson concluded that the markedly differing characteristics and achievements of the A stream, B stream and C stream classes that he documented were not a reflection of natural and inevitable differences in kinds of children, qualities of mind and potential for learning, but were created by the processes of selection and streaming operated *by* the school: the classic self-fulfilling prophecy. Because teachers believe that such differences exist, Jackson argued, and act accordingly, the differences actually come to exist, and so apparently confirm the original belief. We may read Jackson's study today and comfort ourselves that things really are not like that any more; but the advent of the National Literacy and Numeracy strategies has led many, if not most, primary schools to reintroduce ability-based groups and sets, believing the latter to be necessary in order to respond to the considerable emphasis upon whole-class teaching in the teaching methodologies recommended by both Strategies. As teachers respond to what is laid down in the Frameworks for Teaching, planning activities and interacting with groups based on the perceived 'ability' of the group, so the conditions are clearly being re-created for processes very similar to those described by Jackson to recur in the current context.

Much more than a critique of streaming, Jackson's study was seminal because, at a time when judgements of fixed ability were still largely unquestioned, it put back into the picture crucial determinants of learning, internal to the school, that are routinely screened out by ability labelling. It drew attention to the part that teacher judgements and grouping systems play in opening up and closing off opportunities and encouragement to learn to individual pupils, and so in determining the possibilities and limits of individuals' achievement. The study helps us to understand not only the processes through which fixed ability thinking helps to create disparities of achievement, but also how ability-based thinking systematically screens out the part played by school-based influences when it represents the resultant disparities of achievement as a natural and inevitable reflection of measurable differences of inherent ability.

Jackson's study also drew attention to the possibility that the processes of selection, grouping and differentiation of curricula discriminate against particular groups of children. Although teachers' conscious intention is to treat all children fairly, there is persuasive evidence that the fixed ability template encourages hierarchical styles of thinking that perpetuate many injustices, both at the level of judgement and at the level of practice. As many other studies have done (for example, Douglas 1964; CACE 1967; Ford 1969; Taylor 1993; Gillborn and Youdell 2000), Jackson identified class-based inequalities in the selection and allocation of pupils to different streams. Comparisons across schools in terms of parental occupation suggested that children with fathers in the semi-skilled or unskilled manual category were disproportionately represented in the lower streams. A summer-born effect was also noted, whereby children born in the autumn or winter were more likely than their younger classmates to find themselves in the top streams. The practices and patterns of allocation and achievement associated with fixed ability thinking that Jackson identified in his study have been corroborated in an accumulating body of research that has continued to the present day. Acknowledging inequalities of 'race' and ethnicity, as well as social class, this further work has helped to show that the idea of fixed ability perpetuates inequalities at two levels. First, judgements of ability always work to the advantage of some pupils and to the disadvantage of others, because they inevitably reflect socially and culturally situated views of what counts as ability and achievement. Second, by naturalizing patterns of achievement, judgements of ability disguise the inequalities of access and opportunity that exclude and disadvantage some pupils.

An important and influential ethnographic study, carried out by Shirley Brice Heath (1983), provides further illustration of how this happens. Heath spent three years living and working with three communities living in close proximity in the USA. She found significant differences in the values and cultural practices in the home that led each community to emphasize, value and promote different linguistic and intellectual abilities. Since these differences were unknown to the teachers, and their judgements of ability were rooted in their own values and cultural practices, children from backgrounds different from their teachers tended to be compared unfavourably to other children and to have their different, culturally situated abilities overlooked. Heath's work offers a complex and sophisticated analysis of how disparities of achievement come to be constructed in school contexts. Her account avoids simplistically locating blame with teachers and schools for ignoring cultural and linguistic differences; it also avoids representing cultural and linguistic differences between young people's home backgrounds in deficit terms. It reveals the fallibility of judgements of ability and the fallibility, therefore, of the differential treatment provided on the basis of such judgements. However, its message is a potentially empowering one: like Jackson's, Heath's study is not just about understanding but about the possibilities for change. The extended final chapter of the book describes how teachers used the insights provided by Heath's study to rethink their judgements and practices and to develop strategies that would help to overcome the barriers of access and opportunity that they were now able to understand more fully.

The work of Tizard and Hughes (1984) offers a similarly telling example of the fallibility of the judgements that teachers use to inform and justify differential treatment and provision. The researchers tape-recorded 4-year-old girls talking at home with their parents and carers, and at nursery school with their teachers and assistants. They found that the working-class girls, in particular, asked far fewer questions, especially 'why' questions, at school than at home. Talk in the home, in both working-class and middle-class families, was characterized by what Tizard and Hughes call 'passages of intense intellectual search'. No such passages were recorded at school. The working-class girls tended to be monosyllabic in their answers to teachers' questions, and appeared lacking in animation in their communications with staff. Whereas at home there was a more or less even balance between the number and duration of adult contributions to talk and those of the children, at school it was the staff who did most of the talking and who kept conversations going, largely on topics of their own choice.

Teachers' judgements of the girls' abilities were inevitably influenced by the evidence available to them regarding the children's use of language and questioning at school, which made the working-class girls appear 'particularly unassertive, subdued and immature' (*ibid*.: 219). Basing their interactions on this evidence, they adjusted their responses to the young people accordingly. For example,

> they made less frequent use of language for complex purposes when addressing the working class girls than the middle class girls. They were more likely to initiate conversations with working class girls by questioning them, and their 'cognitive demands' were pitched at a lower level. They gave a more restricted range of information to the working class children. They were also less likely to ask the working class children for descriptions, and more likely to ask them intellectually easy questions concerned with labelling objects and naming their attributes, 'What's that called? What colour is it?'
>
> (*ibid*.: 222)

Tizard and Hughes use the evidence from their study to show how such unwarranted differential treatment, based on misleading evidence, can become a factor in working-class pupils' underachievement. They argue that, 'If, as we found, teachers respond to [children's] apparent rather than their real abilities, they will tend to underestimate what the children can achieve and present them with inappropriately low-level tasks. An initial setback of this kind can soon become cumulative' (*ibid*.: 225). The accumulating effects of such differential treatment can eventually create the disparities of achievement that appear to confirm the original judgement.

Like Tizard and Hughes, the French sociologist Pierre Bourdieu (1976) powerfully redirects the focus of our attention to understanding what is happening in schools. Whatever social group young people come from, he argues, they develop complex skills, understandings and habits relevant to the culture of that group, just as Shirley Brice Heath found. However, only the learning of those from the dominant social groups is valued, he contends, or even recognized in school, so only young people from these groups have the 'cultural capital' necessary for success at school. Bourdieu's argument is, strikingly, that the problem arises because the knowledge and understanding needed for success in school-based academic learning are not explicitly taught in schools. So those who succeed are those who come already equipped with this essential cultural capital by virtue of their backgrounds. Such differences, however, are not inevitable. Instead of naturalizing them as differences of ability, schools can take up the task of explicitly teaching young people the knowledge and understanding that they need in order to succeed.

The implications for classroom pedagogy that we draw from Bourdieu's ideas also connect with Benjamin Bloom's work on 'mastery learning'. On the basis of his own research and his review of others', Bloom (1976) challenged the dominant accepted orthodoxies of his time (and ours) that there are good learners and poor learners, or fast and slow learners. He saw these differences, and their tendency to increase as learners get older, as the result of a system of schooling based on ideas of fixed differences of ability. Such a system, he persuasively argued, was quite unnecessary because all the factors – cognitive, motivational, instructional – that influence how effectively students learn at school, how quickly they learn and how motivated they are for further learning are *alterable*. In Bloom's theory of mastery learning, evidence of students' difficulties in grasping new ideas and concepts, or in developing new skills, is treated as a sign that they lack the prerequisite knowledge, understandings or skills needed in order to take these new steps in their learning. The educator's expertise lies in the ability to analyse the 'cognitive entry behaviours' necessary for successful learning, to structure learning activities so that these prerequisites are taught, if not already acquired, and so to create conditions in which all students can experience success.

According to Bloom, then, the so-called ability range is not a natural and unalterable fact of life. Under favourable conditions, the majority of students could, in principle, reach levels of attainment previously thought to be achievable only by a minority. Support for this thesis has been provided by a more recent experiment in science teaching. Barbara White and John Frederiksen (1998: 5) set out to challenge the widespread belief that science is 'an abstract and difficult discipline that is accessible only to an elite subset of the population' – namely, to high-achieving students over the age of 13 who, it is argued, are the only ones capable of the abstract, complex reasoning processes needed to learn and do science.' They were convinced that the failure of the vast majority of students to engage meaningfully with science, and particularly with physics, was caused by traditional modes of teaching that did not instruct them in the kinds of thinking that would enable them to be successful. White and Frederiksen set up an experiment to test this hypothesis by actually teaching pupils, as part of the regular physics curriculum, how to 'construct conceptual models of scientific phenomena and how to monitor and reflect on their progress' (*ibid.*: 5). They involved three teachers working in two urban schools in the USA, who, between them, taught the experimental programme to 12 classes (grade levels 7–9). The outcomes showed some dramatic differences in performance between the control groups (taught by the same teachers) and the groups taught by the explicit methods. On *all* the measures of physics learning, those originally selected as 'low achievers' performed much better in the experimental groups compared with the control groups; furthermore, they closed the gap between themselves and the designated 'high achievers'. Moreover, on some measures, the *low* achievers in the experimental groups performed as well as the *high* achievers in the control groups, challenging the argument that prior achievement is a reliable predictor of future performance, and demonstrating the power of pedagogical inventiveness to bring about significant changes in existing patterns of achievement.

The findings of this study demonstrate once again how learning can be impeded by the mind-set created by the template of fixed ability. If we assume that current patterns of attainment are a fair reflection of young people's inherent abilities, we will not be prompted to teach them what they need to know and understand in order to transcend existing limits. So it is not a real lack of ability, but our *belief* in their lack of ability – for instance, to tackle tasks requiring complex reasoning skills – that holds some young people back, because they are not offered the chance to develop the complex modes of thinking that they have not so far demonstrated.

Evidence of how opportunities to learn offered by teachers vary according to the perceived ability of the group is provided in a synthesis of research by Laura Suknandan and Barbara Lee (1998: 29). They summarize a study by Hacker *et al.* (1991), who reported noticeable changes in the 'type' of instruction that teachers gave when they moved from teaching a high-ability to a low-ability class. In high-ability classes, there was an emphasis on acquiring concepts, learning principles, applying concepts to problem-solving activities and working independently. In contrast, teacher–pupil interactions in low-ability classes concentrated on the transmission of factual information through statements made by the teacher. Similar variations in instructional practices were reported in a number of other studies (for example, Oakes 1982, 1985; Boaler 1997a, b; Boaler *et al.* 2000).

The fixed ability template encourages us to make the assumption that manifest differences in young people's characteristics and performances as learners are stable and permanent, rather than a function of the opportunities and experiences to which young people are routinely exposed. In a fascinating article entitled 'The acquisition of a child by a learning disability', McDermott (1996) argues that we need to stop focusing on who learns more or less of particular, culturally well-defined fragments of knowledge and 'ask questions instead about what is around to be learned, in what circumstances and to what ends' (*ibid.*: 277). What can happen when we do ask such questions is graphically illustrated by Adrienne Bennett, a teacher of pupils designated as having 'moderate learning difficulties'. She describes how the link between classroom experience and the typical characteristics displayed by the young people with whom she worked came to her attention when she changed her approaches to teaching mathematics as a result of attending a course of professional development (Bennett and Williams 1992). She found that changes in her practice brought about changes in young people's engagement with activities, revealing qualities, characteristics and skills she had not previously thought them capable of. She writes:

> I have found that the pupils designated as having moderate learning difficulties ... can: concentrate for long periods of time; sustain protracted investigations; be systematic; reason logically; find patterns and relationships; make tests and predictions; generalise; record and explain their findings. I have found them working in ways I had never expected them to be able to. What they couldn't do was perform meaningless calculations and relate them to situations which were equally meaningless to them. But then who can?
>
> (*ibid.*: 74)

Consequences for school curricula

Fixed ability thinking is not, of course, simply an idea in the minds of individual teachers; it has an institutional reality. The legacy of theories of IQ and intelligence testing still permeates the whole of the education system, its structure and organization, curriculum content, pedagogy and modes of assessment. New teachers are inducted into an established system and set of conditions that place specific expectations upon them and limit their freedom of manoeuvre. In the study discussed above, Nash (1973) describes, for example, how the syllabus he was expected to work from, as a new teacher of English teaching a bottom stream class, stressed the need to have 'limited aims', to 'attack relentlessly' areas such as correct usage of commas, full stops and capital letters. The endemic pessimism about the capabilities of those deemed less able comes through in the choice of language used to describe the kind of repetitive teaching required, and in the lowering of teachers' pedagogical horizons to no more than 'hammering in' the basics. In this syllabus, the idea that these pupils might be capable of experiencing any excitement or fulfilment in their learning, or that the teacher should try to make such experiences possible, is clearly not entertained as a realistic possibility.

Nash's account reminds us how ideas of fixed ability have been used to justify offering a restricted curriculum to some pupils on the grounds of their presumed ability; and how these ideas have justified selecting priorities for these pupils' learning that deprive them of the very kinds of opportunities that might actually challenge and stimulate them to learn more success- fully. It is worth noting, however, that the restricted opportunities that decades of research have associated with ability grouping do not just affect students allocated to supposedly average or less able groups. Nel Keddie's (1971) seminal study of how teachers' ideas of ability shape their know- ledge of students, and inform their interpretations of students' contribu- tions, reveals what those deemed more able have to do, and what they sacrifice, in gaining and maintaining their ability status. According to Keddie, those who are perceived as bright are those who are prepared to take on ready-formed teachers' definitions of knowledge rather than ques- tioning these and making sense of them in their own terms. Indeed, Keddie concludes, rather depressingly, that 'it would seem to be the failure of high- ability pupils to question what they are taught in schools that contributes in large measure to their educational achievement' (*ibid.*: 156).

While it can be argued that, in different ways, fixed ability thinking and grouping impose limits on all young people's learning, the negative consequences are potentially much greater for those in the low-status groups. In their synthesis of research on the impact of ability grouping, Suknandan and Lee (1998) note the widely reported phenomenon of inequalities in the staffing of ability-based groups. A number of studies found that teachers are not randomly allocated to teach pupils of different ability levels. Instead, 'those teachers who have the greatest amount of experience and who are more highly qualified (i.e. heads of department) are more frequently allocated to teach pupils of high ability'. This practice is not lost on pupils, as Boaler *et al.* (2000) discovered when interviewing students about their experiences of learning maths. One student com- mented that 'they don't think they have to bother with us. I know that sounds really mean and unrealistic, but they just think they don't have to bother with us, 'cause we're group 5. They get say a teacher who knows nothing about maths, and they'll give them us, a PE teacher or something. They think they can send us anybody' (*ibid.*: 637).

Educators committed to the development of a fully comprehensive education system campaigned for many years to abolish the inequalities of provision associated with ability labelling, selection and differentiated cur- ricula. The establishment in 1988 of a statutory curriculum, intended as an entitlement for all young people, could have been an important milestone, creating a common curriculum and conditions within which all young people's learning could be given equal support and encourage- ment. However, many of the conditions known to perpetuate inequality of opportunity and experience have been *built into* the new statutory curriculum.

For example, the content, structure and differentiated framework of the National Curriculum leave in place the longstanding limitations of curriculum breadth and balance that result from restricted ideas about ability and what counts as worthwhile learning and achievement. David Hargreaves's (1980) critique of the one-sidedness of the school curriculum is no less relevant to the National Curriculum as currently defined than it was two decades ago. According to Hargreaves, the traditional grammar school curriculum stresses one form of ability, which he characterizes as the intellectual-cognitive, at the expense of 'other forms of valid ability, knowledge and skill (in particular the aesthetic-artistic, the affective-emotional, the physical-manual and the social-interpersonal)' (Hargreaves 1980: 33). Differential patterns of attainment reflect this in-built bias, and so when we use the ability template to make sense of differences, the effect is to naturalize and legitimate this narrow view of curriculum and so perpetuate existing patterns of learning and achievement. In the National Curriculum, the split between core and foundation subjects also tends to reinforce this bias. As Robin Alexander (1984, 2000) has pointed out, making a powerful distinction between what he calls 'Curriculum I' and 'Curriculum II', the separation of core and foundation subjects, is merely an updating (with science added) of the traditional divide between the basics (Curriculum I) and the rest (Curriculum II). The division, he says, 'is fundamental: it is one of time allocations, priority, seriousness of purpose and quality. Curriculum I is safeguarded, Curriculum II is vulnerable' (Alexander 2000: 147). Moreover, the imbalance in status – and therefore in relative emphasis – between core and foundation subjects has been given further endorsement through the introduction of the National Literacy Strategy and National Numeracy Strategy in primary schools.

It is the ten-level structure of the curriculum, however, with its underlying 'ladder' model of teaching, learning and achievement, that has perhaps done most to restrict the potential for widening opportunity and reducing inequalities that was opened up by the establishment of a common framework and the principle of universal entitlement to participate in and derive benefit from a broad and balanced curriculum. The framework of levels of attainment in terms of which the National Curriculum is constructed quite deliberately echoes the idea of differences among pupils being reducible, at least within a subject, to a single dimension: the relative levels pupils have reached on the curriculum ladder are quite explicitly expected to reflect their relative levels of ability. Teachers are explicitly encouraged to formulate teaching objectives and targets for particular groups in terms of where pupils are judged to be on the 'ladder' and to measure progress in terms of movement up the ladder. The assumption, underpinned by the template of ability, is that, while it is the task of teaching and learning to move everyone up the ladder as far as possible, there are reliably predictable limits on how far any particular pupil is likely to go.

The potential for teachers to organize and develop their practice on the basis of richer and more empowering models of teaching, learning and curriculum is inevitably reduced by the statutory requirements to teach, and by pupils' entitlement to experience, the National Curriculum as currently organized and conceived. The inadequacy of the construction of learning as an inexorable movement forwards or upwards – with success determined by how fast individuals move to the top – has been repeatedly exposed. Harvey Goldstein and Richard Noss (1990) make a useful distinction between a model of learning as the ascent of a mountain, and a model of learning as a visit to an exhibition. In the first, there is only one way to go and the point is to get to the top. In the second, there is a logic to the arrangement of exhibits but there is no inexorable order. Visitors can stop as long as they like at particular exhibits, and return to them again and again, with new purposes and fresh interests.

As long as teachers are held to a ladder model of teaching and learning, underpinned by assumptions of differential ability, it is likely that teaching will continue to privilege psychometric knowledge over the details of individual biographies and knowledge of what Robert Hull (1985) refers to as 'the living actuality, the contours and pressures of individual minds', available to teachers through classroom dialogue. In the conclusion to his powerful study, *The Language Gap: How Classroom Dialogue Fails*, Hull discusses the limitations of psychometric information, which, though apparently scientific and objective, is none the less 'remote and imprecise ... of no immediate dialogic use in a teaching relation'. Yet this knowledge has institutional currency in a way that teachers' own daily observations do not. For Hull, the knowledge available to teachers through direct contact with pupils is infinitely superior and illuminating, and it is this knowledge that is necessary if the teaching-learning relationship is to be more than a monologue, more than the transmission of supposedly objective knowledge from teachers to learners. 'When the actuality of children's minds is given expression', he explains, 'teachers have something to say which is part of a dialogue ... A dialogic relation clearly depends on knowing children and their minds in a different, more precisely human way, and on drawing continuously on this knowledge' (*ibid*.: 228).

History has shown Hull's insight to be more than a little prescient, as secondary schools, in particular, have increasingly, over the past decade, turned to psychometric measurement to help them to make predictions about young people's future achievements. Most schools now administer cognitive ability tests (CATs) to each new Year 7 intake and use this information, along with National Curriculum assessments, to inform teaching and monitor progress. CATs claim to predict examination outcomes several years ahead with 80 per cent accuracy. If the school 'adds value' significantly, everyone's achievements should improve, but the pattern of performance relative to the prediction should stay the same. Experience may well appear to demonstrate that these predictions broadly hold good. However, based on the evidence of this chapter, our argument is that the stability and predictablity of patterns of achievement is brought about not because these patterns are a reflection of immutable laws of differential ability, but because the social processes that produce and perpetuate current patterns, and disparities, of achievement continue to produce their effects unacknowledged; consequently, patterns of achievement remain unchanged.

There is nothing fixed or immutable about existing patterns of attainment, as we have demonstrated in this chapter. They are the outcomes of complex processes in which ability labelling, and other influences both internal and external to schools, play a central, not peripheral, role. Our analysis has identified many subtle and not so subtle ways in which ability labelling imposes limits, directly and indirectly, on the curriculum, on teachers' thinking and on young people's attitudes and expectations for their learning. It shows that we could, and why we should, commit ourselves to an alternative improvement agenda, dedicated to the task of freeing learning from the limits imposed by ability-led practices. We cannot yet claim to know with certainty what young people might be capable of, if their experience and learning were not subject to these constraints from their earliest days in what we now call the Foundation Stage. But we can assert with confidence, on the basis of this analysis, that young people clearly are capable of achieving very much more, and in ways different from those suggested by current patterns, if their experiences in school are not shaped and constrained from the outset by the visible and invisible effects of ability labelling.

Towards classrooms free from ability labelling

From the compelling evidence reviewed in this chapter, we conclude that it is not possible to fulfil our professional commitment to treating all young people fairly and to giving them all the best possible start in life as long as school organization, curriculum, pedagogy and assessment practices continue to be permeated by ability labelling. In the interests of justice and entitlement, and indeed in the social and economic interests of our whole society, educators must take a resolute stance to set aside the template of fixed ability and take active steps to free young people from the limits that it imposes on their learning.

To follow this conviction through into practice, however, is more easily said than done, for the concept of ability is not just a way of making sense of differences; it is actively used by teachers to accomplish the essential tasks of teaching. Evidence from the 1960s to the 1990s suggests that ability tends to be the characteristic of their pupils that is most salient for many British primary and secondary school teachers in their perceptions and classroom decision-making (for example, Morrison and McIntyre 1969; Brown and McIntyre 1993; Cooper and McIntyre 1996). These teachers use their perceptions of apparent differences in ability, as we have seen, to set expectations, design tasks, adjust the content and style of their interactions with young people, assess work and evaluate their teaching. For these teachers, ability is a central organizing category around which their pedagogy is constructed.

The analysis in this chapter demonstrates the potential, indeed the necessity, for teachers' work to be informed by the kind of understanding we defined at the start of this chapter: a much more complex, multifaceted and infinitely more empowering understanding of teaching and learning processes and of the influences, internal and external to the school, that impinge on learning and achievement. However, it does not explain how this understanding translates into a coherent, principled and practicable pedagogy. The pressing question that must be addressed, therefore, if the template of ability is set aside, is: what replaces it? How do (or might) teachers construct their practice, fulfil their essential tasks and respond to evident differences, if not with reference to ability? Indeed, *can* they do so and still fulfil statutory requirements and expectations?

We are in no doubt that there will not be a sufficiently radical change to the damaging effects described in this chapter if the idea of fixed ability is just replaced with a less deterministic concept of ability, such as the performance or comparative view that we discussed in Chapter 1. We know teachers who admit the limitations of the concept of fixed ability, who do their best to mitigate its negative effects, but who say that they still use the language of ability as a convenient, and benign, shorthand way of referring to differences for practical purposes. However, we believe that the threefold effects – on young people's experience, on teachers' thinking and practices and on the school curriculum – described in this chapter are no less likely to be produced by more descriptive or shorthand uses of ability labels. Teachers cannot control the messages they communicate to young people through this shorthand. What teachers mean and intend is not necessarily what young people pick up and internalize, as we have seen in this chapter. Whenever the language of ability is used, there will always be ambiguity about what is meant, and potential for misinterpretation – by other adults and by children – as long as ideas of fixed ability are pervasive within our culture. And if perceived differences are used to divide children into permanent groups and sets, or to justify systematic selection and provision of different tasks and learning opportunities, the unintended effects of ability labelling on young people's self-perceptions, expectations and hopes for their learning are likely to be broadly the same whatever interpretation of ability teachers have in mind. Indeed, even when used in a purely descriptive or shorthand way, ability labels divert the focus of teachers' attention to differences in children's attainments and the need to respond to these differences, and away from the processes that *produce* these differences, and the need to respond to the limits those processes put in place.

Focusing on the practice of experienced teachers

We were and are convinced that the priority is to articulate in a generalized way one or more models of teaching that do not rely upon ability labelling in any form in order to carry out the essential tasks of the teacher. One strategy that we considered was to identify alternative models of pedagogy in the existing literature and invite a group of teachers who had themselves rejected ability labelling to examine and assess their practical potential (Hart 1998). In the early years of schooling, for instance, there has been growing interest, indeed excitement, in applying pedagogical approaches based on the work of early years professionals in Reggio Emilia, Italy, whose commitment to a particular view of children's capacity to learn is strikingly free from any concept of inherent ability (Edwards *et al.* 1998). We knew as well of current work exploring the application of Howard Gardner's theory of multiple intelligences to practice in primary and secondary schools, which has aroused much interest (Gardner 1983, 1999; Chamberlain 1996; Jack 1996). One member of the university team also had previous experience of working with teachers to explore the potential for applying Bloom's (1976) theory of mastery learning, discussed above, with teachers in Scottish secondary schools.

We decided against this research strategy, however, because we thought that the most powerful and persuasive models would be those developed by teachers themselves. The experience of other projects (for example, Quicke and Winter 1996) suggested that externally derived models tend to run into difficulties, either because they do not mesh readily with teachers' theories of learning and practical repertoires, or because they are difficult to reconcile with external pressures and requirements that fix the parameters within which teachers must operate. From our own experience in schools, and from our day-to-day work with experienced teachers on courses of professional development, we knew that many teachers are uncomfortable with ideas of fixed ability and avoid overt differentiation by ability. Some refuse on principle to refer to differences in the terminology of ability, preferring to refer to lower and higher *attainers*, or more and less *experienced* readers, in order to avoid implied predictions relating to future performance. We were confident that we would find teachers who shared the aims and values of the project, and who would be prepared to work with us in articulating alternative models of teaching. The advantage of this strategy, we thought, was that, unlike theoretically derived models, the approach to pedagogy developed by each teacher would already have proved itself to be workable within the practical constraints and pressures of schools.

In this chapter, we have explained why we believe the task is such an important one and why we are convinced that commitment to tackling it is long overdue. In the next chapter, we explain how the research was carried out, before moving on, in the remainder of the book, to describe the practices of the teachers we studied and what we learnt from them about the ideas and principles that make teaching free from ability labelling possible. In this work, as we explain, we were guided and inspired by the words of George Kelly, who wrote, back in 1970, that 'even the most obvious occurrences of everyday life might appear utterly transformed if we were inventive enough to construe them differently' (cited in Thomson and Thomson 1996: 31).

3   The Learning without Limits project: methods and approaches

If teachers reject ability labelling and approaches to teaching based on it, what alternative ideas do they use to inform and construct their teaching? How do such teachers organize their classrooms to engage, inspire and liberate the learning of young people with widely differing experiences, backgrounds, interests and attainments? On what basis do they make all the essential decisions that teachers have to make in order to create a workable, purposeful and productive classroom environment? What adjustments or creative compromises do they make in order to fulfil statutory requirements and expectations? Are there some common principles that underpin the work of teachers who have rejected ability labelling, or are there different principles and approaches that can be identified? And how do the schools in which they work support them in their efforts to liberate learning from the constraints of ability labelling?

As we explained in Chapter 2, the strategy we chose in order to investigate these questions was to bring together a carefully selected group of experienced teachers who identified themselves as having rejected ability labelling and who had been actively working to develop their approaches to teaching in accordance with their values and beliefs. Our plan was to work collaboratively with them, first to discover and document what each of them was doing individually, and then to compare and contrast the similarities and differences in their personal approaches. From this comparative analysis of individual accounts of their teaching, we hoped to be able to identify and elaborate some of the distinctive characteristics of pedagogy free from ability labelling.

Creating a team

The first essential task of recruiting the team presented us with some interesting challenges. How would we be able to check – on the basis of written application and interview alone – that the teachers who expressed interest in joining the project had not just rejected ability labelling but really had developed successful practices consistent with their ideas? And if they had, would we be in a position to make that judgement before we had carried out the research? A further problem was that we could not necessarily expect the teachers we interviewed – however expert in teaching free from ability labelling – to offer an instant articulation of their theories and practices. Previous research has indicated that teachers often find it difficult to make their thinking explicit, because so much of their knowledge and expertise is tacit in nature (Brown and McIntyre 1993). In this case, we would expect it to be particularly difficult since the whole point of our research was to articulate explicitly approaches to teaching that we believed had not previously been adequately and convincingly theorized.

Our advertisements in the national and local press drew many expressions of interest, including from headteachers and from people working in special provision, such as pupil referral units, but we felt that the research approach we had chosen required, at this stage, that we work with people who were full-time mainstream class teachers. We invited 17 people for interview.

To help us plan the interview, we drew on George Kelly's work on personal construct psychology (Kelly 1955; Bannister and Fransella 1976; Salmon 1988, 1995). Revolutionary in its day, Kelly's theory is that we each construct our own personal ways of seeing the world – our personal construct system – and that this system defines the understanding by which we live. This does not mean that we each invent our own individual meaning systems independent of the societies and cultures in which we live. It does mean that we can only know the world we live in through the personal interpretations, or constructions, that we make of it. In making our personal interpretations, we of course draw on the cultural resources and understandings available to us through our membership of particular social worlds; but the meaning systems that we construct on the basis of our interpretations of experience are always, inevitably, personal. Moreover, the systems so constructed can be reconstructed; change is always possible, though it is fraught with difficulty because all the parts of the system are interconnected. Any change, or learning, in one part calls into question all the rest.

For the purposes of this initial interview, we used a technique that Kelly had developed to assist in probing and identifying people's personal construct systems. We did not use the full 'repertory grid technique' (Fransella and Bannister 1976), which involves prioritizing as well as identifying pairs of opposing constructs. Instead, we asked our interviewees to bring with them a class list and to write the names of 12 of the young people in the class on separate pieces of card. We then asked them to select three names and talk to us about the ways in which two of the individuals were alike, and how they were different from the third.

We interviewed each teacher in pairs, so that one interviewer could make notes, and so that two of the team had met each person to assist in the final decision-making. This was a difficult process; everyone we interviewed impressed and moved us by the values, convictions and commitment to young people that they so abundantly demonstrated in the course of the interviews. The final decisions were mainly made in the interests of balance, bringing together a team that reflected different phases of primary education, and different subjects in the secondary phase. Although three out of five secondary teachers selected were English specialists, the teachers were working in schools in very different locations and with very different student populations.

Collaborative research: a fundamental principle

Our intention was that, once the team was constituted, the research would be carried out on a fully collaborative, or partnership, basis. Every member of the team would be actively involved in developing the methodology and methods of data collection to be used, and we would engage together in the analysis and construction of models of teaching free from ability labelling. Over the first year, we met on five occasions, mostly for a day at a time and, during the analysis, for two days together. Initially our main priority was to build the relationships, common understandings and purposes that would make genuine collaborative research possible. Soon, we were able to progress to joint construction and elaboration of the methodology of the project, and eventually to collaborative analysis of the common themes and differences within individual accounts. Since the first year, project team members have been actively involved in a further development and dissemination phase of the work, trialling dissemination activities in their schools, leading INSET sessions in schools, making conference presentations, contributing to seminar discussions and sharing in the writing of this book.

Overview of the research

The processes of data collection and analysis were designed to take place over one school year, and were divided into three phases. Eight of the teachers worked collaboratively with a member of the university team, who visited each school seven times, three times each in Phase 1 and Phase 2, and once in Phase 3. The ninth teacher worked collaboratively with her students as co-researchers to investigate and generate an account of her practice. The methods and approaches she used are described in a separate section later in this chapter.

In Phase 1, our main aim was to develop a preliminary, descriptive account of each teacher's thinking and practice. We observed the teachers teaching and interviewed them before and after lessons in order to discover the key ideas – about learners, learning and teaching – at the heart of each teacher's personal construct system, and the relationship between these key constructs and their classroom practices.

In Phase 2, we began to delve deeper into the teachers' thinking and to explore the relationship between their constructs. Our aim was to try to understand how these constructs worked *together* to create each teacher's distinctive pedagogy. As part of this second phase, teachers chose up to five individuals in their classes who became the focus of sustained observation, analysis and conversation. The teachers kept journals in which they recorded their ongoing observations of these five individuals, and their reflections on their learning. Through this focus on individuals, we hoped to move beyond a generalized understanding of the teachers' philosophy, and their approach to teaching and learning, to reach a fuller understanding of how the teachers conceptualized individual learning and fine-tuned their strategies for enabling learning at an individual level.

In Phase 2, we also developed specific strategies for probing the thinking and experience of young people. The teachers used a range of imaginative activities to encourage the pupils in their classes to articulate their sense of themselves as learners and what they felt it was important for a teacher to know about them individually. As well as observing them in class, we interviewed them, individually and in groups, to discover if their experience of being a pupil in these teachers' classes did indeed seem to correspond to what their teachers themselves said was important to them, and to what they were trying to achieve.

A third dimension of our research in Phase 2 was to begin to explore with the teachers, in our team meetings, through individual interviews and through journal entries, the relationship between their approaches to teaching and learning and the wider context of the school within which they were working. The mainstream schools in which our teachers worked were all affected by expectations and pressures arising from current national policies. All were subject to Ofsted inspections, to the pressures of repeated testing, target setting and league tables. We wanted to understand how our teachers reconciled their own values and beliefs about ability and learning with this agenda, the compromises they had to make and the ways they found of creatively mediating external expectations and requirements. Most importantly, we wanted to understand in what ways, and to what extent, features of the school context in which they were working actively supported them in developing teaching free from ability labelling.

As the main outcome of Phase 2, we wrote some lengthy appendices to the preliminary accounts produced in Phase 1. The appendices summarized what new insights and understandings relating to the teachers' thinking and practice had emerged from Phase 2. They included a much fuller elaboration of existing constructs, the identification of additional constructs, and an attempt to articulate the mechanisms whereby these constructs worked together to create a workable, successful and distinctive pedagogy. They included an analysis of the pupils' comments set against each teacher's personal construct system. They also included an account of how teachers responded to external expectations and pressures, and how these responses were reflected in their thinking and their practice.

The first task of Phase 3 was to develop fully elaborated accounts of each teacher's thinking and practice. Alongside this work, we also took steps to deepen our understanding of the school contexts by interviewing the head or a senior member of staff in each school. We drew up our interview questions, in consultation with each of the teacher members of our team; they helped us to identify fruitful lines of enquiry and their collaboration was important in ensuring that this interview was ethically acceptable. We asked them to talk about how they thought the school context lent support to the teachers in the team, enabling them to work in the ways that reflected as closely as possible their values and beliefs. We also asked them to identify what they thought were the greatest constraints that prevented them from offering fuller support.

In our team meetings, we then moved on to a further phase of analysis in which we looked across all the accounts, identified common themes and explored differences. At the start, we did not know whether the teachers would have anything in common, apart from their commitment to the learning without limits ideal. They might all have sought to realize that ideal in different ways. This part of the process was much more demanding of time and collaborative work than we had allowed for in our original plans. It took another six months, and several more meetings, before we had worked on all the material in sufficient depth for the one key idea to emerge that enabled everything else to fall into place and that became, after further elaboration and discussion, the basis for this account of a distinctive pedagogy free from ability labelling.

Methods for eliciting teachers' thinking

In developing our procedures for gaining access to teachers' thinking, we drew on the insights and techniques used in previous studies of teachers' thinking carried out by Sally Brown and Donald McIntyre (1993) and by Paul Cooper and Donald McIntyre (1996). As the authors of those studies had done, we decided to focus our efforts to understand teachers' thinking and practices around selected lessons in secondary schools, and selected periods of activity (sessions) in primary schools. We recognize that this was not an ideal approach to the understanding of primary teaching and learn-ing, the more fluid rhythms of which are not comfortably encompassed within such clear-cut boundaries. Nevertheless, our reasoning was that a common focus and shared experience between teacher and researcher would stimulate a detailed conversation, with in-depth examination of specific actions by the teacher in response to specific circumstances and events. We wanted to be sure that our methods would enable us to go beyond values and espoused theories to an understanding of teachers' thinking as it was reflected in observable classroom practices and learning experiences. Keeping the focus of discussion on particular periods of classroom time when the researcher was present allowed the researcher to be more proac-tive in supporting the process of recall, to offer prompts and ask questions that would help teachers to reconstruct in their minds events and interactions that might otherwise have quickly faded beyond the reach of memory.

While observing, we kept narrative field notes in which we tried to capture as much as possible of the appearance and feel of the various class-rooms, what the pupils and teacher were doing moment by moment, ver-batim dialogue between teachers and pupils, what was written on the board and what kinds of work pupils produced. We kept examples of learning materials and made photocopies of young people's work. We tried to record as much detailed description as possible to match against teachers' accounts, and to assist in the elaboration and illustration of the system of constructs as it emerged. These observations provided the focus for the dis-cussion after the lesson. Interviews were all recorded and transcribed, and the interview transcripts sent to the teachers for validation, further comment and amendment of anything that they felt did not represent their thoughts fully or adequately.

Exploring young people's thoughts and perspectives on their learning

We thought it was vital, as an integral part of the research, to include young people's perspectives on their own learning and classroom experiences. We wanted to know if – and to what extent – the key ideas and constructs that the teachers identified as being important to them were received, recog-nized and internalized by the young people in their classes, and how their sense of themselves and their learning was affected by them. What had these ideas, and the practices that embodied them, become at the level of pupils' classroom experience? Had they appropriated them, acted upon them, rejected them, ignored them?

We thought that it was important to build a picture, at least to a limited extent, of the perspectives of *all* young people in each of the selected classes. How the group as a whole thinks can have an effect on how individuals within it perceive their own capabilities, as we noted in our discussion of Nash's research in Chapter 2. At one of our team meetings early in Phase 2, the teachers worked together to explore imaginative ways of encouraging individuals to express their thoughts about themselves, their learning and their classroom experience to use as part of a whole-class activity.

Narinder, for example, a teacher working in a small inner-city primary school with a mixed class of Year 5 and Year 6 pupils, created an irresistible sense of drama, donning a stormtrooper mask and acting the role of a messenger freshly arrived from outer space. The planet Earth is on the brink of destruction, she announces, but 'my master the War Lord is in merciful mood. He wishes you to leave your knowledge and advice to all future generations of children so that they may build an excellent education system.' The pupils listen, breathless with excitement, as the teacher shows them the time capsule in which their completed reports on an ideal education system will be projected into space. Then, with a flourish, she hands each pupil a large, sealed, named envelope, in which she has placed the materials from which they will create their reports: a set of open-ended questions and sentence completion tasks, a selection of cartoon figures from the *Clip-Art* computer program, a digital snapshot of each pupil, blank speech bubbles for spontaneous additional comments. One or two pupils look around at the observer to check whether she appreciates the joke, and then they open their envelopes with glee, and fall to work on the first page of the report, which begins: 'To my unknown friends in deep space, answers to these questions may help you ... '

Another primary teacher, Alison, asked her Year 5 class to draw a picture to show learning, encouraging them to use metaphors to express their thoughts and feelings. Non, a secondary teacher, asked the students in her Year 11 class to write a letter to a member of the university team describing themselves as learners and explaining what classroom conditions and strategies help and hinder their learning. We recognized that asking young people, in school, to discuss their school experiences raises sensitive ethical issues, so we made it a rule not to mention by name any teacher in the school apart from the teacher team member.

In addition to the involvement of the whole class, we also carried out post-lesson interviews with the young people who had been identified by their teachers as the focus for more in-depth study in Phase 2. As with the teacher interviews, we used observations of the lesson/session to guide and prompt recall, helping interviewees to elaborate their responses without (as far as possible) leading them towards specific kinds of responses. We also used statement cards, specially prepared for particular classes, as a stimulus to discussion. For example, in Narinder's Year 5 and Year 6 class, the small group interviews with pupils were structured around a sorting activity. The young people were invited to use the headings 'All the time', 'Some of the time' and 'Never' to sort a set of statements about their feelings, which included:

I feel safe in this classroom.   I can learn anything in here.
This is a fair classroom.   Listening is very hard work.
Mrs B is on my side.   Mrs B cares about us and we care
                                             about her.
I know all the classroom rules.   Learning can be very exciting.

These statements were all based on issues that had arisen in the interviews and discussions with the class teacher, and had been negotiated with her. They reflect some of the important things that this teacher said she was trying to achieve with her classes, as they might be experienced and expressed by young people. The cards provided a focus and stimulus for discussion, exploring young people's reasons for placing cards under a particular heading. The statements used in this group interview were all expressed in positive terms, though the pupils had the opportunity to reject them, by placing them in the 'Never' and 'Sometimes' piles. In the whole-class activity described earlier, the pupils had been offered a range of negative and positive statements with which to describe their feelings, such as:

I never know what to do.

I feel frightened.

Wasting my time.

Lonely.

A small minority of the class expressed feelings of this kind but always tempered them with other more appreciative comments, such as:

My teacher listens to me.

I understand the work …

Most young people were forthcoming and articulate in the interviews. Perhaps some students put an unambiguously positive gloss on their experiences, out of loyalty to the teacher, but the way in which they were able to offer concrete illustrations to back up their points suggested their claims were reliable and authentic. A detailed analysis of these interviews, and other aspects of the students' perspective, is presented in Chapter 15.

The use of the teachers' journals

Towards the end of Phase 1, we asked teachers to select up to five young people as the focus of detailed study during Phase 2. We left the criteria for selection open, in order not to impose preconceived notions of significant differences between pupils on the writing of these case studies. Teachers were invited to begin their journals with a thumbnail sketch of each individual and some explanation of why he or she had been chosen for close study. Since our opportunities for detailed observation and interview were limited, the journal was to be the principal means through which we hoped to gain access to teachers' thinking about individuals over time, and how this thinking informed their teaching.

Teachers agreed to keep their journals for ten weeks and to include in them:

- significant incidents involving the case study individuals
- how these incidents fed into planning and pedagogy
- how the teacher's knowledge of each individual grew and changed
- reflections on the relationship between what was happening with individuals and what the rest of the class were doing or learning.

Teachers were also asked to use their journals to record their ongoing thoughts about how features of the school context where they were working supported them (or otherwise) in developing their teaching in the ways that they considered to be most effective. We outlined the questions that we were keen to explore with them, through entries in their journals and through interview, as follows:

- To what extent do you find yourself able to achieve your aspirations?
- What are the circumstances and conditions of your particular context that are supportive of your teaching?
- What are the constraints? Could anything be done to address these?
- What do you think are the necessary conditions for the success of your practice?

Engaging pupils as co-researchers

For a number of reasons, one member of the teacher team, Non Worrall, who was very experienced in carrying out research in her own classroom and school, opted to examine her own practice and generate her own account, with students in her Year 11 English GCSE class working collaboratively with her as co-researchers. She was able to take this decision to involve the young people actively in the research because of her previous involvement in school-based research in which young people had taken an active role as co-researchers. She was able to build on this experience to construct an approach specifically tailored to fit the purposes of the Learning without Limits project.

Approaches to collaborative analysis

With the exception of Non's study, the first stage of analysis was carried out in dialogue between individual teachers and the member of the university team working with them. Preliminary accounts of teachers' key constructs were created, drawing mainly on the teachers' own words, taken from the interview transcripts. The teachers then gave their feedback on these draft accounts, which were amended in the light of their comments.

For the analysis in Phase 2, we drew on all the data to extend and elaborate on the preliminary accounts. Again, the teachers were asked to make amendments to these more developed accounts, which explored the interconnections between constructs and their relation to practice. Although we took the lead in writing these accounts, we tried to portray authentically the teachers' own perspectives on their practice, rather than our interpretations of them.

The continuing challenge, in the analysis, was not just to capture the essence of teachers' thinking and its relationship to their practice, but to capture what was distinctive about it as a pedagogy for Learning without Limits. It was not enough to describe and celebrate these teachers' work as 'good practice'. We had to keep the analysis focused on trying to reach a closer understanding of how their distinctive approach to their teaching (both thinking and practice) was inseparably connected to, and followed from, their rejection of ability labelling. To this end, we devised activities for our team meetings in Phase 3 that encouraged the teachers to articulate these links themselves, and make them explicit in their own terms.

For example, in one extended discussion activity, we asked the teachers to draw emotional and metaphorical maps of their classrooms; we gave them a set of statements summarizing some of the problems of ability labelling that had been previously raised and discussed within the group; we asked them to select those that reflected their own values and beliefs and to add to or change the statements, so that they would reflect their own thinking as closely as possible. Then we asked them to match the statements to their classroom maps and record for us the links that they themselves identified between these values and their classroom practices. The teachers then described their maps to one another and explored similarities and differences between the ways in which they sought to translate their beliefs and values into practice.

In the next part of the book, we present the accounts of each teacher's thinking and practice that we wrote, in collaboration with the teachers, as part of Phase 3 of the project. We present them here exactly as we wrote them before we developed the key ideas about teaching free from ability labelling that we discuss in the third part of the book. We made a conscious decision *not* to re-write the accounts in the light of our emerging model of teaching, because we want to retain and foreground what is fresh, different and distinctively individual about each teacher's work from which this model was developed. By presenting them in this way, we put readers in a position similar to the one we were in ourselves, as we tackled the task of trying to extrapolate, from these separate accounts, key ideas and principles that would encapsulate what is distinctive about teaching free from ability labelling.

Nevertheless, we know we are taking a risk in doing so. While we hope and expect that readers will be impressed and inspired by the accounts, they may also find themselves wondering what, if anything, is particularly different, special or noteworthy about these teachers' work. As one head-teacher of long experience memorably asked, at our first dissemination conference, 'Isn't this just good practice?' We are well aware that many of the methods and skills used by the nine teachers would be recognized by many experienced teachers as similar to their own. It is the overall approach that we believe to be distinctive; it is the core ideas, purposes and principles underlying their work that demonstrate why and how theirs is not *just* good practice (minus ability-based judgements), but practice dedicated to learning without limits.

PART 2
Accounts of the teachers' practice

Introduction

Part 2 of this book is made up of nine chapters describing the work of the nine teachers who collaborated with us on the Learning without Limits project. In the first eight of these chapters, we draw on our detailed observations in the teachers' classrooms, and the many hours we spent with them, in interviews and small discussion groups. We analyse their distinctive philosophies and priorities, and identify the key constructs at the heart of their work. Chapter 12, the last in Part 2, is rather different. Non Worrall, the teacher whose work is presented here, wrote this chapter herself, drawing on the collaborative enquiry into her own teaching that she conducted in a Year 11 GCSE class. This was a partnership project; we described briefly in Chapter 3 how Non and her students worked together to investigate the impact of her teaching on their learning.

We imagine that while some readers will want to read straight through all nine chapters, others will want to treat this section of the book more selectively, choosing to concentrate on teachers in either the primary or secondary phase, or selecting particular subject specialisms from the secondary teachers' chapters. To help readers to find their way through this section, there follows a brief description of each of the nine teachers and the school and classroom they were working in during the fieldwork period of the research (October 1999 to June 2000). The chapters are presented in order according to the age of the children they feature, with the youngest class appearing first.

Chapter 4: Anne Reay was teaching a Year 1 class in a large infant school with a nursery class, in West Yorkshire, in a small town on the edge of the Yorkshire Dales.

Chapter 5: Claire Conway was the literacy coordinator and curriculum/ assessment manager in a primary school of 220 students in a large village in Lincolnshire; she was teaching a Year 4 class of 36 students. In May 2000, Claire became the teaching head of a small rural Church of England primary school, where she worked with a mixed-age class of Year 3 to Year 6 students.

Chapter 6: Alison Peacock was deputy head of a primary school with a nursery class in the county town of a large shire county. She was teaching a Year 5 class of 34 children.

Chapter 7: Narinder Brach was the deputy head of a very small primary school with a nursery class in the heart of a major industrial city; she was teaching a mixed Year 5 and Year 6 class. The school stood in a neglected and severely disadvantaged area, with a high proportion of minority ethnic families.

Chapter 8: Patrick Yarker was an English teacher in a large comprehensive school in south London: the observations were carried out in a Year 9 class of 30 students.

Chapter 9: Nicky Madigan (then Nicky Hancock), Head of English, was observed in a Year 10 class in an 11–16 comprehensive school in west London that served an area with a very high population of refugees living locally in reception centres.

Chapter 10: Yahi Tahibet was a mathematics teacher, working in a mixed comprehensive, which was until recently a boys' grammar school, in a large city in the west of England. He was observed teaching a Year 10 class.

Chapter 11: Julie Marshall was teaching history in a comprehensive school, where she was Head of Humanities. The school served a predominantly white rural community, 15 miles from the centre of a large town in the Midlands. She was observed teaching a Year 10 class.

Chapter 12: Non Worrall was teaching English in a girls' comprehensive school in an outer London borough: her reflective enquiry was carried out in partnership with her Year 11 GCSE class.

4 Anne's approach: they all have their different ways to go

One way of accounting for Anne's teaching is to identify the tensions and oppositions that seem to characterize her understanding of her work. For example, her outspoken dissatisfaction with some of the structures of school achievement is in stark contrast with her equally articulate enthusiasm for the processes and rewards of learning. But another way of seeing is characterized by the connections that can be made within Anne's pedagogy, and by the productive synthesis that emerges from looking at the key constructs in her work as an undivided whole.

In Anne's classroom, and in her thinking, two distinct sets of views come together, in a kind of binocular vision, creating in-depth perceptions and forming a stereoscopic picture of learning without limits. Indeed, the binocular metaphor seems to have a further application. One of the pairs of ideas identifiable in Anne's thinking is the conjunction of detailed knowledge of the children she teaches in the here and now, the small print of their daily lives, with a view of their journeys beyond the present, into time, in their future lives. These two sets of perceptions add up to long-distance vision, in which she sees with great clarity both the people she teaches now ('I think of them as people', she once remarked, in a group discussion) and their infinitely varied trajectories in the future.

As this metaphor began to take shape, it was tempting simply to list the pairs of ideas that seemed to operate in combination in Anne's work, a whole range of concepts united by the discipline of 'and'. Such a list, created from Anne's own words and topics of discussion over the data collection period, would include:

clear planning	*and*	flexibility
a structure	*and*	gaps
school learning	*and*	learning in the world
the Yorkshire Dales	*and*	South Africa
reaching the targets	*and*	sustained personal effort
the safety of making mistakes	*and*	the excitement of a new challenge
awareness of constraints	*and*	awareness of how to deal with them

> the level achieved   *and*   the energy expended
> these children, here today   *and*   other children, my daughters, myself,
>   young people everywhere
>   here and now   *and*   anywhere ('I can teach in a car park')

And so on. However, the task of these accounts is not to generate lists, but to attempt to explain how the key ideas in each teacher's thinking work together to create the conditions for learning without limits. The account that follows is such an attempt.

It seems to be possible to group the key themes in Anne's teaching into three concentric circles or nesting boxes of concerns. At the centre of the model are people: this is the word Anne uses to refer to the young children she teaches, just as Iona Opie does in her captivating book *The People in the Playground* (1993). It is a particularly apt word in this model because it also signifies the adults (the grown-up people) that the children will become; it includes Anne herself, and her view of her distinct, and limited, powers and responsibilities as a teacher. Around this central theme are grouped sets of ideas about structures, the structures of contemporary schooling, as Anne sees them, and the structures of teaching and learning that allow for learning without limits. And around these structures are considerations of the context of the whole, both the world of the infant school, in which Anne and her pupils presently find themselves, and the wider society to which they also belong, as citizens of the world.

Contexts: the Yorkshire Dales and South Africa

This section shows how Anne's teaching takes account of her school and classroom contexts, and how it is located in the wider world, beyond West Yorkshire.

Anne works in a large infant school, on the edge of the Yorkshire Dales. The essentially rural setting was unmistakably observable, on every visit to the school. For example, Anne led an assembly based on the parable of the lost sheep, and painstakingly counted out a hundred sheep into her fold from the excited ranks of infants. The event concluded with lively and expert contributions from the children about the breeds of sheep being farmed in their neighbourhood and further afield. On another visit, a huge black hen was observed in a travelling cage, accompanied by her six or seven tiny fluffy chicks, crawling on her back, hiding in her feathers, crowding under her sheltering body.

One basic element in Anne's approach to teaching for learning without limits is to start with what the learners know best – themselves and their surroundings. For example, Anne taught a science lesson on touch (as part of a topic on 'ourselves' and the five senses). The activities included identifying objects by touch alone, and, consistently with Anne's pedagogical principles, the objects she had hidden in pillow-cases were from the real world (a compact disc, a bottle brush, a clothes peg) not pieces of classroom bric-a-brac. Anne explained how the theme would develop and, how in the sessions on sight, she would invite an ex-parent, a well-known figure in the community, who is blind, to talk to the children and read to them from Braille texts. In the interview in which she described her planning for this session, Anne referred to the QCA documentation that she and her Year 1 colleagues use as the basis for their science teaching, but made it very clear that her own thinking went deeper than drawing up a list of enjoyable activities. She explained her objectives for the theme of the senses in terms of children 'making sense of the world': the world, we note, not the QCA targets, or the Year 1 classroom in which these children work.

In Anne's model of learning, the immediate context of children's lives is where their learning starts, and they experience this living world actively. They paint, draw, model, run and skip, swim and sing, discuss, listen and rise to mathematical challenges as they arise in their talk. (How many Year 1 children can stand on one sheet of paper? Will it be more if we use reception class children? If one child has 20 teeth, how many do 50 have?) In an early interview Anne made explicit this aspect of her work: 'School's a great place for doing things.' By implication, she was identifying the difference between active and passive learning (a theme she developed in later discussions). Doing things, not listening to things, or being told things, or remembering things, or conforming to things, but doing things, with real world materials, that make human sense to the children: these are some of Anne's priorities. In looking at the first draft of this account of her work, in January 2000, Anne was dubious about whether she really always lived up to the description of her on the page. But she was definite about one aspect of the account: 'I would always be certain the children were doing something meaningful.'

For all her commitment to the here and now of the school and classroom context, and her determination that the children should learn from their first-hand experiences, there is no sense in which their curriculum diet is limited to what happens in the fields and streets where they live. Anne is a determined world traveller and brings her travels into the classroom with her. Although some of the children also travel far afield, Anne is not certain that they are helped to make the most of these experiences: 'I think it's tragic when they go on holiday and they haven't a clue where they've been.' She is determined to open the world and its treasures to her pupils: there is a model skeleton to support the topic on 'ourselves'; there are artefacts from China and India; there is a display that documents Anne's connections with a mixed-race community school in South Africa. Anne first made contact with this infant school, in Knysna, about 100 miles from Cape Town, in 1988, when Mandela was still in prison and the rule of apartheid was absolute. Photographs of Anne's visits to the school are an unexpected window on the wider world that opens out from this small Yorkshire town.

Anne often talks to the children about her own daughters, their experiences at university, their travels and the languages they speak. Her view of the world is unrestricted, unconfined, and she aspires to the same for her children. Learning must not be limited to the classroom, however active and meaningful that classroom may be. In a group discussion in Cambridge, Anne put it forcefully: 'There are a thousand things they can learn that Mrs Reay (i.e. herself) cannot teach them, but it's out there to be learned.' Anne assumes that her own appetite for learning and new experiences is every child's, and that she shares the responsibility for responding to that appetite.[1]

In many respects there are parallels between Anne's construction of the contexts within which she works and the model of the school proposed by John Dewey in *The School and Society* (1899). Denouncing what he sees as the isolation of the contemporary school from life, Dewey offers an alternative model, the fully permeable school, which is represented in Fig 4.1. On a less magnificent scale, Anne and her class of learners also reach out to the world around them, and invite its representatives to enrich and enliven theirs.

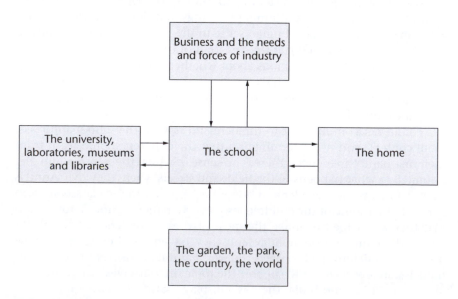

Figure 4.1 The fully permeable school (from Dewey 1899: 75)

Structures: schooling, teaching and learning

In this section of the account, Anne's capacity to accommodate and combine different perspectives within her binocular vision is especially striking. She is always aware, as the interviews and observations testify, of both the structures of school achievement and the structures of learning as it actually takes place. She does not reject the concepts of levels, standards or measures, but adds to them her belief in the importance of spontaneous, unpredictable acts of meaning-making. She talks a great deal about the detail of those quantifiable achievements, about spelling, presentation, left to right sequencing, copying accurately, pencil skills; but she always adds her own priorities into the sum. So, alongside those achievements that appear on pieces of paper, and can be used to measure one kind of progress, Anne sets other values: an emphasis on involvement and effort, on reading for pleasure, not just with accuracy, on interesting ideas, on noticing something no-one else has noticed (in a painting activity, for example, a child noticed and represented in fine detail the veins in a leaf he was studying). 'I want them to *think*', she emphasizes and, on another occasion, 'I honestly think they'll learn to spell when they get older'.

Anne is to some degree out of step with some of her colleagues on some of these issues, but she is in no sense an out-and-out rebel against the system. She is quite prepared to do the work of planning, and equally prepared to be flexible ('The plans aren't that important'). The learning needs attending to, as well as the plan. Of one maths activity she said, 'It's not on the plan, but they are fascinated. Why not let them be fascinated?' To the need for coverage, Anne adds the necessity of interest, and making sustained personal effort. There is room, in the structures of her classroom, for both kinds of endeavour. After a lively activity on alphabetical order ('I've got the letters of the alphabet here and you're all going to get one. When I say 'go', you're going to get into alphabetical order', which they did), the children were given time for activities of their own choice and regulation. Two girls were observed drawing with intense concentration, chatting sociably as they worked. Anne asked them about their drawings; one represented a fox's burrow, the other 'snakes and ice-creams'. Within Anne's discipline of 'and', these two children (and all their peers) can be honoured both for their knowledge of the alphabet and for their spontaneous and unpredictable inventions.

Another aspect of Anne's willingness to combine perspectives, rather than set them up in opposition to one another, can be seen in the way in which her discussion of children and classroom events, particularly in the post-observation interviews, moves freely, without any sense of dysjunction, between minute particulars and general principles. For example, in a discussion of ways in which tasks can be both structured and open-ended,

Anne described some work a small group of children had been doing, over a period of some days, with the magnetic 100 square (numbers 0–99). They had taken all the numbers off it and set themselves the task of reconstructing it. Anne's description showed how attentively she had observed their strategies. After completing the first row, 0–10, she said, 'Michael thought that the best thing was to collect the numbers for the rows, so he collected all the numbers with a 2 in; he got all the twos (i.e. 42 as well as 24 etc.), and then of course he hadn't got enough room.'

After this vivid description of a thoroughly worthwhile error in thinking, Anne goes straight on to define its value in more general terms:

> When they finally do it, they will then understand ... You could have given them a piece of paper and they would never have made ... they would never have made these discoveries on a piece of paper ... but I don't have anything in their books to show for that.

And in the same interview, she pushes the point home: the struggle, the process, the learning by doing, are as important as the achievement. 'Even if I teach them their two times table this week, they will have forgotten it by next week. But if they have learned how to learn this week, they won't forget that as easily.'

Without dismissing the theory of the general, or the activity of theorizing, Anne's keenest vision is trained on the particulars. Of a child's invented spelling of 'rough', for example, she remarked, with admiration: 'Look at it my way; to be able to spell it "ruf" means he has learned a lot.' She looks at it her way, and from other perspectives too, admitting the need to achieve accuracy, in due course, and also the imperative to honour learning in all its forms. In this instance, she also recognizes the determined effort of an individual learner 'going off and having a stab at it' (rather than acting out the dependence of an imperfect speller who checks every word with the teacher). In Anne's classroom the pressure for standards coexists with spontaneity and desire.

Her own synthesis, or summary of the attitudes elaborated here, is probably the best way to bring this section to a close. In the final interview, in June 2000, looking back over the year-long process of the project, and the ups and downs of her journal entries, Anne described what she saw as the most important condition for learning without limits across the school as a whole. 'There has to be a structure, with gaps in, so that today is today. If you have got a structure, you can cope with today.'

A structure with gaps in: is this an adequate or a satisfactory definition of a learning without limits school or classroom? Only if there is an accompanying account of what might fill those gaps; and Anne is abundantly clear and confident about how and why they should be filled – with the children's acts of meaning-making, problem-solving, invention, imagination and discovery. Anne and her colleagues, the constraints of Ofsted, SATs, QCA and so on, may set the structures, but in the gaps, the children take the lead.

People: the teacher and the children, now and in the future

In this third set of ideas, the power of the conjunction 'and' is persistently present. Anne is clear that she has powers and responsibilities, as a teacher, and that there is another side to the story: that however effective her best efforts as a teacher are, it is always the children who do their own learning, who lead their own lives. Although it is Anne who explains the task, it is they who explain the world to themselves. At the very first selection interview with Anne, in the summer of 1999, she made this conjunction clear. Towards the end of the interview she asked us, the interviewers, what we were trying to find out. Our reply was given in terms of teachers and pedagogy; Anne was not satisfied. 'What about the children being responsible for their own learning?' she asked. She went on to emphasize 'There is always more to the process than what I do.' The teacher alone, however wise or insightful, is not a sufficient condition for the learning without limits classroom; there are also always the children, their energies, their desires, and these themes appear regularly in the interview data:

> They must do it for themselves, not just to please me.

> They could become docile learners.

> They need to know there's more than I can teach them.

> I encourage them [to know] that they will learn for the rest of their lives.

Anne's elder daughter Helen, who recently graduated with a first class degree in architecture, was a frequent topic in Anne's interviews. But years ago, when she was attending the school where Anne now teaches, 'She got stuck in a bottom set ... and we knew she could do more.' The history of her daughter's close escape from being labelled a failure, and her capacity to overcome her dyslexia and to learn without limits when the conditions were right, are significant memories for Anne. But even so, Anne is clear about the shared responsibility for Helen's success. Anne and her husband arranged extra tuition for their daughter, but Anne emphasizes that this was only part of the plan, 'Helen wasn't going to be beaten'. The teacher and the child: neither one is an island, alone unto herself.

Anne's view of herself as a teacher and as a person, teaching people, is another interesting combination. There are times when she speaks very modestly of herself, with a marked sense of professional humility, drawing on her own experiences as an unremarkable pupil and college student, and there is also a strong element of pride, courage and conviction. After completing an Open University degree in maths, her preferred subject, Anne's view of herself changed: 'I'm actually quite good at maths! It's taken a long time to dawn on me … It really is only now.' It is not just in the discipline of mathematics that Anne knows she has something to say. In the interview in which Anne reflected on an early draft of this account, she was asked if reading it had affected her teaching. Her reply was forcibly expressed:

> It gave me some sort of conviction that I was right … that it was accepted that it worked this way, and if need be, to stand and argue your corner. It also made it obvious that my views on education as a whole were actually more important than whether or not we all manage to do our two times tables this week.

Anne is positioning herself here as both fox and hedgehog. She knows many little things about schools and children and how to teach the tables, and she knows one big thing: big ideas are more important than little ideas. Her unbounded confidence in every learner's potential is one of the very big ideas.

Another significant aspect of Anne's thinking about the people she teaches is her capacity to see them as they are now, in all their individuality and difference, and also to see the variety in their future trajectories, 'because they all have their different ways to go'. Her emphasis on the significance of the future in the present is in complete harmony with Dewey's formulation of the same insight in *The Child and the Curriculum* (1902: 14): 'Everything we see in children is transitional, promises and signs of the future … not to be treated as achievements, cut off and fixed; they are prophetic, signs of an accumulating power and interest.'

Dewey's almost Vygotskian metaphor (the seeds and buds of future learning) is simply another way of formulating Anne's long-distance vision, her commitment to her pupils as people with futures, who must not be put into boxes, because they all have their different ways to go. Interestingly, this commitment finds an echo in a writer of a very different educational and political stance, Antonio Gramsci, who argued for 'a humanistic school, a school which does not mortgage a child's future, a school which does not force the child's will, his intelligence and growing awareness to run along tracks to a pre-determined station' (Entwhistle 1979: 133).

For Anne, teaching for learning without limits has many dimensions. There are considerations of space and time: only the world is big enough for children's learning, and only the future is long enough for their lives. There are considerations of responsibility, which is always shared (I and they, the teacher and the children); and there are considerations of value. Measurable achievements in mathematics, science and literacy are important achievements, and so are love of learning, fascination with learning, the engagement of the imagination, the energy and enthusiasm of the learners in finding out for themselves and making sense of the world. Anne's capacity for binocular and long-distance vision, in which she sees far beyond the limits of the classroom and the school, unites all these considerations.

Note

1 There is an echo here of Baudelaire's beautiful poem 'Le Voyage':
'Pour l'enfant, amoureux de cartes et d'estampes,
L'univers est égal à son vaste appétit!'

5 Claire's approach: a thinking classroom

There is every good reason why the children in Claire's class listen to her when she is addressing the whole group. It is not because they are afraid of her or she has promised them a treat if they listen, but because each child knows from experience that she is worth listening to. It is an outward manifestation of Claire's philosophy: learning is for all the children in her class, in which there is a powerful sense of inclusion. She often emphasizes that 'every child has something to offer'. While she acknowledges that some children are not going to find learning easy in every respect, she feels it is important to recognize that one 'should always remember that ability can depend on what you're looking at'. The pace of these children, their attention level and their need for more practice are taken account of in her planning but in no way does she see any of them as less important members of the class, less entitled to what everyone has a right to. Everybody is entitled to the same learning experiences, framed to suit their needs, so that nobody misses out on a significant learning opportunity.

The teaching and learning environment

So it was that, whenever Claire's class was being observed – 36 of them, well-built 8- and 9-year-old youngsters, squashed into a classroom intended for 26 – despite the physical constraints, there was always a look of anticipation across the whole room when she explained what they would be doing next. One or two children, pressed up against the back of another's chair, may have looked uncomfortable, but they knew it was a problem that was shortly going to be sorted out. In the meantime, what was being said mattered to each one of them more than this temporary but familiar discomfort. Their experience of Claire was that she brought worthwhile things for them to do and think about. Indeed, it is one of Claire's key principles that one should 'remember that enjoyment and interest has an important place in children's learning, particularly in keeping the momentum going'. Claire herself finds learning interesting and enjoyable and she goes to considerable lengths to extend her children's learning experiences, often taking them on visits to such places as the Viking Museum in York, the Millennium Dome and other more local places of interest. Within the classroom environment she actively tries to keep the children engaged by providing opportunities for enjoyment and interest, 'especially when the task or lesson seems initially boring'. For example, in a literacy hour session, she introduced a card game that the whole class played together with an evident sense of fun, even though it had to do with the revision of a less than enthralling grammar lesson on apostrophes.

The school in which Claire was teaching served a large south Lincolnshire village, and the modern building had recently replaced a nineteenth-century school one. The numbers in the school were rising faster than expected, however, and inside the building the impression was of a small school notably lacking in space. For instance, there was no identifiable library space and the staffroom, for 12, was no wider than a railway carriage and certainly shorter.

Claire had taught in the school for several years and was familiar with its background and its families. Most of these families were employed, largely in transport, light industry and market gardening. Many families had lived in the area for generations, although there were a number of RAF families who only stayed in the district for a few years before moving on. Some children from the school went on to grammar school each year (Lincolnshire still retaining the 11 plus) but the majority attended the local comprehensive.

Claire's classroom was typical of most in the school in that it was newly painted and had bright, modern furniture and space for little else. However, although it was noticeably cramped, Claire always managed to create a room that looked attractive and inviting. The subject of the actual classroom environment, and how she planned for it, did not feature in any of her interviews, although Claire's evident attention to it signified that she felt that part of her professionalism as a teacher was to keep it looking orderly and attractive. This linked in with her views on creating educational experiences for children that were interesting and enjoyable.

Establishing a thinking classroom

The timetable of Claire's day followed the demands of the National Curriculum and the exigencies of availability (for example, hall times), but below the surface, Claire hoped that she was in the process of creating a classroom with more than targets to be met and boxes to be ticked. In her own words, the key to creating learning without limits was and is through establishing what she terms a *'thinking classroom'*. While Claire did not go into detail about her concept of herself as a 'thinking teacher', there is plenty of evidence of her own intellectual exploration and personal reflections. Reference to thinking about her own teaching is a constant and unmistakable theme, and runs through her observations, not only about learning and teaching, but also about the children in her class.

It is how she arrives, sometimes tentatively, at particular conclusions: for example, she said on one occasion, 'It's the stage I perhaps got to in my thinking ...' It is how she tries to make sense of events and plans ahead; she is open to changing her opinions and reconsidering her ideas. A typical statement in this respect was 'It's something I'm still thinking about and trying to work through.' It was noticeable in the interviews that she often said she had 'thought about something afterwards' or 'on reflection I ... ' and 'I hadn't realized that ... ' and 'We need to *look* and think about things all the time.' She used 'I think' or 'I thought' well over a dozen times in one interview in relation to either children or a variety of classroom situations.

It was on the basis of her own reflections about teaching and learning that she arrived at the notion of an inclusive education, which, for Claire, means that learning can be without limits for anyone. As she wrote in her letter of application to the project, 'the principles apply as much to adults as to children. Therefore I assume no limits to individual potential in my dealings with colleagues, family, friends and with myself!' She also acknowledged in the same letter that she has 'an open-minded attitude to opinions and evidence'; it is interesting that one of the constraints Claire perceives as a barrier to learning without limits in a whole-school situation is the presence of other members of staff who do not prioritize thinking in a similar way. For Claire, much of the job of an effective teacher, particularly one who is committed to removing limits on children's learning, lies in those thinking skills that are epitomized by 'planning, adjusting, reflecting, targeting and enabling'.

Like most honest teachers, Claire is aware that not even with considered forethought will everything necessarily turn out as intended. As she cheerfully admits, it is important to recognize those 'occasions where you might need to change your plans midway through a session'. She is not afraid, indeed thinks it important, to share her thinking with the children in her class. 'As I always say to [them], you don't learn anything if you get everything right all the time, do you?'

That is not to say that Claire is unsure of herself: her planning schedules and her class organization reflect her confidence and attention to detail. Instead, there is a sense of there being more to learn: however well organized one may be and however clear about one's objectives, this is not the whole picture, even though, to Claire, the latter is particularly important. She has certain criteria against which she assesses herself. For instance, she says she frequently asks herself: 'Am I using my time wisely? What were my objectives?'

It was not uncharacteristic of her to say about one child's achievements that she had not really thought through what she might have been expecting of him: 'What was I actually asking of him? What [was] I actually looking for?'

To Claire, the term 'the thinking classroom' is deliberately and purposefully inclusive; it applies to the kind of skills and attitudes she wants to be able to develop throughout her class. It is to be a place where each and every child learns to think and to do so in a variety of ways, and a variety of situations. Such thinking includes problem-solving, seeing links or connections and reflecting on what they have done or are about to do. She emphasizes that she wants to be able to help every child to see that these thinking skills are transferable and will help them in all their learning. For instance, on two occasions observed, she invited all the children to 'think out' how they would undertake certain jobs to do with a forthcoming class activity. In recognition that this would need time, she told them they would be given five minutes to engage in this kind of thinking. On the second occasion, the children were asked to 'think out' what they might need in order to undertake particular tasks; this too was accompanied by the reassurance that they would be given a certain length of time in order to do their thinking. This did not seem novel or unusual to the children and they all used the time quickly and constructively, as if familiar to such instructions. 'Thinking', in other words, was a recognized and worthwhile activity in its own right; like other activities it was due its own specified and particular time if it was to be undertaken properly. No one was excluded from this activity and there was an expectation, which appeared to be met, that they would all engage and be able to engage in it.

Claire is aware that there are real risks to the children in seeing their learning as simply an unconnected series of mini-skills. In line with her emphasis on thinking as being 'the key to learning without limits', she considers that this can be greatly helped when the children see the 'connectedness of things'; she sees it as part of the teachers' work to 'support the children in making links – nothing happens in isolation'. She is concerned that 'sometimes I feel that children miss the point because they just don't see the links between what they are doing'. Learning skills can only be seen to make sense if they are presented to the children as 'transferable, relevant and interesting'. It was noticeable that in each lesson Claire would stop the class at various points to ask them if a certain skill seemed familiar (for example, using reference books when they were finding out about mini-beasts or Ancient Egyptians) and to ask them if remembering how to exercise certain skills, like making lists of things they might need, might help them on other occasions.

It is by helping children to make such links that Claire feels they can be helped to move away from thinking that what they do is simply to generate a product. As she says, they think 'doing your best means producing this incredibly neat piece of work', and she wants to move them towards a view that involves process, a view that *this* is the important part of their work: 'moving them away from thinking about learning as just task-ori-entated'. On re-reading a classroom journal she had kept for some weeks during the previous term, she was struck by how much time she had spent on 'trying to get through to the children that it is not necessarily the end product – it's what goes before, it's the transferring of skills and getting them to see the links'.

The children were also asked to think in quite abstract ways about their own learning. For example, following a session in which they were invited to think about themselves as learners, Claire asked the class to think about how 'we are going to change the situation to make learning easier for you'. The children's answers showed that they were very ready to think about such questions. To Claire, enabling children to think for themselves means releasing them from dependence and passivity, particularly those who had been deemed less able and who had consequently taken on this judgement as meaning *'unable'*. In her own estimation, Claire had been pleased to think that she had now managed to get the class to the stage 'of being quite good at working independently'. She felt confirmed in this observation by the fact that when she left the school, the teacher who succeeded her com-mented more than once on the children's improved attitude: 'I think Vicky was quite surprised at how independent they were – she was expecting the worst!'

Expectations of learners

On moving to a new school Claire realized quite quickly that she could not assume that her new class was at the same level of independence as her pre-vious one and that she would accordingly have to make adjustments: 'I just don't think they've been given time to think.' That her previous class had learned to do so, in Claire's estimation, was largely a matter of expec-tation. As she said, 'I felt that I got to the stage when I was quite clear in my own mind what I was expecting and they [the children] understood what I was expecting.' She made no exceptions to this, the expectation was one she had for all the class; all the children could, in their own ways, become more independent, more competent thinkers than they had previously been. To Claire, to give them such skills was, and indeed is, to give children the key to removing limits to their learning. Other kinds of expectations, too, play an important part for Claire, and she commented on more than one occasion that it was necessary to keep them high, 'bearing in mind that one can sometimes expect too little'. Likewise, experience had also told her that one 'can expect too much'. It is a continual matter of balance that constantly exercises Claire. She feels there is a certain 'comfort zone' that should be aimed for in which expectations are matched to the individual: '[They] need to feel comfortable and "at home" and at ease – not to the extent that they aren't going to *do* anything though!' She also adds: 'I think [of] "comfortable" in terms of being happy with the teacher's expectations and understanding them.' She was also aware that for the children this included how they felt comfortable 'with their friends as well'. This in its turn raised a certain conflict of interest because, as she sees it, 'feeling comfortable in relation to their peers could also induce a certain complacency'. As she admits, 'It is quite a deep thing actually to try to get across to them, how to keep the motivation going and then knowing that they can achieve an unlimited level of whatever it might be.'

Connected to this idea of 'comfort' is another of Claire's concerns about potential barriers to children feeling there is no ceiling to their learning. While wanting them to be fully involved and engaged in what they are doing, she knows what can happen if children are made to feel anxious or unduly worried by what they are being asked to do. As she says, 'I would hate to think that I was doing something that made any child anxious.' Indeed, 'quite central to [her] teaching philosophy', she says, is 'getting children away from a sense of failure, or offering them tasks or activities in which there is a distinct potential for failure'.

It seems that Claire's work in this direction had not been in vain, because none of the four children interviewed reported feeling unduly concerned if they did not get things right or did not understand straight away what Claire had asked them to do. Each of them had evolved certain coping strategies for such occasions: for example, Terry said he went directly to Claire if he was stuck; Roxanne said she went to a friend and if that did not work she would have another go at working things out for herself. Kerry had a perennial problem, however, and one with which all learners will surely sympathize. As she said, 'You see, I get all the *questions* right, and then the *answers* go all wrong.' At these times Kerry said she usually asked for a bit of help or waited for Claire to have 'another little talk' with the class, as it was common practice for Claire regularly to review activities and progress during a session.

An occasion at Claire's new school, a much smaller village school with 60 children, illustrated very vividly for her the potential for failure and for lowering vital self-esteem, which could follow on from inappropriate expectations for a child. The situation came about when, at the start of term, she had given all the Year 6 children their Year 6 workbooks, only to be told by other children in the class that although Joseph '*was* Year 6, he didn't do Year 6 books: Miss, he only does Year 4 ones'. Joseph, unsurprisingly, was a boy whose low self-esteem was already marked and in Claire's opinion he required nothing more of this nature that could reduce it still further. She consequently adapted some of the Year 6 workbooks to suit him.

Knowing your pupils

Flexibility in Claire's planning has been touched on above, in regard to both expectations and being able to be adaptable. She sees it as just one element of a classroom in which the limits to learning are removed by various strategies, the most important being, in her estimation, and she herself writes it in capitals: 'KNOW YOUR PUPIL!' If the 'thinking classroom' is, as she says, 'the key to learning without limits', then, for Claire, knowing your pupils is the keyhole into which the key fits.

Claire also stresses that for her it is important to be open-minded about the children in the class and to see them as individuals: '[There's] a danger of having preconceived ideas about children and making assumptions about their previous learning, skills, experience etc.' It is also important to notice the pattern of social relationships within the class and recognize that this is all part of knowing each child. Although Claire often refers to 'individuals as learners' rather than using the term 'individuals', her implicit knowledge of the individual personalities within the class is very extensive and her comments on the characteristics of the four children interviewed were corroborated by what they said. For instance, her comment on Roxanne was that she had chosen her to be interviewed because she felt she didn't 'quite have a full understanding of where she [Roxanne] was coming from'. She seems to 'drift off in her mind and she will sort of say things that aren't linked to what we are doing'. Roxanne, in her turn, considers that Claire knew how she learnt 'sometimes'; when asked if there were times when she thought of Claire, 'Oh – you haven't understood what I'm trying to say', she agreed very readily: 'Yeah, sometimes in my head I do – I don't say it out loud though.' Brian was sure that Claire knew him and how he liked to learn; he commented that (as indeed she had remarked) he preferred working things out for himself and enjoyed learning interesting new things rather than opting for practice work.

Claire's close knowledge of the children in her class seemed to play a large part in the direction her planning took for them; one of the most important influences in this respect was a consideration of children's different learning styles. Over the two terms Claire had been involved in the project, she had become increasingly interested in this aspect of learning and was beginning to see it as having real relevance for how she assessed children's responses and attitudes and her plans for their work. As she said at the time, 'The learning styles thing, I think that is something that I could put more thought to in terms of planning ... it ties in with getting the best out of children.' Knowing the children better as learners has not necessarily been at a conscious level, though. She thought that in fact it had sometimes affected her approach 'subconsciously. I'm not sure I've been very good at *consciously* sitting down and saying: "Right, I now know this, so I am going to make a huge effort to do this that way or the other". But I think subconsciously it does. I think it does affect what you do ... '

Claire found that the concept of learning styles helped in 'looking at overall planning. The balance of activities across a term maybe. And also helping me to remember to vary the approaches within a subject and with different children.' She also saw that there could be a potential downside, of having to be careful to avoid 'pandering to a child's preferred style because otherwise they are only going to be able to learn in one way'. The observations made in a variety of lessons in the spring term showed very clearly how Claire allowed for different kinds of learning; in all the lessons some children were writing, others drawing and making, others studying reference books and others looking carefully at pictures and artefacts. When they were working in groups, for instance, in one lesson when they were making mini-beast booklets, the children were given a wide choice of activity. They decided quite quickly for themselves which aspect of the work they would undertake; for example, creative work, list making, organizing, writing notes. It seemed as though they were already aware of 'what worked best for them'.

Social learning

The high priority Claire gives to thinking skills is complemented by her awareness of the importance of developing the children's social skills. If the class is to 'work' as a unit, there has to be a degree of harmony between the children and the teacher ('The teacher is *not* the enemy!' as she once said); there should be a sense of 'partnership between children and teacher, learning together and from each other'. This is not something she either takes for granted or assumes does not need planning for. If the children do not feel secure and happy, or if they feel socially isolated, there can well arise a barrier to learning without limits as Claire sees it. There should be a sense of 'pulling together in the same direction', and that cannot be accomplished in a situation in which children's social development receives little attention because it is undervalued and its importance is unrecognized.

In an interesting music lesson, prioritizing the development of the children's social skills was uppermost in Claire's aims, as she felt that this particular class needed more experiences of this kind. As a result, the children were not grouped by achievement, nor by their usual friendship group; Claire deliberately placed them alongside children with whom they did not generally work. She felt that, as a whole, they were not a particularly socially mature class and this session could offer them the chance of a positive experience and of widening their knowledge of each other. As she said, 'One of my targets for it was getting them to work in different groups'. Even so, knowing the individuals in the class, she had taken care over the placing of one or two children who, she thought, might find it difficult to work with 'too many people who were unfamiliar' to them. This was characteristic of Claire's practice and supported what she said on another occasion about the importance of remembering that 'One should look out for personality and ability clashes in groups'.

It is characteristic of her teaching that Claire refers to the children or pupils in her class as 'people' quite frequently. As children, they may be less experienced, less mature, but to her that does not make them lesser mortals, and she has a basic respect for them as fellow human beings. 'People' is indeed how she sees them. For Claire, the work of creating the 'thinking classroom' entails helping the people in her class to see the links between what they are learning, to understand that it is the *process* of learning as much as the creation of products that is important and to recognize the need for reflection, problem-solving and thinking things through. Knowing each of them as individuals, understanding their learning styles, accommodating 'where they're at', planning, adjusting, enabling, keeping them engaged and interested are the means by which Claire hopes to arrive at a thinking classroom, and, to restate her aim, thereby fashion the key to learning without limits.

Constraints and barriers to learning without limits

Claire recognizes that there are constraints and barriers to what she would like to achieve. Some, as she sees it, lie within herself; for instance, her need for more ex-perience, the changes in her expectations and priorities, the adequacy of her reflections and observations and her necessarily piecemeal knowledge about the children and their circumstances. These, however, are constraints that she feels can be worked upon, that are open to change and improvement; she is realistic in her recognition that learning without limits is not going to be achieved overnight but is a goal to keep constantly in mind.

Other constraints, though, she sees as being less under her control, and these range from the whole-school setting to the macro-level of government demands. With regard to the former, she cites the problems that can arise from isolation in a school characterized by superficial teamwork and communication and little sense of shared goals or values. Claire is also very aware that physical constraints, such as a lack of classroom space and resources, can often militate against innovation and development. The latter constraint, the overprescription of government demands, includes for Claire, among other things, 'continuous [and unnecessary] demands for justification ... ' and the promotion of a culture that emphasizes 'technicalities and presentation ... at the expense of a wide range of other skills that children can demonstrate'. The new, if hesitant, government interest in thinking and problem-solving skills, which she welcomes, has yet, in her experience, to filter down, and she would like to see it become 'more of an acceptable thing'.

For a teacher like Claire who sees the thinking classroom as being the key to learning without limits, this is not too surprising a wish; in her mind she knows what a classroom based on these principles would be like and she thinks she 'needs to be very clear about what my ideal would be'. Her perfect classroom, besides being large and significantly resourced, 'would be calm, focused and purposeful ... There would be a variety of things going on most of the time; sometimes [the children] may be doing a written task but within that a range of activities may be going on.' Finally, she adds, in this perfect classroom 'The children would all be smiling!'

6 Alison's approach: an open invitation

Alison offers an open invitation to her children: it is an invitation to all comers, an invitation that she hopes they will find irresistible. It is to join her in the adventure of learning of all kinds, an opportunity for the children to extend themselves as far as and further than they may sometimes have thought possible and to do so in an environment of encouragement and interest. As she sees it, accepting the invitation opens the way to a classroom where learning has no limits, and where children feel themselves to be increasingly in charge of their own learning.

At the same time as becoming aware that they matter to her as individual young people in their own right, with their own interests, opinions, uncertainties and achievements, the children are also made aware of themselves as being members of a team, of being a 'learning community'. This is particularly important to Alison, who sees the potential for removing limits to learning in the creation of a genuine excitement around learning in which every one of the children in the class can be caught up.

Whatever lesson of Alison's was being observed, it always seemed to be accompanied by a sense of anticipation, of expectation. It was not only evident in her physical expression and stance, but also seemed to be present in the children. Whatever might be expected of them, there was an almost tangible feeling that they shared Alison's view that 'we are on a kind of journey together' and that this journey would enable them to share the excitement of learning. Indeed, not to share this excitement could be to diminish, to limit even, their engagement with the activity of learning.

Another source of this sense of excitement was the learning situation itself, which for both Alison and the children seemed to hold a sense of unknown potential: while she acknowledged the need for an underlying structure and carefully provided one – as she said, 'making sure you have enough strategies and structures in place' – there was none the less the feeling that this did not preclude an unexpected landfall to their journey. Alison speaks of 'encouraging the sense [among all the class] that "we could do this" or "we could do that"'. One of the lessons observed in Alison's Year 5 classroom was a drama session, which exemplified not only these values but others that she holds to be significant and important in the work of learning. The narrative account of this lesson that follows has been written to illustrate the ways in which Alison's core values work together, in practical ways, for the good of all the children. While Alison herself did not consider it to be a particularly auspicious lesson (and indeed it was spiked by the kind of minor institutional exasperations that can be cumulatively destructive of the best prepared sessions), there can be seen in it many examples of Alison's key constructs, her awareness of the ways in which it is only too easy to place limits on children's learning, and also her great expertise in finding ways of lifting those limits.

The dynamics of the group

The drama lesson took place, as usual, in the school hall. This was the second drama lesson of the term and the organizational side of affairs was not helped by the fact that it ran concurrently with swimming lessons; this introduced a certain unpredictability into the lesson, as groups would be leaving and arriving at the start and in the middle of the drama session. On this particular day there had been an alteration to these groups and a new, hastily formed one, constituting the 'strongest swimmers', had to leave the drama lesson at its start because of a forthcoming swimming gala.

Alison is particularly aware of the implications of the social structure of the class for children's learning and their attitudes towards it, and she observed that the characteristic of this group was that it contained few of the really dominant characters 'and the fact that some of those children weren't there changed the dynamic of the whole group'. The altered situation meant that some children who were naturally rather tentative were unexpectedly placed in roles for which they would not normally have volunteered. This was perceived by Alison as not only being helpful to these children, who were given an unexpected opportunity, but also as giving her the chance to observe what she sometimes refers to as 'the disappearing children', those who normally keep in the background, get on quietly with things, are no trouble but, she feels, are basically unknown to her. This was a chance to get to know them a little better. As the children began to take part in the lesson, which involved trying to recreate some of the stories and events of the Second World War (an ongoing class topic at the time), Alison was pleased to see that these children were beginning to take up the chance to show themselves. She commented, 'The whole point of it is to encourage children, those who haven't done it before, but could this time. That's the whole point of it, isn't it?'

She began with the instruction to find a space, sit down and then, as they listened to the beat of a tambourine, follow its rhythm in any way that suggested itself. Alison could have given a more conventional instruction – that is, to run if they thought they detected a running pattern, or to walk, skip or march depending on the rhythm – but true to what she considers important, even a five minute warm-up like this has the potential to contribute to one of her overall aims, which is to 'get the children to the point where, hopefully, they can see themselves as being part of something, rather than something that is done unto them'. She saw this lesson, even the brief introduction to it, as an opportunity to help children by giving them the chance to feel more noticed as individuals; their need for affirmation, she considers, should be met whenever possible. To fail to do so, as she sees it, is to set a limit on one of the ways in which children's self-confidence and learning can be enhanced.

Taking the lead or being led

As the tambourine rhythm became livelier, so, unsurprisingly, did the children's movement. However, it was noticeable that one or two were becoming overlively and were starting to get engrossed in watching and copying each other's acceleration. Noticing this but without drawing attention to it, 'not having to do things in an obvious way', as she says, Alison brought this short part of the session to a close and gave them the next instruction. Reminding them of the work they had undertaken the previous week, she asked them 'to imagine you're travelling back in time to the topic we've learned about – then I'll come round and ask you who you are, what you're doing, who you are with, the sounds you can hear and so on.' Without hesitation, quite a number of boys lay on their stomachs and wriggled forward on the floor, sighting along imaginary rifles; one girl said she was shooting someone. This was not what Alison had envisaged happening and she realized she had a choice: to continue with what they were doing and take it where it would, or to change direction. She was quick to recognize that the make-up of the group and their level of maturity meant that she was 'going to have to control it more than I would want to … because I feel the group need management … They were slipping back into a stereotype view rather than anything they had learned about [and] I didn't want to go down that road.'

Alison did not criticize what the boys were doing; instead she settled on the activity of one girl, Kirsty, who was evidently doing something different. It transpired that she was imagining herself having just been evacuated to the countryside and was looking around her to see if she recognized anything. The children were then instructed to follow Kirsty's lead and Alison widened out the opportunities for them by asking them to imagine the different situations they might find themselves in if they were evacuees, something they had studied quite extensively in the classroom. If she felt she had had to curtail the work developing in one direction, she opened it up for them in another. Two children quickly showed by their movements that they had each thought of something and Alison asked Natalie, who was crouching down and alternately rubbing her eyes and stretching out her hands, to explain who she was to the rest of the class: 'I'm a three-year-old and I'm lost and nobody's with me.' A boy, Shaun, who was walking slowly backwards and bending down as he went, straightened up to explain he was being Mr Freeman, who had recently been invited as a visitor to the school to tell the class what it had been like in the 1940s. Shaun as the young Mr Freeman was now walking down some steps into a small bomb shelter. Alison acknowledged their contributions and then developed the small beginning of Kirsty's, as she judged it to be the best way to take the class forward on that particular occasion: 'I took the idea of the evacuation because the children who were able to talk about being evacuated [out of that group] were the ones that came across as having some sort of empathy with what it could have been like, which wasn't necessarily something that I envisaged doing but it was the closest to what they were able to be part of'.

This awareness of the need to shape what she was doing to the nature of the child or the group is a recognizable theme in Alison's approach to learning and teaching. It can be seen in her forward planning but it can also be seen in the decisions she has to make quickly, as in this situation. Her long-term aim is, in either event, 'to give them the opportunity to come in at the task where they are most comfortable and then maybe to move on quickly or stay there and consolidate ... It's a way of ... you know, they don't need to feel failing in any way.'

Judging that the children had probably gone as far as was profitable in the first part of the drama exercise, Alison brought them back together by using the tambourine once more, to mark a move into a more focused activity. Once they were together again, they were invited to imagine that they were all just about to be evacuated. She reminded them of the work they had done in class about evacuation and how often the evacuee children did not know where they were going or who they were going to stay with. Thus they were to imagine that they were such children; Alison told them that after a few moments she would stop and ask them questions such as what they had chosen to pack, what they were looking forward to and what they were feeling scared about.

Transcending limits

In her original planning for this drama session, Alison had considered that it was a necessary link to the work they had been doing in class; they had read stories and had had discussions in which a number of quite difficult issues had been raised, so she thought it was necessary and appropriate 'to give the children the opportunity to play out some of the things that they have heard about'. She recognized they might have had a need to do this but at the same time she has a particular concern for children's emotional lives in school and feels they have to be carefully handled. As she says, 'I think we have to be very careful [about children's feelings]. You have to take care not to prod at something that's a bit too sensitive.' Alongside this, to fail to recognize or meet children's emotional needs for affirmation could also be to set a limit to one of the ways in which children's self-confidence and learning could be enhanced. Even so, she considers that in creating situations in which she has tried, as far as possible, to avoid such pitfalls, children can experience 'a sense of security, of being safe ... which can free them up'. This sense of freeing children, of releasing them from the ceilings that are so often placed upon them and that affect the way they see themselves as learners, is a continuous thread running through Alison's practice. With the provision of appropriate experiences, support and encouragement, she believes that children can take themselves to places they did not feel would ever be their territory. This is one of the reasons why she feels drama is such an important experience for children, as well as for her as a teacher. She feels that 'some of them come to life in drama in a way they do nowhere else ... [It] enables children to open up in a way that they would not normally do in school'.

After five minutes, Alison stopped the class and asked them to 'freeze' in position so that she could ask the 'evacuees' some questions and the other children could hear their answers. They all admitted to feeling scared and a number said they were going alone. Their body language spoke of a genuine seriousness and the children became increasingly quiet during the exercise. She now asked them to imagine that they were on their way to school on the morning of the evacuation and that their parents would be there with them: they were to play 'playground' games until one child (nominated as the teacher) would ask them to line up in lines of girls and boys and read out the register, to which they should respond.

Learning about individuals: expanding opportunities

In the event, Stephen, the child chosen as the teacher, found it difficult to manage the role but Alison thanked him for his efforts. Although he looked pleased at being relieved of the position he did not seem disheartened; in fact he gave something of a skip! Later, Alison commented that she did not regret having chosen him; she was aware that she 'probably took most risks in choosing children she didn't know [so well]' but it represented an opportunity for Stephen that he might not otherwise have had. Her sense of justice runs deep, and she firmly believes that 'It wouldn't really be equitable – to choose the same ones you know will perform.' Offering opportunities was one of Alison's priorities, and she constantly worked to ensure that 'I provide opportunities all the time; ceaselessly having opportunities there that children can show you [what they can really do].'

Looked at in one way, Stephen's contribution in the role of teacher might not have been considered successful but because of Alison's tactful handling of what was happening and the way she brought his particular involvement to a close, before he started to flounder, it did not develop into an identifiable situation of failure. Alison is very aware of what this feeling of failure can do to children and, as we have seen, takes great pains to plan and structure the children's work groupings and experiences so that as far as possible they do not experience it. Although much of her teaching in this particular session had to be an immediate response to the situation, rather than following her intended plan, she was aware all the way through that she wanted them to be able to take something positive away with them; when the session finished she said she felt that 'when they went out of the hall none of them had failed', despite unforeseen hiccups.

The next child she chose to be the teacher was Jakinder, a girl of Indian origin, usually a very quiet, unassuming child who 'never asks to be singled out' and one who 'could make herself completely disappear'. In this lesson, rather to Alison's surprise, Jakinder was 'obviously wanting to get involved in the drama'. For instance, she was taking different poses and trying out different voices, 'so I thought I would give her her moment'. This was consistent with much of what Alison has to say about the importance of noticing individuals within the class (as well as seeing them as part of a team) and also giving those individuals the chance to try out things they might not otherwise undertake. As she said, 'it's always looking for ways in which to make things better for individual children'.

Jackie was another ostensibly 'quiet girl, who used to be a very softly spoken type who wouldn't speak out'. It was only by observing her in a drama lesson that Alison realized 'how much more there was to her character … I could see a totally different side to her character then, a very lively side that I had never witnessed before.' Such experiences alone would have justified the use of drama as far as Alison was concerned, but she also claims that it helps the children to gain a greater insight into themselves and that 'It's another way in, isn't it? And we ought to be exploring these.'

Revising expectations

As the drama lesson continued, Alison noticed that some boys were starting to follow the undesirable example of another youngster who was beginning to push through the queues and argue with the 'teacher'. She drew them back to the activity by inviting the children to imagine what it must have felt like to have been going off on a train, perhaps for the first time, and that they should now check their labels and say goodbye to their parents.

Alison reminded herself that 'You have to go from where they are ... if they are not ready for it, they find it very difficult ... and you have to take a step back and say, right, this is too hard, we'll try something easier [to begin with] ... If their response is inhibited, they need more time.' It was noticeable that she did not blame the children but that she considered it was her professional responsibility to reflect upon what she herself might have done to bring about the situation and how she might correct it on another occasion. This flexibility and willingness to use and learn from such situations in order to improve the learning chances of the children are strong and constant themes throughout the whole of Alison's commentary and classroom decisions. It was characteristic of her approach in general that she said: 'I try to see where we go next and if my expectations are too high, it doesn't mean we won't get there, it just means I need to take them much more slowly.'

Pacing it, timing it, finding something in which the children are interested so that they keep their involvement in learning: all help, in Alison's view, to heighten the sense of possible and potential success. It may be that she has to fine-tune her particular expectations from time to time for certain groups and for individual children, but that in no way diminishes her sense of the importance of her expectations: as she maintains, 'It's all about expectation, isn't it?'

Once the children seemed together again, Alison moved them on to another part of the unfolding drama, asking them to imagine that they had arrived at their destination and were being walked up to a village hall where people would meet them who might choose them to be their children. Once they had arrived in the hall she chose a child to be 'the lady' who interviewed the children before they went off to their prospective parents. There then seemed to arise one of those moments when a silence becomes almost tangible; all the children appeared to be deeply involved in this situation and looked towards the 'interviewing lady' with real attention. The chosen girl, Aisha, then went quickly across to Alison and asked her if she could add something to the questions that it had been suggested she could ask the 'evacuees'.

This was a development that particularly pleased Alison. In her original planning for this session she had hoped to start off by 'sort of managing the situation … and then they, the children, walk in and take the story wherever they want to take it'. Her long-term aim for drama sessions is that 'It's on the basis … of the sort of structure within which the children can work, rather than outcomes.' She dislikes and distrusts the idea of having a pre-set story in her head 'because it wouldn't be anything to do with what they wanted'. Her aim is 'for it not to be led by me'. Having said that, she acknowledges the need for an initial framework for the class so that 'they don't feel intimidated or inhibited or singled out in any way'. However, in some instances, like this particular lesson, she had to maintain that framework for far longer than she would have done normally. The fact that Aisha wanted to take on part of the story and develop it in a particular way was therefore encouraging evidence that at least one of the children had felt confident enough to take control.

Children were then chosen by those who were acting as substitute parents and the new family groups went out of the village hall, with those acting as children spontaneously bending down or semi-squatting, as if by making themselves smaller they could demonstrate their role as young children. Those who were not chosen looked disconsolate. Although it had taken nearly the whole session to reach this point, the children were now undoubtedly identifying with the drama and their place in it. Alison recognized that there was a need to bring them out of it gently before returning them to real life: 'At the end, I just felt that I wanted to lift the mood because [although] it was very interesting, I didn't want it to go on for too long.' She did not want them to leave the session feeling they were unable to throw off the feelings of sadness that might have been engendered by the imagined situation of wartime evacuation.

Valuing and affirming achievement

Throughout the session Natalie's behaviour had presented Alison with certain choices and she had had to draw on her considerable knowledge of her in order to take the decisions she did. Later, she described Natalie as a girl who was having a particularly difficult time at home; unsurprisingly, this was having an observable effect on her behaviour and concentration in school. Alison had recognized from the start that much would depend on the quality of the relationship she could build up with Natalie, and this was something that was going to take time. It is one of her key beliefs or constructs, though, that 'children need to be noticed as individuals' and in this case 'notice' was going to have to take a variety of forms.

Alison realized that Natalie's problems were making it harder than usual to create a constructive relationship but she was persevering. 'I think in a way we are forging a relationship, but it's going to take a little while and she is a tough nut to crack because she has got so much else [going on in life] so she needs to be tough, but basically I think we are beginning to make a friendship.' Observations of Natalie in other lessons verified what Alison said: although Natalie would ostensibly object to just about anything that was suggested in any lesson, it was noticeable that at the same time that she was making these forcible objections, she was also busy organizing the very resources she needed in order to get on with the suggested activity – perhaps one of the 'little glimmers' that Alison said she was beginning to see as the term progressed. Indeed, in her opinion much of the success with and of individuals and the class as a whole depended on the growth of a 'trust relationship with the class and with me'.

As she drew the children out of the final phase of the wartime scenario and into something less demanding, Alison recognized that Natalie was actually taking part, even though it was at a very simple level; the class were instructed that 'They were [now] coming back to the present day and they were to mime something they would like to be'. In fact, to Alison, the choice Natalie made of doing something at such an elementary level was in itself significant: 'She needed to be doing something that was very minimal … something that somebody would be able to guess straight away so then she would get the success of it [very quickly].' That she accepted Natalie's mime, for all its self-evident simplicity, reinforces what Alison says elsewhere about 'accepting children, where they're at', and is part of the professional judgement she brings to a whole range of teaching situations. In this instance, Alison could have challenged Natalie to have done something more exacting, and indeed she might well have done so to another child, or to Natalie at another point later on in the term, but she also recognized that Natalie taking part at all was an achievement in its own right and she thought it was important at this point that she gained the attention she needed from the class. By doing so, Alison felt she had, to a certain extent, satisfied the expectations she had of herself: 'It wasn't a question of, if Natalie can't join in, it is not Natalie's fault. [Instead] it is, how can I find a way in for her?'

Moving on to look at the performances of the other children was a deliberately planned part of the session and Alison had purposefully left time for the group to 'share each other's ideas and value each other's contributions'. On this occasion she had reservations about the quality of some of the contributions, but because she considers it important to 'stop and evaluate what the children are learning', she gave time to considering why this might have been so, returning once more to the general emotional immaturity of this particular group of children: 'If they are not up to it, then it is up to me to look at what I'm giving them to do.'

Flexible groupings, flexible tasks

One aspect of the session that had pleased her was that 'nobody had laughed at anyone else', and she saw that as an example of something she was constantly working towards, a mutual respect: 'That is something that I'm trying to build up with the children, that they are tolerant of each other and accepting of each other, no matter who does what or what was said.' In the classroom setting this emphasis on respect extended to how and when she organized the children into groups and the kind of work she set them. Her groupings were consistently and deliberately flexible and often depended upon the demands of the task. Groups were often self-selected, friendship ones, or if she thought the nature of the task needed a variety of skills and approaches she would deliberately, but temporarily, assign particular children to particular groups. On other occasions she would group, or simply pair, more confident children with those who were less so. If any of these groupings eventually proved difficult because of personality clashes, she quietly moved children around, but only after having given them the opportunity to sort out the problems for themselves. Social learning was one of Alison's priorities, but she recognized when a situation was in danger of becoming destructive and creating another kind of sense of failure.

Alison recognized that not all children were going to learn at the same pace or in the same way but her solution was not to offer differentiated work to different ability groups. It was to offer a wide range of differentiated work to everyone in the class. For example, at the start of a maths lesson she explained the nature of a range of tasks and invited the children to choose where to begin. It was a genuine invitation to start wherever they felt most comfortable and then to move on to something that, in their own estimation, they considered more challenging. It did not matter to Alison if the more confident started with a comparatively easy task. As she saw it, perhaps they felt the need to consolidate or revise some previous learning, but in her experience they rarely, if ever, shied away from progressing to more difficult tasks. In her opinion it was mistaken to assume that those who found academic work easier had no need for security or reassurance. Quite a number of them were children already made anxious by parent and public pressures as they approached the Year 6 SATs.

The invitation to learn

In Alison's classroom there was no assumption of a ceiling for anyone; nor had it been decided how far and how fast anyone should go. If problems arose there was a common understanding that the children were expected not to flounder but to discuss them with other children or with Alison. One of the important ways in which she tried to reduce potential difficulties was by varying the tasks so that they would appeal to those who had problems with 'pencil work', as Alison calls it, but who could show their understanding in other ways. The example of Bill illustrates the significance of building in variety. Bill, a 10-year-old who still found considerable difficulty with reading and writing, chose a maths problem on volume that could be solved in a number of ways, including a practical one. Not surprisingly, he decided on the practical approach and managed to solve the problem more quickly than anyone in the class. His readiness to take up the challenge was a response to the perennial and irresistible sense of open invitation in Alison's classroom. It was an invitation to all comers to have a go, to see where they could get to. However, Alison's ambition for her class did not stop at this point: she also managed to get across the feeling that every task they took on was a beginning, a first step into something else. As she said on another occasion: 'I'm working towards all of them having the feeling that what we are doing now is actually a bloomin' good thing and can *even* be better'.

This optimism, this feeling that things 'can *even* be better', is a strong strand in Alison's approach both to herself as a teacher and to the children as learners. In reviewing the drama session she felt that it was only a matter of time before 'things got better', and although she recognized that 'they haven't got a lot of experience [yet] ... I think they are capable of going such a long way with this. They are very willing and very cooperative.'

Her belief in all the children and their potential is one that is transparently without limits.

7 Narinder's approach: the promise of tomorrow

This account of Narinder's classroom, where she works with a mixed Year 5 and 6 class, attempts to show how the key constructs in Narinder's thinking come together in her teaching: the way her teaching works, rather than a list of the elements of which it is composed. Narinder herself uses the metaphor of cogs: 'the cogs that must engage' for learning without limits to follow.

A model of active learning

At the heart of Narinder's teaching is a complex model of active learning, which is made up of three components, interrelated and interdependent: the social, emotional and intellectual correlates of learning. In order to see more clearly how they fit together in the wholeness of each individual pupil's life as a learner, it is worth disentangling them, temporarily, and examining them in turn.

From the outset of this project it has been clear that Narinder sees learning as an activity with an *emotional dimension*. She frequently uses terms from the emotional domain, and talks of children engaging with energy and passion in the work of learning. She talks of 'lighting them up' and of how she works towards 'a lot of firing of emotions and giving them the experiences within that'. On another occasion she argued that 'You have to get to the heart of something for them to feel the emotion of it, for them to respond to it.'

On the wall of her classroom is a poster that illustrates the word *listening* in Chinese. Apparently, this composite character is made up of four other characters that represent the words ear, eye, mind and heart: the four human organs involved in listening. Narinder's comment on the work of the heart in listening was this: 'We talk about where the heart comes into this, if you are not listening properly to somebody ... you can't feel the emotion in the words, so you can't respond in the way that you should.'

The pupils' emotional involvement seems to drive their sustained engagement. As Narinder says to them sometimes: 'I can tell when you are in tune.' She is clear that feeling in tune, being emotionally engaged, is an essential aspect of effective learning. She compares their classroom experiences with their lives outside the school, in the rundown heart of a major industrial city:

> the root of their lives is, you know, fighting, violence, burglaries, break-ins, broken homes. Their whole lives are turmoil, and for them to come to school, they have got to see some purpose in it, and that purpose has really got to be built in by us very quickly, because not only have they got to have a purpose but they have got to have some success and they have got to enjoy school to come in next day, to see what was the pleasure of it.

Narinder is equally emphatic about the *social dimension* of learning, and specifies the kinds of learning that she sees as important here. 'Learning to resolve conflict, tolerate each other, respect and be respected, social skills ... these are all the foundations of learning on which acquiring academic knowledge can take place.'

In her classroom, the pupils are learning what it is to be members of a community, of a team (a term Narinder often uses). As she demonstrates to them the principle of solidarity ('I am one of them, I am on their side') they learn the lesson of solidarity with one another. For Narinder, the pupils' learning cannot be isolated from their social relationships: it is by living together that they learn. She sees this as a necessary condition:

> As they walk through the door, they must have a sense of belonging. The school is theirs, decisions are taken by them, not for them ... They have to feel that it's their environment [the classroom] ... They are the ones that make the rules and the charters about what is acceptable. They are the ones that organize the classroom in the way they feel is best ... They make the decisions, they decide ... on rules, rights and responsibilities.

'Greater learning', she maintains, follows from the pupils' work on these salient features of their classroom environment, than through acquiring subject knowledge.

But, for all her emphasis on social and emotional aspects of learning, in no way does she marginalize or trivialize the *intellectual dimension* of learning. At the heart of this work, she sees her pupils' acts of making meaning. Understanding is always prioritized over coverage, recall and regurgitation. 'You can throw subjects at them, and curriculum, but if it doesn't mean anything in their lives, it is, you know, quite pointless.' The act of making meaning is, for Narinder, essentially and necessarily an active one: it is the pupils who construct their understanding from the open-ended opportunities she gives them to apply the concepts and the ideas that are being explored. They make their own decisions, formulate their own expectations; they extend the task to whatever level they wish, and so develop a sense of ownership of their learning.

So, for example, reviewing a mathematics lesson, Narinder singles out the two most important aspects of what she was teaching: 'numbers mean things' (and understanding what they mean is the priority, not the algorithm or the right answer) and 'my aim today was to get them to reason about numbers'. The tasks set in this lesson were open-ended and capable of many interpretations, but all of them required the work of making meaning and reasoning. As we shall see in more detail later, Narinder uses many terms from the domain of metacognition, both in her interactions with the pupils and in her interviews. The intellectual exercise that her pupils take in the course of her lessons is not concentrated in the verb 'remember', but extended to 'connect', 'explain', 'put it together' and 'understand'.

Although these three aspects of learning have been presented as if they were separate and discrete, they are, for every individual pupil, bound together by what Narinder sees as virtually a congruence between learning and living. She frequently emphasizes this relationship:

> [Learning] doesn't happen if it doesn't mean anything in their lives.

> It's important that they don't feel it is a task as opposed to a life-skill.

> These are the things that are going to be their life-savers, aren't they... ?

> These are the life chances I am giving them.

> I am going to add value to their lives.

Narinder's model of learning, then, is a representation of her aspirations for the lives of her pupils, rather than for their levels of attainment, their reading ages or their test scores (see figure 7.1 p.92).

The conditions that support learning

This tentative model of Narinder's understanding of learning is the starting point for understanding the conditions that effective learning requires. For

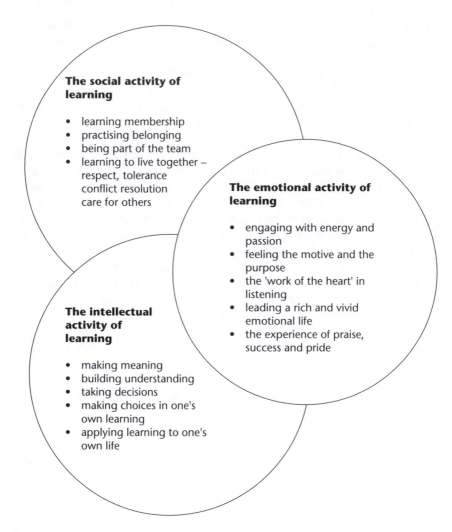

Figure 7.1 A model of active learning: three overlapping kinds of activity

each of the different aspects of learning outlined above, it is possible to identify the ways in which Narinder and her pupils work together to establish the 'totally supportive environment' for learning (a phrase used by Bruno Bettelheim (1950), to describe the Orthogenic School in Chicago, a school for severely disturbed children, who needed, in his view, total support).

First is the emotional domain. Narinder stresses the need for the classroom to be a place of safety, where the pupils know they are trusted and also know they can trust. 'I give you a guarantee that you are going to be safe', she says, but the guarantee stands or falls by the pupils' corporate responsibility for the quality of their emotional environment. And we have already seen how this responsibility is built into Narinder's expectations of her pupils: 'They are the ones that make the rules and the charters about what is acceptable.'

But there is more to a totally supportive emotional environment than rules and charters, however safe they make the pupils feel. There are also humour and playfulness, in abundance. There is the work of circle time, where the ethic of care is made explicit and its practices are discussed. For example, Narinder described an incident when a pupil, Jake, brought cigarettes and matches into school, and another pupil, Tony, told her about it.

> And Jake said [to Tony] 'I'm going to kill you'. So we talked about why Tony told me. I said, Jake, it is because he is worried about you and that is what we do when we care about somebody. We worry about them. We worry about their health, we worry about the dangers ... we have got to protect all the children within our care ... And we talked it through as a class, what courage it took for Tony to do that ... So that, in the end, Jake saw that Tony was a caring person, that he had told me on the basis of care.

This sensitive attention to individual pupils and to their intimate and personal stories appears over and over again as Narinder describes the process of making the class safe for every individual. Her determination to 'bring everybody with me' is tempered by her knowledge of individual quirks:

> I don't like putting children on the spot ... people like Sarah, who will always hide behind somebody; people like Thomas, who will always hide near the radiator, things like that. They are symptoms of something and I have tried to see what the symptoms might be, and I try not to direct the question at a child who is going to find it difficult to answer.

Another key element in the structures of feeling that Narinder sets in place is respect, a concept that frequently appears in the interview transcripts and observation notes. Narinder deliberately sets out to foster this sense of being respected, of being expected to respect others. 'I am constantly thanking them for their efforts, for coming to school, for their achievements. I think it is very important they have a feel-good factor.' When Narinder thanks them, and praises them, she is not acting up to a role she has prescribed for herself. Her emotions are heart-felt. 'I am so very, very proud of them', she says, and means it. In an early interview, before the observations began, she described her class with genuine admiration: 'We do a lot of talking about their roles and responsibilities, and they leave me astounded with their thought, with the depth of their thought and their perceptions of what they are able to effect. It is amazing.'

Narinder works just as hard to create the conditions for the social activity of learning. For example, sometimes the children select their own groups or partners for a particular task; they work with their chosen colleagues in ways that strengthen their capacity to give and receive support from their peers. At other times, Narinder forms groups of particular individuals, basing her selection on the kind of support each person needs and/or is well qualified to give. So in a task where a written record of the children's thinking is needed, but is not the priority in terms of learning, she will group children who worry about writing correctly and neatly with other pupils with more confidence in their advanced writing skills.

One lesson observed was explicitly described as an exercise in team-building. Narinder used parachute games, dance and music to foster the pupils' sense of what it is, and how it feels, to work as a team. And it is a team of which she is a member, rather than a leader, as was made very clear in more than one of the pupils' interviews. As one student said, 'Mrs Brach is on our side. All the time. She always tries to help us, whatever the situation. But if we don't cooperate, then she can't help us.' In another interview, one pupil made an interesting distinction, in terms of sides and teams. He was adamant in claiming that his teacher never sided with one individual against another. Her commitment was to the whole group: 'She's on our side, not on my side.' This work of modelling solidarity and supportiveness is just one way in which Narinder creates the conditions for learning membership and citizenship.

The conditions for the active intellectual work of making meaning and creating understanding are equally important – another set of 'cogs that must engage'. There is evidence of a strong emphasis on relevance, purpose, making connections, and personal meaning. There are many opportunities for pupils to see how subjects fit together in terms of big ideas: there are mathematical ideas to explore in the history lesson, and the concepts of evidence and reliability appear in both history and science lessons. The pupils are given opportunities to apply the ideas they are studying in ways that make sense to them as individuals. In their history work in the spring term, for example, the concepts of time, period and dynasty were explored through the pupils' work on their own personal time-lines, family trees and an outline account of their 'period at N School'. Tasks are set with built-in choices to be made, with minimum expectations that everyone can successfully meet and with opportunities for expansion and extension, directed by the pupils themselves. The kinds of thinking that are asked of them are named and defined. The power of explanation is frequently modelled, and the pupils are regularly asked to explain their thinking, their working, their insights and conclusions.

In both whole-class and small-group discussion work, Narinder offers her pupils, by analogy with the supportive 'writing frames' in use in many primary classrooms, both *thinking frames* and *speaking frames*. She often refers, for example, to 'private thoughts' and 'shared thoughts', making it clear what each task, or segment of a task, demands. She uses explicit terminology to explain what kind of thinking she expects of them: connect, explain, definition, views, points. In a lesson building up to a formal debate on animal rights, Narinder prepared prompt cards to support the pupils' presentations. The cards included phrases such as 'with respect', 'another way of looking at this', and 'finally'. There is evidence in the pupil interviews that this aspect of Narinder's teaching was not wasted when one pupil closed down a disagreement with the comment 'Look, in this debate you've got a good point and so have we'.

What distinguishes Narinder's work, as a learning without limits teacher, is that these conditions are framed to support learning for everyone. Narinder works to secure unlimited access to learning for all her pupils, so the classroom has to be governed by what we later call *the ethic of everybody*. The progress of individual pupils, at their own pace, meeting individual targets, is not Narinder's main concern. It is the learning of everybody to which she is committed: the classroom environment, the necessary conditions, the pace and the processes of her teaching, all have to support the learning of everybody. Everybody must experience emotional safety and membership of the team; everybody must be lit up by the learning, must be listened to and recognized as a learner; everybody must contribute to the intellectual work of every aspect of the curriculum. Everybody collaborates in shaping the conditions for learning, because the ethic of everybody dictates it.

Although, as we have seen, Narinder is sensitive to vulnerable pupils, to individual quirks, and, in a sense, differentiates by person, the main subject of the key verbs in her classroom is everybody. Everybody will engage, everybody will connect, everybody will contribute, everybody will be heard. Narinder will add value to everybody's life.

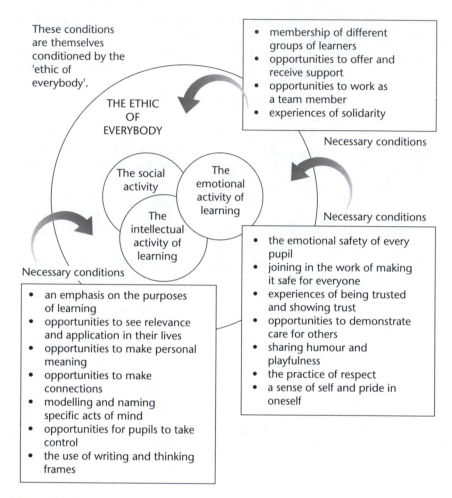

These conditions are themselves conditioned by the 'ethic of everybody'.

THE ETHIC OF EVERYBODY

The social activity

The emotional activity of learning

The intellectual activity of learning

Necessary conditions

• membership of different groups of learners
• opportunities to offer and receive support
• opportunities to work as a team member
• experiences of solidarity

Necessary conditions

Necessary conditions

• the emotional safety of every pupil
• joining in the work of making it safe for everyone
• experiences of being trusted and showing trust
• opportunities to demonstrate care for others
• sharing humour and playfulness
• the practice of respect
• a sense of self and pride in oneself

Necessary conditions

• an emphasis on the purposes of learning
• opportunities to see relevance and application in their lives
• opportunities to make personal meaning
• opportunities to make connections
• modelling and naming specific acts of mind
• opportunities for pupils to take control
• the use of writing and thinking frames

Figure 7.2 The conditions that support learning without limits for everybody

The synthesis: learning, conditions, processes, the ethic of everybody

In a chapter called 'The Rhythm of Education', A. N. Whitehead (1932) describes the cyclical nature of learning, which, he claims, must pass through the three consecutive stages of romance, precision and generalization (or application, the putting to use of what has been learned). In a helpful commentary on this hypothesis, Entwhistle (1979) explains that Whitehead extended this cyclical theory to apply not only to the entire educational lifetime of any particular learner, but also to a single learning experience, such as an individual lesson, which should in itself manifest all three stages of the cycle. This model can help us to see, in the rhythms of Narinder's teaching, the synthesis of her views of learners and learning, and her beliefs about the conditions that are necessary for the learning of everybody. There are four, rather than three, stages that can be identified, but there are striking similarities none the less. In the first stage, which Whitehead calls romance, glossing it with words such as 'excitement' and phrases such as 'a ferment ... stirring in the mind', and which Entwhistle calls a 'mood of adventure, of liberation', we can see the equivalent of Narinder's determination to engage her pupils emotionally, to fire them up, to help them to get to the heart of the subject, for them to feel the emotion of it.

The second stage, of *precision*, of attention to what Whitehead calls the 'grammar of the subject', and Entwhistle 'the thrust towards mastery and skill', also seems to have a very close parallel in Narinder's classroom when, once her pupils are emotionally engaged, she too teaches the grammar of the subject. She teaches the big ideas, the key concepts, on the one hand, and, on the other, the distinctive ways of thinking that a particular topic demands, the acts of mind, the intellectual skills that she aspires to in her pupils. She teaches the grammar of the subject in terms of nouns (concepts) and verbs (the things the pupils do).

Next, Narinder typically sets a task, or sequence of mini-tasks, in which the work of generalization (Whitehead) or praxis (Entwhistle) is carried out. Now the pupils are offered the opportunity of putting to use what has been learned, and, in Narinder's classroom, they are also offered multiple opportunities to reflect back, to their teacher and to one another, the substance of what they are doing, always with an emphasis on explanation and understanding, rather than on memory. At this point, without abandoning her role as teacher (of the grammar of the subject), or her full-time work of supporting learning, Narinder also attentively listens to her pupils, listening for their learning in order to name it to them, reflect it back to them, praise them and thank them, thereby closing a cycle of positive feedback.

But the rhythm of Narinder's teaching is not yet concluded. Observations of a number of Narinder's lessons show that after the third stage, of individual and small-group application (or generalization, to stick with Whitehead's term), there is a fourth, in which the individual learners, or small groups of learners, reconvene as a whole, to review as a class, as a learning community, what they have learned. At this stage, too, the ethic of everybody prevails: everybody is invited to contribute, everybody's learning is valued and listened to, everybody is present as a practising member of the team. There are opportunities too for connections to be made, with past experiences, with personal meanings, with other topics and curriculum areas. And, significantly, connections are made with what lies ahead, with the pupils' future learning, with what we may call the promise of tomorrow, a promise Narinder seems to give her pupils after each day's learning, assuring them that the purposes for which they worked today will still be alive, worthwhile and engaging, on the following day.

In emphasizing the continuity of her pupils' learning, from day to day, as well as between subjects, Narinder offers her pupils a promising future, an assurance of their capacity to move into the space that Vygotsky calls the zone of proximal development. It is as if Narinder's closing of the daily cycle (or cycles) is intended to remind her pupils that the purposes of learning continue, that there is a worthwhile reason for their returning to the classroom, that the life they lead together will continue to make sense. For example, reviewing a literacy lesson, Narinder says 'It's best to leave them thinking and wanting to do it so we can pick it up tomorrow and work from there.' The life of the team, the classroom learning community they have shaped together, cannot be reduced to the subjects listed on the weekly timetable. Their work together is a continuous movement, a steady progress, not a list of curriculum areas. The continuity of hope offers each and every pupil the promise of continuing progress as a life-long learner, truly a learner without limits.

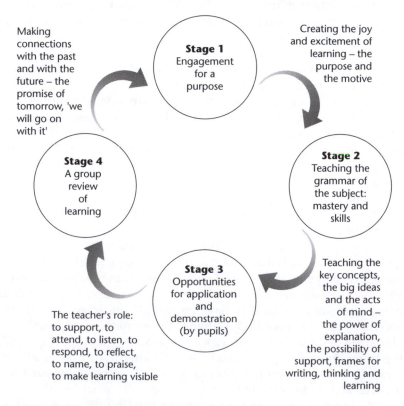

Figure 7.3 The rhythm of Narinder's teaching

The rhythm of Narinder's teaching: a narrative account

Narinder's classroom is high up under the pitched gables of the ultra-Victorian building. This cold November afternoon, the views across the red and black tiled rooftops are dim and misty, but the classroom feels warm and welcoming. Narinder brings the children in from the cloakroom, chattering and relaxed, and they all go over to the carpet, where the Year 5 children sit, while the seven Year 6 children sit on chairs around the edge. 'It's giving them that little extra bit of respect', Narinder explains, though she also uses the privilege of the chair as an occasional reward or encouragement for the odd individual who also seems to need something 'a little extra' (an example of Narinder's sensitivity to the differences between persons). The register routine begins, with a request for silence expressed in terms of thinking: 'While I'm doing the register, I want you to be having private thoughts, not shared thoughts.' Narinder nominates a pupil to call the names on the register, and the pupils answer in a variety of tongues: 'Bonjour', 'Guten Tag', 'Buon giorno' ... a tiny expression of freedom of choice, a familiar routine enlivened by an act of personal meaning. The lesson plan is outlined on the flipchart, with the key ideas to be covered: 'We are looking at the Tudors, but more about the skills of discovering evidence in history, that's what today's objective is about, what we look for, when we're looking at history.' Narinder checks through the lesson plan with the whole class, emphasizing the vocabulary they will be using (chronological order, evidence, reliability) using examples from their own lives and experiences to illustrate the definitions that she and the pupils both contribute.

The first activity is a worksheet, prepared in advance and structured so that every pupil will achieve some success with it: it shows a number of dates, from 1485 to 1605, which are to be arranged in chronological order. Narinder increases the pace of her instructions as she prepares them for this sheet, until they are excitedly waiting for the dramatic word of command 'Go!' They rush straight to the tables and start. Before the lesson began, Narinder commented on the need to engage and enthuse her class: 'When I plan a history lesson, obviously the style of teaching is very important in relation to the type of children I have ... Very much I have to keep the whole thing alive. I have to keep it so that boredom doesn't set in ... So that is the first feature of any lesson.' All the children are indeed engaged with their sheets. Some have quickly spotted the pattern of dates, and have moved to the second part of the task, which is to explain their thinking, using the words millennium, century and decade. Seeing that some children are finishing their work, Narinder calls them back to the carpet where she has a set of the same dates prepared on individual pieces of paper laid out on the floor. These too are to be arranged in chronological order, this time as a group activity, in which everyone can participate. The earliest date, 1485, is Blu-tacked to the flipchart, and then the second and third. At 1505, Narinder stops them and asks for an explanation using the word century; six or seven pupils enthusiastically volunteer explanations, for which Narinder thanks them. They practise the use of the word century as Narinder points to the different dates: 'What century is this?' A boy volunteers: 'At the moment we're in the twentieth century!' Another rejoins: 'Like Twentieth Century Fox!' Hands keep shooting up and pupils comment as the chronological list grows longer. One boy's comment contains the key words 'dynasty' and 'period', which have been the focus of earlier lessons. Narinder is delighted, and says so.

Now the chronological list is replaced with a time line (1485 – 1509 – 1547 – 1553 – 1558 – 1603) and a list of monarchs to match to their respective reigns, a task that is completed as a class activity. Next the children are asked to calculate the length of each king or queen's reign. Narinder models the process using Elizabeth II, and sends the class away in pairs to work on one of the possibilities. After only a few minutes, the class regroups around the flipchart to hear individual pupils work through each example. The mathematical skills and concepts being taught and practised here are an important part of Narinder's approach. 'We do a lot of cross-curricular activity ... part of this history lesson you might term as a maths lesson.' She states her reasons explicitly: the principle is making meaning, making connections, seeing that learning makes sense. 'We look at where links can be made so that for children, [each lesson] is not something in a vacuum, it is not sort of in a black hole, and they can't relate to anything.'

Now there is a change of theme and a change of activity. The class is set the question: 'Where do we get evidence?' After a few contributions are collected from the class, the task becomes an individual one. The pupils begin excitedly to write and draw in their books, talking about the question as they do so. Their ideas include books, videos, computers, clothes, go to a museum, ask people, jewellery, do an archaeological dig, tombstones and coins. The individual task, although there has been considerable sharing (or purloining) of ideas, is followed by a quick class session of 'brain dumping' in which all contributions are acknowledged and welcomed; some pupils are invited to extend or rethink their suggestions.

Next comes a group task. Each group is given three items to consider: a picture postcard reproduction of a monarch, a replica of a Tudor coin and a short piece of prose prepared (by Narinder) about Henry VIII. Two questions are set: is it true? Is it reliable? Narinder reminds them of class guidelines for working in groups and sets them off. She spends the next ten minutes with a number of individual pupils, supporting and extending their thinking. At the end of the time allocated Narinder calls them together again and reviews their work. Several of them have perseverated with the previous task, writing in their individual books, rather than thinking together as a group, and Narinder points this out to them, firmly and distinctly, but without rancour. There is an expectation that has not been met; in the interests of honesty and fair play, Narinder identifies it (and, besides, the capacity to work in a group is a key part of her overall strategy). But, at the same time, Narinder preserves the emotional security of the class. It is still a safe place to be.

The plenary continues: Narinder focuses on the coin. She teaches the phrase 'date of accession', and moves on to the Latin text: 'What does that tell you?' Preliminary answers include 'Rome', 'Greece', 'Italy'. Narinder waits for individual contributions to slow down and invites them to move into explanation and connection. 'Douglas, can you put it together for me?' Douglas does not know the textbook answer, but he knows what putting it together means: 'The Tudors grew up in Rome?' And another pupil: 'Rome is where the Tudors were?' The time is getting short and Narinder seizes the moment to build a bridge of connection and explanation across to their next lesson: 'That's what we're going to find out next week, the connection between Latin and the Tudors.'

The last five minutes of the lesson (which has lasted for over two hours) are taken up with a lively whole-class discussion of the short prose extract, in terms of the concepts of truth and reliability. The liveliness is considerably increased by Narinder's introduction of football reports as a contemporary example of the ideas she is teaching. The example sets the discussion alight: the distinction between opinion and observable fact is immediately made familiar and accessible to many of the pupils. Narinder adds, and not as an afterthought, 'It also happens every day in school, when two people tell different versions of the same incident ... ' Once again the discussion is energetic, vivid, personal, meaningful. This is cross-curricular indeed. Is it a history lesson? Or a moral enquiry? Or a lesson in harmonious living? Or all of the above?

Narinder is on playground duty: two flights down the steep stone stairs and out into the grey drizzle. The hot coffee does not compensate for the cold or the series of incidents that Narinder has to sort out, some of them serious infractions of the safety rules (staff and visitors' cars are parked in the playground and the rules around this hazard are very strictly enforced). Back in the classroom, Narinder confronts the behaviour issue, and speaks very plainly about her feelings, as well as identifying, most explicitly, what and who had been at fault. And, typically, she concludes with a tribute to the ideal that she never loses sight of: 'And lastly a big thank you to the people who helped to make the playtime a pleasant one, not just for themselves but for other people.' Nominations of particular pupils are made, and justice has been done.

The lesson plan Narinder had drawn up for the afternoon session included a period for role play. Many teachers would be inclined to abandon this part of the plan in the light of the group's unruly and disruptive playground behaviour. But not Narinder. In a few words, while they still sit close to her on the carpet, Narinder sets the class a scenario: a portrait painter, a king or queen, the palace guards and courtiers. 'You've just received your portrait – how are you going to respond?' She groups them, sets them a time limit and sends them off into their own space, their own inventiveness. The rhythm has quickened again, and she has let them go: the observation notes show how persistent this pattern is: the quickening and slowing of the pace, the pulling in of the pupils, and the letting them go, the support, the structure, the scaffolding – and the freedom, the open door to imagination and personal meaning.

The groups are immediately at work, eager and purposeful. Even the least engaged of pupils (when there are written tasks set) knows all about being a royal guard. There are five minutes of rehearsal time and then the performances: some brilliant monarchs, improvising their lines, every inch the ruler, and fine supporting casts with obsequious portraitists, flattering courtiers. Narinder asks the boldest and most articulate players a range of extending questions, probing their feelings, their motives, their chosen expressions. The class spend 20 minutes in this exhilarating activity, with unwavering enthusiasm and commitment. Narinder listens, responds, praises, makes their achievements visible.

There is just time left for a brief plenary, recapping the big ideas, the *grammar* of the lesson: reliability, evidence, sources of information, correct vocabulary. All the pupils' contributions are acknowledged and accepted as part of the work of learning that the whole class has engaged in, singly and collectively. The final activity has an ingenious format: every pupil is given a slip of paper with a question and an answer (to a different question) on it. This is a completely egalitarian activity: everyone contributes, everyone succeeds. Nicola, for example, has a paper that says:

Century
What are the names of two of Henry VIII's wives?

She waits until Seymour reads out his question ('What's the correct word for a period of 100 years?') and answers proudly: 'Century!' Then she reads her own question, answered from somewhere else in the circle of attentive, engaged pupils. And then the lesson and the day are over and Narinder is saying goodbye, to the class and to individuals. It is time to let go again.

In a brief review of this lesson Narinder gave one of her most explicit descriptions of her priorities in teaching for learning without limits. The discussion focused on her emphasis on conceptual understanding rather than on factual knowledge, and the observer commented: 'They don't really need to know when Henry VIII came to the throne.' Narinder took up the theme with gusto: 'They'll never remember that! But the ideas, the language, these are the life chances we are giving them!'

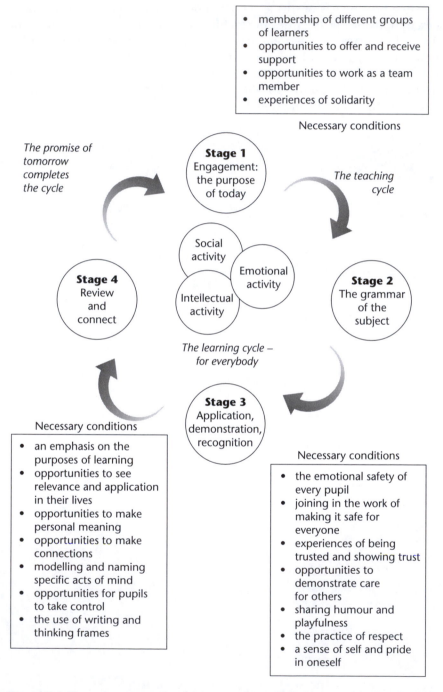

- membership of different groups of learners
- opportunities to offer and receive support
- opportunities to work as a team member
- experiences of solidarity

Necessary conditions

The promise of tomorrow completes the cycle

The teaching cycle

Stage 1
Engagement: the purpose of today

Social activity

Emotional activity

Stage 4
Review and connect

Intellectual activity

Stage 2
The grammar of the subject

The learning cycle – for everybody

Stage 3
Application, demonstration, recognition

Necessary conditions

Necessary conditions

- an emphasis on the purposes of learning
- opportunities to see relevance and application in their lives
- opportunities to make personal meaning
- opportunities to make connections
- modelling and naming specific acts of mind
- opportunities for pupils to take control
- the use of writing and thinking frames

- the emotional safety of every pupil
- joining in the work of making it safe for everyone
- experiences of being trusted and showing trust
- opportunities to demonstrate care for others
- sharing humour and playfulness
- the practice of respect
- a sense of self and pride in oneself

Figure 7.4 The cogs engage, the elements work together

8 Patrick's approach: only connect

Patrick, an English teacher, worked in a large comprehensive school in south London, where he had taught for 17 years. Patrick has strong political convictions that shape his identity as a teacher, his sense of what he is trying to achieve and what it is possible to achieve within schools in the current social, political and economic conditions. While recognizing 'the inevitable constraints imposed by education under capitalism, the historical limits', he is at the same time trying 'to hold a conception of what socialist education might or could be like and endeavouring to make it real'. Despite the drastic curtailment of professional atuonomy that has occurred in recent years, he believes that it is still possible to 'go some way' towards creating the kind of learning environment and learning experiences to which he aspires.

Beliefs about education, teaching and learning

Patrick's view of education is based on a fundamental belief in *all* human beings' natural propensity to make sense and to learn. 'You cannot but encounter the world, engage with the world, make sense of the world. My bedrock position is that you do so in school and out of school in the ways that make sense to you and that is why I teach in the ways that I try and teach.'

This view of learners as 'active, critical makers of their own meaning' shapes Patrick's perception of his own role and responsibilities as a teacher. Rather than the effective delivery of a predetermined curriculum, it implies a view of teaching and learning as a process of *exchange* between teachers and learners; what learners bring and contribute is as important to the learning that takes place as what the teacher brings and contributes. Learning is built out of these exchanges, shaped both by the contributions of learners and by the teacher's responses to them. Although Patrick does have a sense of the direction that he expects and intends learning to take in a particular lesson or over the course of several lessons, and of the kinds of engagement with ideas, texts and techniques that he envisages the activities will foster, the outcomes are unpredictable, because what happens once the lesson gets under way is shaped by students' contributions. As Patrick says, 'Their talk/work and not just my lesson plan takes us places.'

The kinds of tasks and activities that Patrick chooses are critically important. As far as possible, they must be 'open and available' so that they allow and encourage all students to contribute, to feel that they have relevant experience to offer; there must be 'space inside the tasks' for them to make their own connections, to respond in their own way.

> The E. M. Forster line about 'only connect' is the kind of root of my teaching ... the best lessons that I think I have ever taught have been lessons that work through creating intellectual connections with students, providing them with ways that they can make their own connections and seeing that happen. That is often around literature or some kind of text.

Through their contributions, Patrick is able to see the kinds of connections that students are making and what is taking their interest, and this helps him to decide what direction the discussion or activity might take from any given point. 'You see who responds to what kinds of things, you see who doesn't, you try to encourage, you gauge what everybody needs and then adjust the next thing you do or the thing down the line that you do, to try and suit that.' One important measure of success is that a lesson has provided scope for the unexpected, and unplanned for, to occur.

This interpretation of teaching and learning provides a lens for understanding what is going on, moment by moment, in Patrick's classroom. In his exchanges with students, Patrick is simultaneously both engaging with students' contributions in the immediate situation, in such a way as to help to move learning on, and negotiating the conditions that will, in the longer term, secure students' continued willingness to engage and to contribute actively to the collective learning endeavour.

Opening moves

Patrick has worked with his Year 9 class since Year 7. During that time, his relationship with them has developed to a point where 'they feel secure with you, they have a sense that you are somehow doing the right thing by them.' Knowing this, Patrick expects that the majority of the class will arrive ready to join in and contribute. So he gives them time to calm down, settle and focus at the start of the lesson, convinced that, if the choice to engage is self-initiated rather than imposed, 'They will listen more and be more attentive and be more in tune with what I want them to do.'

In line with his core belief that 'students are in charge of their own learning', he allows them to choose who to sit with and who to work with.

> If students are to own their own knowledge and own their own learning, to what extent do they own a space that they can do that in? To what extent is it their classroom as well as mine? And a huge part of that is who they sit with and who they work with. I personally prefer them to choose, although I will intervene in that for various reasons.

Patrick draws the students in with initial activities that he thinks will be fun and that he is confident everyone will be able to do; for example, sharing words or ideas arising from a poem, or an intriguing puzzle to challenge their ingenuity where there are no right or wrong ideas.

> I think it is one of the things that should happen all the time in school, handing over to them and saying 'What can you make of it?' 'What you make of it is interesting and important' and 'How ingenious can you be?' and 'What things strike you?'

In one lesson, for example, Patrick gave the class two numbers and asked them, alone or together, to think of all the different meanings that might be attributed to these numbers; for example, bus numbers, house numbers and ages. The two numbers came from a class text that the group was currently reading, and the activity helped to provide a focus for the next chapter they would be reading, where the significance of the two numbers would be revealed.

As individuals offer ideas, Patrick responds warmly, praising and thanking them for their contributions.

> I have a sense that they are not thanked very much in the school. ... Thanking them genuinely for taking part and contributing is something that I try and do with everybody ... I say 'That's brilliant, you have worked really hard.' I have asked them to do things and they have done things. They have been properly responded to.

These initial contributions are vital, indicating to Patrick how students are feeling and their readiness to engage: 'It's them coming to meet you. It's them expressing themselves. It's them finding their voice, believing they've got something to say, feeling safe enough. It's people listening to them.'

Through the way that he responds, Patrick communicates to students his belief in their competence and creativity as thinkers and learners, and his trust in the value and relevance of what they have to contribute. Through the ways that he makes use of their contributions, not just praising them, but incorporating them into the resources for group learning in a visible or tangible way, he reinforces the students' sense that

> they will be taken seriously as learners, in talk and in writing (i.e. my writing to them). ... What they bring is ... germane and [will] be made constructive use of: personal knowledge, ideas, perceptions, responses, attitudes, jokes ... I trust them to have interesting, reasonable, relevant things to say and to try to construct a situation in which they feel safe to present and give that.

To contribute, the students need to feel safe not only with the teacher but with one another. Through his responses, Patrick models the respect for individuals' ideas that he expects them to show for one another. 'The feeling in the room is that you don't do down what other people say; you might not contribute yourself, but you don't mock, cast aspersions, talk over, laugh; [the awareness that] actually that's serious and important.'

Patrick responds not merely by praising or recording their contributions but by adding information of his own to complement what they have said, or encouraging them to add to what they have said, to defend their ideas, to push their thinking further. He also models processes of listening to and building on the ideas of others, reinforcing their sense of what they can learn from and with one another, demonstrating that they can be actively learning, within the collective learning process, even when they are not actively contributing.

As the initial tasks or activities gather momentum, Patrick does not simply remain at the front of the class; he continually circulates, helping by his movement and his presence to 'warm up' those areas of the room where there is less sign of active participation. This response is less a disciplinary move than a signal that everyone's learning is important, and that everyone has a part to play in the collective learning of the group.

> I think one of the things that I try to do is create a group rapport and a whole-group sense ... where everyone is basically on board and going the same way; and a reliable few will always offer, but everyone else, who isn't necessarily so vocal, at least feels part of the process ... They're all in the same boat, all got something to do. They're all part of it.

This sense of having a place, of contributing to a collective endeavour, where everyone has something to learn from everyone else, is nurtured by the kinds of tasks that Patrick chooses and his beliefs about differentiation:

> I've always been more interested in finding ways to make the shared text or object of study available to any and everyone ... This is partly survival, but it's also to do with my core belief that anything's accessible, available and interesting if you can find the right way into it ... I'd deliberately chosen a 'challenging' text to give everyone (though pairs had different extracts depending on what I thought they might be especially interested in), because I hoped that what they were reading about would in itself grip them enough to offset some of the difficult vocabulary.

He resists attainment grouping because of the negative effects that this can have on students' perceptions of their capabilities and the learning opportunities open to them:

> Students aren't stupid. They will understand that they are being labelled in some way, and all the attempt to say 'This looks just as interesting' won't wash. Students will live up or down to the expectations that people have of them, in particular their class teachers ... And the other thing is, of course, that teachers get it wrong ... The fallibility of [the] judgement undermines the whole basis on which the judgement might be made, which is that people can do things that you didn't think they could do, and if you say 'You are this' you will put a lid and a ceiling on their achievement and what is possible for them.

Choosing tasks where 'everybody can share the same thing' not only enables people to learn from one another's contributions, but allows the momentum of the group to carry along those who are perhaps more reluctant to commit themselves. The students' readiness to contribute to collective work is affected by an awareness and appreciation that their teacher 'always tries to set work where everyone can get involved'. It is important to them to feel that opportunities for active participation and contribution are offered equally to everyone. Patrick takes conscious steps to ensure equality of participation for both boys and girls. He strives for a 'general balance' by taking contributions from boys and girls in turn; and will deliberately wait on occasions 'if only girls' hands are up' until a boy offers to contribute.

Patrick's concern to ensure equality of participation for everyone has a class as well as a gender dimension. He makes a special effort to reach out to working-class students, because he believes that the 'middle-class ... nature of the curriculum and what's valued' in schools make it more diffi- cult for working-class students to feel a genuine sense of belonging, of having a personal stake in school learning.

> I try to learn from them, about the kind of situation that they are coming from. What do they go home into? Are they likely to be able to sit and do this kind of homework? Are they likely to be able to go to the library? Are they likely to be able to bring stuff in? How would they feel about being asked about certain aspects of their life? I try to make decisions around that. Then you try to do what you can to alter the way the institution responds to those pupils.

To help to reinforce the value of *all* students' contributions, Patrick regu- larly chooses activities that he knows will place all students in a position of being equal experts, in the sense that everyone has relevant experience to contribute (for example, a discussion of the pros and cons of McDonald's food), and no one's knowledge or experience (including that of the teacher) can be considered superior or inferior in the ensuing discussion. He also creates activities in which students' research will necessarily put them in a position of being more knowledgeable about one particular topic area than anyone else (including himself).

> I would be very surprised if I can answer a lot of their questions [in a particular research task] and I think it is important for them to see that they are the experts ... they know stuff that I don't know ... I think it creates an atmosphere where people feel more able to contribute and more secure in contributing.

Keeping the intellectual engagement moving

Patrick's responses to students' contributions in the early part of the lesson are critical in laying the foundations for sustained engagement. At its most basic, engagement means making the choice to opt in rather than opt out of the formal learning activities of the class, choosing to come 'on board' with everyone else. Patrick recognizes that it is a choice that learners can only make for themselves; that patterns of engagement are inevitably variable for all learners, throughout a lesson; and that students will only routinely make the choice to engage if they know from experience that they are likely to find personally relevant and satisfying ways of making meaning within what the school has to offer. To be worthwhile, though, engagement has to be sustained. Engagement in its fuller sense involves

active, intellectual effort, thinking, making connections, taking thinking
further, building, constructing, taking ideas forward.

Patrick judges from students' responses when the time is ripe to move
on to other activities that will enable them to develop further ideas that the
initial activities have begun to open up. He adjusts his plans for the lesson,
taking into account the nature and quality of students' contributions, the
mood of the group and their willingness and ability to remain focused
around certain tasks. If an activity does not take off as he expects or intends,
he switches to a different kind of activity that enables students to engage
more successfully, rather than 'having a rant' at them, which 'is demeaning
for everybody. And you don't help people to grow by demeaning them.'

Transitions from one activity to another can lead to a loss of momentum, particularly when the switch is from whole-class work to group work.
Patrick makes a point of moving around the room, approaching each group
in turn to find out how they are doing, knowing that in this way he
becomes more available, that they are more likely to ask him things if he is
in their immediate proximity. As he circulates, Patrick also discusses with
students the purpose and value of their tasks, in the belief that they are
more likely to sustain engagement if he makes explicit and discusses with
them his expectations for their learning, and helps them to understand the
kinds of thinking and learning that he values:

> What the teacher wants is critical, and if I want them to think for
> themselves, and reason, and support what they say, and listen to
> each other, the more I can reinforce that by what I say, by smiling,
> by setting it up so that they can make it happen, the better.

These individual exchanges provide scope for responses that are personally
tailored to validate, develop and challenge individuals' thinking. They also
contribute to pupils' sense of being known and valued as individuals. They
are greatly appreciated by the students, who know from experience that 'If
you don't understand it, he will come to you personally.' 'He will explain it
really well.' 'He tries to make it real.' Students feel comfortable asking for
help. Through these exchanges, they not only receive specific help with
their work and suggestions for improvements, but also realize that 'He
makes me feel that I am good at what I am doing, and makes me feel more
confident'.

This personal dimension to Patrick's relationship with students is also
fostered through the students' ongoing task of maintaining a reading
journal, to which Patrick provides an individual written response. Through
this medium, Patrick develops a personal exchange with individuals around
the books they are reading, which provides strong reinforcement to students
that they each matter to him individually.

Individuals taking control

In his exchanges with individuals, and when he is working with the class as a whole group, Patrick strives for a relationship of reciprocity, 'mutual guidance of the educational process by teacher and learner', where the teacher both leads and takes the lead from students, so that both parties shape the learning that takes place.

> The whole thing about being in charge is in a way paradoxical because I have a sense that I give them direction, there's probably a lot of time when I'm leading them places. So in a way they're not really in charge ... it's more about creating a communal sense that yes we do want to go that way or we can get there ... And the way we're going isn't entirely the way I'd envisaged it or imagined it because they will bring and add stuff to it. So it becomes their space and they show me things I hadn't already seen.

The importance of reciprocity in the exchanges between teacher and students is highlighted by the educators in Reggio Emilia, through the metaphor of throwing and catching a ball. They stress the need to 'catch the ball that children throw and throw it back in such a way that makes children want to continue the game with us, developing perhaps other games as we go along' (Edwards *et al.* 1998: 217). How students' contributions are received and responded to determines whether or not they want to continue with the games they have begun, or move on to any further games.

Within the collective learning experience, it is also important to provide space for individuals and groups to pursue their own interests and develop the ideas and connections that they are making in personally meaningful ways. Patrick tries to offer some choice of tasks, or choice within tasks, so that students are able to exercise more control over their learning. 'Negotiation is welcome, though I don't build it in nearly enough. [Students] may be able to influence the pace of the lesson, for example, by being asked if they need more time. They may be able to move to another activity they or I suggest should the initial one not be what they want to do.'

Students are able to exercise control over the shape and direction of learning, both when they are working collectively as a group and when they are working in smaller groups or individually. The organization of the learning environment allows them to make choices about who to work with, about how to approach a task. They can make suggestions about how to organize the layout of the room, or what tasks they would like to do, if what has been suggested does not appeal or they have other ideas, and can be sure that they will be listened to. There needs to be flexibility for individuals and groups sometimes to determine and shape their own learning paths. On one occasion, for example, during a discussion on the pressures faced by Lord

Capulet, a student remarked that, in her view, Romeo and Juliet were under far more pressure than Lord Capulet, and she chose to pursue that line of thinking when the group moved on to record their own thoughts in writing.

Another lesson towards the end of the spring term was identified by Patrick as exemplifying this flexibility particularly effectively. The class were working in groups on scripts for a Radio Verona phone-in relating to their work on *Romeo and Juliet*. The task was designed to help the students to review what had happened, consider culpability and work in role. The task provided a great deal of scope for personal interpretation and development of ideas, as well as the opportunity for groups to choose where they wanted to focus their efforts and develop their work at their own pace. One group immediately announced that they had finished their script. One individual who had not completed any 'serious writing' for weeks suddenly produced a five-page piece for homework. The group decided to go off and tape-record their script to play to the rest of the group later in the lesson. The remaining groups made their own choices about how to spend their time. Patrick circulated, listening for a time to what each group was discussing and spending some time acting as a scribe for one group who were struggling to sustain writing. Patrick noted in his journal that this was the lesson that came closest (of those recorded for the purposes of the project) to what he is trying to achieve: 'The lesson was adjusted for different groups as it went along, and we came together for the final ten minutes ... I really enjoyed the lesson today and the way the class had helped shape it.'

Expanding the possibilities for learning

In Patrick's approach, the exchanges between teacher and learners out of which learning is built in the immediate situation are also building the foundations that will continue to support and extend the possibilities for learning in the future. This involves negotiating with students, and continually working to build their desire to engage and to learn, because of the intrinsic interest and worth of the activities that they are invited to engage in; their sense of security in taking the risks that genuine learning requires; their sense of belonging, of being known and valued for who they are and for what they have to contribute to the collective; and their sense of personal power as thinkers and learners, their sense of the relevance of their own knowledge and ideas, their confidence in their ability to engage successfully with tasks, their understanding of what is expected and their capacity to use all the resources available to them to develop their understanding and skills. 'The learning model or the model of teaching and learning that the classroom will try to present will show that learning is good in itself, and to be valued; that it is worth doing and that they can do it.'

Students' willingness to engage actively in the exchanges out of which learning is built in each lesson is shaped by the extent to which each of these conditions obtains for them individually. This in turn determines the limits of their capacity for learning in the classroom context. 'How you feel about yourself and the place and what you're doing impacts fundamentally on your ability to learn, your willingness to learn and how much you learn.'

While Patrick's commitment to reciprocity means that he will lead as well as take the lead from students as he responds to their contributions, it also means that he cannot lead them to places where (judging from their contributions) they will not be able to follow him and continue to play a genuinely reciprocal role. 'Each group gives you what they give you', he says, and while he works hard to create conditions where they choose to engage and give more, the learning that is possible within the group is both shaped by what they give and always, necessarily, limited by what they give.

In one lesson, for example, when the class was studying a Wilfred Owen poem, Patrick had anticipated that the various activities planned might move on to more sophisticated discussion of the language used in the poem: 'Ideally I wanted a big discussion about why this language is being used. What did it do? What was the effect of it? What kind of impact did it have and how was it different from the letter?'

However, taking his lead from the group, Patrick judged that the time was not right in the latter part of the lesson to try to move the learning on: 'It is the kind of discussion that if it is going to be real, they have to have most of it. If I say "Isn't that language different?", they will go "Yes, the language is different, sir", but they won't really take it on board.' In one sense, then, it could be argued that the students imposed their own limits on the learning that was possible in this lesson. Yet Patrick's commitment to teaching as a process of working with students' contributions also means knowing when to hold back and accept what has been achieved as worthwhile, knowing that attempting to impose a particular agenda is unlikely to be a productive strategy, either in the immediate or long term. He could have forced their acquiescence to his agenda, on this occasion, by 'having a rant' at them, but he could not force their learning.

> Every class gives you what they give you, and it's hard. Unless, it seems to me, you're the scary teacher. And if you're a scary teacher, you probably don't have any discipline problems at all. But you lose what you lose. And what you lose is too valuable to want to be the scary teacher to stop the other stuff.

Although, in this lesson, Patrick chose to take the lead from the students regarding the limits of what could be achieved in the immediate situation, the group's capacity to sustain concentration and constructive engagement with one another's ideas during whole group discussion was an area that Patrick was actively working on with this class. His fundamental stance towards students' responses that fall short of his aspirations, and particularly when difficulty in sustaining concentration on the part of some students functions as a 'sheet anchor' upon the learning of the rest of the group, is that the way things are is not necessarily the way they have to be, and that it is possible to take action to change things for the better.

Later in the year, during a unit of work on *Romeo and Juliet*, things came to a head with a group of students who were increasingly choosing to opt out or remain on the periphery of classroom activities. 'They are unprepared to participate in the work of the rest of the class, staying silent in class talk or conducting their own conversations when given group work, habitually avoiding engaging in the class activities.'

Although Patrick is firmly committed to the idea that students are in charge of their own learning, he does not simply accept the choice to opt out. His response is a creative one: to try to change the dynamics of the situation and inject new opportunities for learning in ways that might encourage and enable them to make a different choice. After half-term, he altered the usual routine and took them out of the classroom to the hall to walk through sections of the play. 'This immediately gave people space to do what they wanted in their groups, or by themselves, and as such at least took pressure off those who aren't at ease in the classroom.' The drama work on the play produced some good responses from the group as a whole, including the disaffected group:

> They came up with good and creative suggestions, but had little scope truly to explore the scene and make it their own as drama. Maybe a slower start to the lessons, allowing them to do something unscripted and free in the new space, would have set up a different dynamic. On the other hand, in terms of mending fences and moving on happily from the pre-half-term lesson, the week so far has gone very well.

As part of his strategies for changing the dynamics, Patrick also changed the organization of desks in the classroom: 'I have built a three-cornered square around the central tables. This is supposed to underscore a sense of togetherness, but of course the downside is precisely that it makes group work harder.' Students in the Year 9 class interviewed shortly after this new arrangement was introduced had mixed responses to it, but understood and were appreciative of what Patrick was trying to achieve.

Patrick stressed that he had no illusions that the problem of re-engaging the disaffected group would be easily solved. No classroom is an island, and there are so many external pressures and influences affecting these students' responses to school learning that it might not actually be possible to effect change at this point. Moreover, Patrick believes that teachers have to be careful about the strategies that they use, because: 'it's possible to prevent people learning things later by how you deal with them at the moment ... '

It is important 'to keep the doors open as long as possible'; not to 'write them off' but to go on believing in the scope for change, and to keep working to create conditions that make such changes more likely to happen. 'I suppose the daily task remains by forethought, preparation, example and practice to hold open a more than instrumentalist view of education, to lead out of each individual student the most of which they find they are capable and to lead them out of a delimited view of themselves and their possibilities.'

One student summarized how her thoughts had changed about her own competencies after working with Patrick's class as follows: 'Now I have realized that I can be clever if I want to ... If you see yourself improving then it makes you feel to yourself, "Yeah, I am clever, I can do it." It makes you push yourself, it gives you so much self-confidence.'

9 Nicky's approach: step back and look at the children

'Sometimes we are just a group and we are seen as a whole class or we are just seen as people, but *most* of the time we're seen as individuals with our own ideas and stuff.' This is how a one member of a group of 15-year-olds sees the teaching approach of their English teacher, Nicky. It validates how she sees herself teaching English to them and also how she makes learning accessible to all her students. In her view it is how she tries to create learning without limits: individuals matter.

To Nicky, labelling young people by ability, instead of seeing them as individuals with their own unique, diverse and distinctive characteristics, is at best an irrelevance, at worst a perpetuation of a whole range of negative and, ultimately, destructive attitudes: the attitudes of students towards themselves and their learning, and the attitudes of teachers towards their students. She is equally opposed to the increased use of different kinds of test scores and the misplaced importance that is attached to them as a basis for setting or streaming pupils. To her such practices serve to encourage an attitude that quickly leads to treating children and young people simply as numbers, not people.

Nicky included these thoughts in her letter of application to the Learning without Limits project. In the course of the selection interview, she explained that she was becoming increasingly bothered by the degree to which children 'were [coming to] be judged by data ... you need to step back and look at the children.' The evidence that Nicky herself looks at the children was later borne out in no uncertain way, in subsequent interviews and in the observations that were made of her practice in the classroom.

Knowing and understanding young people

As a secondary teacher, it is not always easy to think deeply about individual students because the timetable usually militates against seeing the same group more than once or twice a week; usually what is gained, understandably, is a general impression, but this is not to describe Nicky's approach. Her knowledge of individual students, their strengths and weaknesses, their potential and their achievements was detailed and impressive. Understanding the individual student also had considerable bearing on how she saw and organized groups within her class. She used her observations of both groups and individuals to plan for the kind of work that would, in her view, lift the limits to the students' learning. In addition, Nicky recognized and accepted the significance of their different backgrounds and previous experiences. For example, a large number of pupils in her class had come from countries such as Somalia, Sierra Leone and Eritrea, and had been caught up in wars and famines; some had even witnessed family and relatives being murdered. For others the issue was of lifestyle, many coming from distant nomadic cultures, which offered little if any schooling.

The following is a characteristic example of Nicky's verbal description of one student from a troubled background, a boy of 16, who had only recently arrived in England and become a member of Nicky's class. She had not had a great deal of time to get to know him, yet, as this extract from a recorded interview shows, she had noticed and found out a considerable amount about him.

> Yahni's never had any formal education – both his parents died in the war and he got refugee status and moved to England with his grandmother, but shortly after they got to England she died and he now lives with his sister. When he arrived, he didn't speak any English ... He's come so far in such a short space of time – but I worry that he does too much; he does a great deal of background reading and he's also got family responsibilities as he's taken on the role of the father and looks after his sister.

The school Yahni attends and where Nicky worked at the time is in an urban area. Situated in the western outskirts of London, it is near reception centres for refugees; the school accepts a considerable number of students from these and from the families who have settled nearby. The school serves a vast housing estate, built largely in the 1930s, which has gradually absorbed a number of small towns and villages to the west of London. The estate once served mainly English and Irish families who came to London in search of work, but the demographic shift that started in the late 1940s and 1950s means that it has become increasingly multicultural. At one time there were mostly West Indian, Pakistani and South-East Asian families, but now over forty nationalities have been recorded at the school, including Turks, Kurds, Koreans, Chinese, Bangladeshi and Nigerians. Even the official DfES form that lists all the languages that might be spoken in schools does not include several that are used by a number of students as their first language.

As Nicky began to talk about her students and her approach to teaching and learning, it quickly became evident that detailed knowledge of individuals and their learning, including how they function in groups, is the foundation of her practice. For example, in describing Niall in an interview, she mentioned a wide range of characteristics, each of which had some bearing on Niall as a learner, and which Nicky felt were significant in this respect.

> Niall's attention span is probably shorter than the rest. He is improving, though. My criticism of Niall is that he would always switch off about quarter of an hour into the lesson. He *can* be very, very good and very, very keen but he always needs a shorter lesson and his work – well, he always writes the minimum that he can get away with – although I've noticed that his short story was actually quite a lengthy piece of work ... he would like you to think he was very mature and very hardworking but actually he will switch off ... he's into 'I'm hard', I think it's because he's so small for his age and he tries to make out that he's really 'a toughie'.

This is a short description of a pupil that took up less than three minutes of an interview. Yet in it Nicky touches on eight important features about Niall and his learning, which all affect how she plans for him to succeed, and to avoid the kind of failure that could contribute to his seeing himself as an unsuccessful learner.

Adjusting and adapting teaching strategies

The potential for Niall to fail in some way was not difficult to perceive; as Nicky observed, 'His attention span is shorter than most'. Another teacher might have found such a constellation of attitudes and behaviour quite irksome and have responded negatively to Niall. Niall could simply have been written off as being perennially inattentive, someone who was more involved in 'mucking about' with his mates and the cause of tiresome and time-wasting interruptions. But Nicky was prepared to persevere. What she had also noticed, in addition to all the traits that could make for eventual trouble, was the fact that he could also show, in brief interludes admittedly, evidence that he could be 'very, very good and very, very keen'. This was something that Nicky wanted to build on and if she had to adapt her teaching in order to maintain that keenness and develop it, then she was prepared to do so: it was one of the ways in which identifiable and possible limits to a pupil's learning could be lifted.

Nicky also made the observation, one that pleased her considerably, that while Niall 'usually wrote the bare minimum he could get away with … he won't push himself', he had none the less recently written quite a lengthy short story. Usually, if he wrote anything at all, she observed, it was in a task that involved filling in boxes or, sometimes, a writing frame: 'If you gave him a blank piece of paper and said "Do something", he wouldn't do it.' Nicky also commented, in another interview, on how competitive Niall was about everything, always 'thinking about competition and TV'. It was an element in his make-up that she recognized as something she needed to take into account when considering appropriate and attractive learning situations for him.

Was this how Niall saw himself, though? As it happened, Niall was chosen by Nicky, on another occasion, as one of a group of students to be interviewed. Three students took part in this particular interview, and the other two were, in comparison to Niall, quite voluble. He had to be asked a question quite directly before he gave an opinion on anything, but there was no doubt he was listening to what was being said by the others. He certainly took any question about learning seriously and he tried to answer in like vein.

Were Nicky's strategies having an effect, based as they were on what she considered she knew of Niall? In terms of understanding what was being asked of him in class, Niall had no hesitation: he felt that not only did he now know what was being asked of him in lessons but if it ever came to a point he failed to understand, he knew that he had only to ask Nicky for clarification; if she was busy he could ask his friends. He seemed to have no anxiety that he would lose face or be criticized for not listening properly and he felt that others in the class would not be put down either.

Somewhat ruefully he had to say that he did not always offer his own best effort; he admitted that he 'sometimes got easily distracted'. Even so, he thought he was much more confident than he had been before he came into Nicky's class and that, besides being the 'best teacher' (out of five previous English teachers that he said he had had), she didn't seem 'to have a *bias* against me like some of the others'. He also appreciated that in English they got 'a wide scale of things [to do] – learning lots of different things' (corroborating Nicky's knowledge of his learning preferences and her provision of such activities).

Niall was aware that Nicky was in control of the class and that 'She doesn't just let us do what we want, yeah?', but at the same time he acknowledged that 'If we have an idea, yeah, she lets us have our own ideas and opinions of things and she respects them.' This was important to Niall, as was the fact that he saw Nicky as having 'helped me a lot'. Dropping his tough stance for once, he even detailed an example of this that went some way to explaining his increased effort when it came to short stories, which according to Nicky, had usually been 'a scant two pages' when he had first come into the class.

> You see, when I was writing stories and things, like, I *never* used to put detail into the work but this year Miss Hancock has given us a writing frame of things, to help us learn exactly how to lay out things and when she normally reads out a story or something or whatever, it has the detail like how each part is describing things and that and I take that in now.

Niall, who was written off as a potential drop-out and recommended for the bottom group, is now happy to say that although PE will always be his first preference, 'actually English isn't bad', and even confesses to finishing English lessons 'feeling quite happy'. Niall is an example of a student who could have seen himself quite differently if Nicky had not taken steps, based on her observations, to accommodate to him as a particular individual with particular needs in his learning. By so doing, she was able to remove what she perceived as the possible limits to his learning.

It was interesting to contrast the adaptations and adjustments Nicky felt were necessary for this student with those she made to Beata, another student in the same class. Beata was a lively, confident girl who had lived in England for about seven years. Beata's attitudes to learning were in striking contrast to Niall's: she wanted to learn all there was to learn, particularly in English, and she was enthusiastic and responsive. Nicky noticed that because Beata was 'verbally excellent', it was easy to misjudge what she could do, to assume understanding, rather than probe the limits of her understanding and offer support. Beata endorsed this observation when being interviewed, saying 'Teachers think you can do things and actually you can't, you don't really understand it yet and *they* think you can.'

Nicky was aware that similarly inaccurate assumptions could easily be made if only cursory observation was relied upon; her own routine of always asking herself questions about her practice and the students in her class is an important part of the continuous process of observation that she is engaged in. For example, she said, 'I'm often asking myself: are they taking it all in? It's only too easy with someone like Rakhi – she's one of those girls who could slip through the net, people like me assuming that she knows a lot because she's very sensible and very nice and you *assume* a lot about what she knows.'

Many other examples could be cited of Nicky's close observation of individual students; it is quite marked how these observations include so much that is outside the remit of tick boxes, percentages and test scores, yet all the knowledge that she gains is absolutely pertinent to the maximizing of their learning. Indeed, she has very little time for test scores and other standard measures. As she says in relation to these, 'How *do* you judge a child's potential and how do you judge who you put where, because what are you judging them on? I just find it so inflexible.' As she said on another occasion, 'It's so dangerous to label individuals or put them into particular categories. This can just limit expectation and prejudice ideas about potential.' To Nicky, how children get on with each other, which ones have leadership skills, who needs to be given space, who needs to feel successful, be challenged by others, be away from certain other individuals, or who will have an energizing effect on others have a real bearing on how she organizes the learning experiences for her class.

Observing and organizing: complementary approaches

In most of the lessons that were observed during the project, the class was organized into groups, although Nicky used other forms of organization as well, depending on the kind of work that was being undertaken. The reasons for the groupings were various but never depended on achievement, which, as noted in the beginning, Nicky found both unacceptable and, in practice, counter-productive. This was a difficult stance to take in a school that was organized around streaming and setting by ability. As she said:

> My big problem when I first arrived was that I had to put these students into groups and I first of all felt I was selling my soul and then I said [to my manager] 'what criteria do you use?' and was told 'potential' but, in English, what are you talking about, 'potential' orally or 'potential' of written work? And what it boils down to ultimately, I think, with *all* setting, is simply spelling and presentation; we try desperately *not* to do that in our department.

Nicky and her supportive colleagues in the English department are as flexible as they can be within this rigid system by having only two sets: one ostensibly including the most proficient and another set of mixed ability. The first group includes some 'who are orally excellent but whose literacy might be terrible'. As an instance of this, Nicky quoted a boy whose verbal skills were sufficient but who, because he did not come from a book-based culture, found writing, with all its various demands, a difficult task. 'The system is against him as it just wants him to produce his ideas on paper.' Niall was also in this group, because Nicky felt that he would respond better in a set where he was challenged.

Nicky not only knew what the individual children were like and what they needed in order to succeed, she was also willing to interpret, even subvert, the system as best she could in their interests. She said, 'Strictly speaking, if you stuck to the data and just did it *according* to data, as we're supposed to, Hussan wouldn't be in there, Joseph probably wouldn't be either, also Chan. Strictly speaking, they shouldn't be in there but they all benefit from being in there.'

All the knowledge that Nicky acquired about her classes by watching them as she did and by providing for them accordingly could count for naught in her estimation if the students themselves became disheartened, most particularly by being publicly considered as 'less able'. An accompanying disadvantage of setting, in her opinion, was that those who were lauded for being in the top group had another, different, kind of attitude problem. 'It breeds arrogance and it breeds complacency', in Nicky's experience.

At the end of the project Nicky considered that she had come to have a wider and deeper notion of what learning without limits could mean, having originally thought of it simply as a form of mixed-ability teaching. None the less, she still feels that streaming and setting are some of the most pernicious organizational practices to be used in schools, practices that impose far more limits on the majority than they ever lift for the minority. As it is, she thinks that 'every class is a mixed ability class', regardless of whether they are set or not. In Nicky's view, setting, or seeing 'ability' as the only consideration that matters, ignores a whole range of issues that should be considered in relation to children working in groups. Some of these issues have already been mentioned. Nicky's observations of children's behaviour in groups are an extension of her observations of them as individuals and serve the same end: to create conditions in which their learning can more fully and effectively flourish.

Taking account of gender

One of the issues that Nicky feels should be considered when placing children in groups or assessing their work and attitudes is gender. Although, as she said, she had an aversion to any kind of generalization, she had to admit that there did seem to be some identifiable behavioural characteristics of boys and girls, once they were placed in groups, and if the most was to be gained from them, these were worth bearing in mind when planning activities. For example, she mentioned two boys, Hussan and Sam, whose attention had been caught by a particular practical task. As she commented:

> I know it does tend to be a generalization but it does tend to be those kinds of boys ... that if you give them a hands-on task, things to look at and things to think about [those are the ones] who respond better than to something to read and write, whereas the girls, that group of very quiet girls, they respond better if you give them something to write down; they are quite happy with that.

She also recognized that some of the girls needed to be challenged in different ways as, she felt, some of the high-achieving girls particularly are, stereotypically:

> more concerned with presenting their work beautifully with pictures and things like that and they have been conditioned to think their work is brilliant ... but they're missing the real analytical side to it ... getting them to write discursive essays and analysing texts has been good in that sense because it stops those girls becoming too concerned about the way their work looks.

Another factor that Nicky takes into account when forming groups is potential leadership skill; she uses this in a number of ways and feels it 'important to recognize class and group leaders and to remember this in planning'. In one of the observed lessons Nicky had placed a rather diffident boy with a group of girls who had much greater leadership potential. He was placed in this group not because Nicky thought he would have a comfortable time and just be carried by them, but because when he himself was put in a leadership role he found the responsibility all too much and he achieved very little. As Nicky had hoped, by being placed in this particular group, he first watched what the successful girls were doing and then gradually began to work on his own with a noticeable degree of confidence. She also noticed that Chan, a 'hardworking boy', had a positive influence in his group, and that Sam and Niall, who could not always be relied upon to concentrate, had done so under Chan's leadership: 'He was quite a good role model for them.' Not all the groupings in that session worked out as successfully, in Nicky's opinion, but they all managed to achieve something and there were also other things that were gained: for Nicky, observing the dynamics of the groups gave her additional and valuable information on which to draw next time she was deciding on how to group the class. The observation of individuals did not end with getting to know them as separate people, but extended to trying to know them in relation to others.

Learning from each other

One of the insights Nicky considered that she had gained from noticing and observing the students in her class was the extent to which they learned from each other. By no means did she see all their learning as being mediated through her, nor would she have liked to think this was so. Indeed, she was glad to say, that she felt 'that they *do* learn [from each other]. I mean, if you watch children who come in to this school and don't speak any English ... I mean they don't learn any English from me ... but they soon pick it up from the other kids in the class.'

She thought that this form of language acquisition was very often underestimated by the school management but formed a very valuable part of their learning: 'There's this lack of recognition of how much the kids will learn from each other.' Nicky also remarked that she thought this lack of understanding extended to the children themselves. 'I don't think they recognize enough how much they learn from each other … I'm always saying – help each other!' In nearly all the lessons observed, Nicky would frequently put the students into situations where they could capitalize on 'recognizing and making use of the importance of them learning from each other'. The students confirmed this, saying in interview that 'We already know that we can ask each other for, like, help with work, yes. That kind of thing.'

Recognizing diversity

We have seen how important it was to Nicky to understand as much as she could about the individuals in her class in order to create conditions that were optimally enabling for each student; she thought the students, too, benefited from understanding about themselves and one another as learners. She noticed that the more they acquired such insight, the greater had been their change of attitude towards learning, and she constructed a number of activities they would find helpful in this respect. She herself gained from activities designed to help the students to find out about their preferred learning styles. She maintained that 'It's something I really try to keep in my head now when I'm planning lessons.' This additional information meant that she could devise a range of different tasks and activities that she thought would cover the range of learning style preferences that had been revealed in her class. She thought that such knowledge also helped students to recognize why some tasks were more to their liking than others and to appreciate why she planned such a range of activities for them. She acknowledged that 'you can't please all the kids all the time' but she hoped it demonstrated to the students that they all learned in different ways. As she said to them, 'You are all going to have to bear with it if the lesson doesn't switch you on; it might switch someone else on and later on there might be one that switches *you* on.'

Nicky found these useful activities to refer back to with her class from time to time and they had evidently made an impression on the students who were interviewed. One boy explained that he only liked certain aspects of an activity they were doing in English (looking for particular descriptive words in *Romeo and Juliet*), but that he accepted that 'Different people learn in different ways – if you like talking and Miss is talking then you will remember, but if they watch things, then they can remember different sorts of stuff.' Two girls in the same interview also agreed with him and said it was very useful to know about your learning style, 'because it gives you, like, you know, it says if you're this kind of learner, you should try *this* or *this*'. One student recorded in her journal: 'I have learned that everyone has their unique learning style and we all learn in different ways and I have come to understand this by watching the rest of the class sometimes and see what and how they are learning.'

Noticing and responding: a continuing process

Careful observation of the individuals in her class, watching how they interacted with others, considering their various characteristics, interests, attention span and learning styles, provides Nicky with a constantly growing fund of information that enables her to further her students' learning and remove any potential limits to their learning. She uses it to inform all aspects of her planning and her moment-by-moment responses in the classroom. Nevertheless, Nicky felt an increasing frustration that it was becoming less and less possible to offer her students what she felt would benefit them most. The kinds of lively lessons and activities that Nicky undertook with her class were the very ones she thought were most likely to fly in the face of the additional testing, exams and new targets that were being introduced into the school timetable. Repetitive revision lessons were soon to be the required diet in place of the imaginative ways Nicky approached the teaching of English. Role play, 'hot seating', word hunts, dictionary races, making up competitions, writing short stories and poems, devising literacy maps, examining different illustrations to the same poems, having discussions, watching videos, using the Net and putting on presentations were all part of the varied diet she offered her students. The chief emphasis was on work that required student input and engagement. In between such lessons Nicky was able to fit in the necessary revision and secretarial practice tasks the children needed for their exams and tests and, because of the balance she created, the students tolerated such sessions with a degree of acceptance and realism. As one girl wrote in her journal, 'In the past few lessons we have been getting ready to do our essays – it wasn't that fun, but I mean, is it meant to be fun?'

In either kind of lesson, Nicky monitored, through her close observation, the success or otherwise of her planning as the lesson progressed; in her interviews she often referred to ways she would alter this or modify that next time she tried them. For instance, she said of something she had tried out for the first time, 'I think I should use that technique again', 'Next time I ... ' and 'I think looking back I would probably ... ' It was most noticeable that such observations were made in relation to the responses of individual students, and they were still very much in Nicky's head when she was planning future work. She is very sure that the quality of such planning has a direct effect on the success or otherwise of a lesson and she is conscious of 'the difference it makes to all the students if I've had time to plan properly – a massive difference'. As Nicky was then head of the English department she was very aware of the huge increase in demands on her time, and felt they were beginning to act as a constraint on such detailed planning.

Even with such detailed and thoughtful planning, often fine-tuned to the needs and interests of individual students and groups of students as she had come to perceive them through her observations, Nicky realized the necessity of being flexible. A racist remark about the Irish, a group that was ironically one of the least represented in the school, once prompted the abandonment of a planned lesson and the beginning of a serious discussion: Nicky sees limits as applying to the learning of attitudes as well as to academic success. Students seemed to appreciate such events, as one of them remarked in an interview that 'Most of the time Miss does organize her lesson but [sometimes] it just happens that people *have* to express themselves and then Miss Hancock says "Well, we'd better get this idea out and then other people might learn from it".'

Whatever was being observed, it was clear that, for Nicky, one of the most powerful ways in which she could encourage and enable learning without limits was by knowing the individual students as well and in as many ways as possible: observing them continuously in a variety of situations, such as in groups, and undertaking a range of activities. However, observing individual students is not used by Nicky just as a tool for effective planning, however committed she is to seeing that as a means to lifting the limits on her students' learning. Nicky is genuinely interested in them and respects them as people in their own right. In one interview, a student was asked why they did not muck around in Nicky's English lessons as they claimed they did in other teachers' lessons: 'Well, it's *different*, you see' was the answer. 'Well, you see, we *respect* Miss Hancock and she respects *us*.'

10 Yahi's approach: raising the level of trust

Rote learning, dictation, memorizing, repetition: all these were the unchanging ingredients of Yahi's own maths education. Discipline was very strict and the teachers, though respected, were regarded for the most part as distant and unapproachable. Yahi recollects all this and the constant tests and exams and feels that to reproduce it in his own teaching would engender little in the way of positive attitude towards the subject. Indeed, it would be to limit the learning of which he believes his students are capable. As he says, 'When I was at secondary school you would often have unexpected impromptu tests, just to see who, you know, had the equation for quadratics. Things like that, and you would be assessed on that. But I don't want to put them [my students] through that.'

Working with the culture of cool

At the same time, Yahi recognizes that there were identifiably positive aspects of his experiences that could still be useful to his present-day students, particularly if he could convince them of their relevance. One of the obstacles to the achievement of this end, probably common to all those who teach Year 10, the age group with whom Yahi was observed, is the existence of an anti-academic 'youth culture'. For Yahi himself, there had been an unquestioned acceptance of the goal of excellence, but he recognizes that this is no longer the case for many of today's young people and that it is a limiting factor in its own right: 'You know, excelling is not "cool".' Yahi is not going to be defeated by such things, however. In his reckoning, a good teacher tries to think around problems like these and Yahi has a sense of pride and professionalism not only in being a teacher but also in being among those teachers who improve their skills and insights by actively seeking out ways in which to do so.

Yahi sees that rejecting this 'culture' outright would not gain him anything; while he admits it has considerable strength, he feels that the situation can be partly redeemed if he approaches it in a positive way and seeks to get behind it: 'I need to tap into it because you need to understand where they're coming from.' Yahi also argues that the same attitude acts as a limit to their mathematical development: 'One of the limits I come across really is challenging them to build up that intense curiosity that takes you to the library to look things up ... but, as they say in French, it's not *le monnaie courant*, it's not the currency, it's not the done thing at the moment.'

Around Yahi's classroom is evidence of some of the ways in which he tries to counteract the youth culture of adopted disaffection; for instance, displays of geometric problems and designs and various kinds of mathematical patterns, all mounted in ways that could catch the interest of students, besides evidence of the work of the students themselves. Without such interesting and lively displays, the classroom would look quite dispiriting. The school has historical foundations and was rebuilt in the 1930s as a boys' city grammar school, and although certain areas of the school have received attention by way of modernization and decoration, classrooms were not a priority. The school is now in the process of becoming a mixed comprehensive school, specializing in the arts, and the nature of its student intake is changing.

The school sets for maths and English but there is evidence of movement between the sets; in Yahi's class of 14- and 15-year-olds, which is deemed a 'middle' set, there seems to be considerable diversity in achievement. Yahi tries to devise ways of engaging the commitment of the whole class, not just those who already see themselves as successful. One strategy is to move away from the students' usual expectations of a maths lesson. For example, in his very first lesson with the class observed, Yahi took an unexpected approach. There was no mathematics teaching in the lesson. Instead, he told the researcher:

> We spent time just talking about issues relating to why they were here, why I was there and what we were going to do together. So we embarked on setting some sort of rules. Agreeing, you know, to what we were going to do together. I spent some time trying to share my background with them, telling them a little story about a holiday around home and my kids – bringing myself to some sort of human rapport with them.

One of the strategies that Yahi uses, on a regular basis, to counteract the anti-work youth culture is to introduce some fun into the maths lessons. Apart from anything else, he maintains that maths should not be seen as a solemn undertaking; serious, perhaps, but an area of learning that admits a degree of fun and interest. As he says, 'I tend to do things in quite a different way. Anything that helps me catch the kids' imagination, I'll use it.' He perceives 'a need [in maths] for more vibrancy and interaction'.

To one student, a Russian boy who had just recently arrived in England, the approach was quite novel, but it was something he appeared to appreciate: 'To help make us learn [it] is good sometimes; the teacher try to make it fun.' Another student, Melanie, said in an interview: 'He's funny and that helps to make everyone happier ... it's generally his personality; makes jokes and stuff like that.' She especially appreciated the benefits of this approach as she did not consider herself very strong in the subject: 'I suppose if it's fun it's more relaxing because maths is very daunting [so he helps us] by making it fun, by explaining it, using examples.' She recollected one occasion when Yahi's approach had been particularly helpful to all the class: 'It was before a test, it was really good actually, we were really nervous for this test because it was quite hard stuff, but Mr Tahibet brought in a little rubber duck and he patted it and it quacked and then it was all quiet and everyone was laughing!' Then, as another student added, 'he said "Good, well, you can get on with your maths test now because you're not stressed".'

The rhythm of the lesson

It is characteristic of Yahi's approach to problems that, instead of meeting them head-on in a confrontational manner, he side-steps them; not in any sense of avoidance but in the sense of neat footwork in a dance. To borrow a phrase from Professor Colwyn Trevarthen, he has 'a teacher's musicality' – a feeling for the rhythm, the ebb and flow of his class. It could be a coincidence, but Yahi is very interested in dance and dance forms and holds a regular after-school dance club. His awareness of the rhythms in learning, and how they can be made to work to a teacher's advantage, can be seen in two regular events that are part of all his lessons. He recognizes that the students need a certain predictable pattern to their lessons and that they have other needs as well if they are to gain the most from their maths periods. So, in order that they can focus on their work calmly and without the internal clamour that might have been produced by the previous lesson or events, Yahi insists that when all the students have come into his classroom and found a place to sit, they shut their eyes for a few moments and concentrate on thinking about something pleasant or peaceful. Yahi considers this time to be vital to his students, 'because they need to be able to unload whatever baggage they've got before coming into the classroom'. He sees that the effect of being preoccupied with this 'baggage' might be to prevent the students concentrating and thereby creating 'their own limits' at a critical point before the lesson has even started. As he observes, 'On the emotional side, if there's somebody who comes in with something that's on their mind ... it's very difficult to reach them and get them to work to a good standard ... It's something, a technique, that they need to learn ... to try to think about something positive.' He tells the students that 'It's just for you to be able to really focus on what you are going to do because otherwise your mind is elsewhere and you know if your mind is elsewhere I can't teach you.'

The second routine that Yahi has introduced into his lessons, in response to what he sees as the natural rhythm of the students' attention level, is a five-minute break in the middle of the session. Yahi recognizes that the students need a high level of concentration in maths if they are to get the most out of a lesson, but that it is unrealistic to expect this to be maintained for forty minutes. Once their level of attention begins to drop, a potentially serious limit to their learning is created, but Yahi sees that it can be largely prevented by adopting his strategy. In the break, students can get up from their seats, stretch, talk to their friends or Yahi and generally relax. According to the students who were interviewed, this practice is not used by any of their other teachers but they seem to appreciate this way of working, as their comments showed. Michaela, for instance, agreed that it was very rare to have a break in the middle of a lesson, and although it didn't exactly count as working 'it's better to have, like, a breather. Everyone likes that and it probably does help people more.'

The emotional dimension of learning

Although Yahi's awareness of what can influence his students' achievements takes in a wide range of factors, these examples demonstrate his particular emphasis on emotional factors. As he reports himself, this awareness has grown in the past few years, not only as he has come to notice the significance of the emotions in the behaviour, attitudes and achievements of his students but also because he now has young children of his own. His observations of them and the way that they respond to events has, he says, 'made a difference; I am much more aware now, of the emotional dimension. I tell my own little boy, "I learn from you" but he's still too young to understand!' Yahi's initial training as a maths teacher was shaped by the expectation that maths teaching is simply the delivery of a subject, and so such considerations are still novel to him. Even so, Yahi admits that they have a significant influence on the way he now sees teaching and the way he sees students and their behaviour: 'These other things have tremendous importance on their performance.' He also adds that 'It is important for teachers to try to tune into it.' The recognition that 'these other [emotional] things have such a tremendous importance for their performance' has led Yahi to see them as setting real limits to his students' learning. He wants to be able to help his students to overcome these and he realizes that he needs to be better informed about the whole area of emotional development. To be the better, more effective teacher that he would like to be, he feels he needs to know more; indeed, Yahi was registering to take a course in the summer holidays, which he hoped would help him to see how he could further 'develop that other side' and incorporate it into his teaching.

An example of this growing sensitivity is an experience of Yahi's with a particular student, a girl who usually had no problems with concentration or understanding. He was only a few minutes into the lesson 'and I thought [to myself] you are not here today'. In his estimation, something had probably happened prior to the lesson 'and it was still there; something was niggling her'. So she had switched off. Yahi said that before he had begun to think seriously about the emotional dimensions to learning, he would have reacted quite differently to the situation: 'You know, whereas before I would say "Come on, what do you mean you can't do it? OK, just sit down and get out your books".' Now he says he often responds quite differently. In the case of this particular student he recognized that his old approach would probably have been counter-productive. His present reaction is to try to assess such situations and consider what might be the most appropriate response. On several occasions with this student he has 'let her spend the whole lesson doing very little – and then she has ... talked to me, she'll say "Oh well, you know, this happened at home".' Yahi said that by 'giving her space' he hoped that she would recognize that it was being given to her deliberately and that 'next time she'd pay me back by working harder, which in the event is what she did'.

Using feedback from the students

Knowing his students well is not just a matter of picking up incidental knowledge about them as the year progresses. Such knowledge is also deliberately sought, using a number of strategies. Yahi considers that getting feedback from the students is one of the most important in this respect, and he deliberately asked this class, at the end of his first term with them, to write down any comments or observations that they might like to make about him or his maths lesson. The students could respond anonymously, but in the event not many did so. He discussed with them why he needed their comments: 'I keep telling them, I need feedback! Otherwise I can't improve the way I do things – I need feedback in any shape or form in order to adjust.' It was a two-way exercise: the students could let Yahi know something about themselves and the way they saw maths, information that they recognized he would treat respectfully and act upon. Yahi saw it as knowledge that would mean he could offer himself to them as a more effective teacher. Some teachers might see this as a somewhat risky enterprise, in which students would take the opportunity to make personal remarks, but

Yahi said this had not happened. On one occasion, the researcher arrived in his classroom when he had just gathered up these comment slips, and he passed them across to her sight unseen. As he had anticipated, there were no comments of a personal nature, but there were plenty of thoughtful observations. Some of these might have made for somewhat uncomfortable reading, but none the less all seemed to have been offered in a constructive manner.

One student, for example, wrote, 'I am finding it easier to stay on track now. I think your class is very demanding and sometimes you move too fast.' The pace was appreciated by another student, though, who wrote: 'I think your speed is just right now and I understand what we do.' Yahi's style of teaching was enjoyed by quite a number and a typical comment was 'I love your style of teaching – maths is fun now but it is not my favourite subject so I know I must try very hard.' This student added that Yahi's style of teaching was 'helping me to understand' but she was also one of those who said she would 'prefer it if you went a *little* bit slower'. Yahi said afterwards how useful he had found the students' feedback; it seemed to fulfil what he said earlier about trying 'to see where there is a link between student and teacher. How the students see the teacher and how much they are willing to open up and take in.' He saw the class as 'willing to be helped now, which is the crucial thing. Every time I mark their books, I try to put constructive comments in their books. Just turn anything into something positive.'

By means such as these, Yahi recognizes that he can now bring individual students 'back on track' and that he is increasing his skill in being able to do so. He acknowledges that individual students approach maths in a variety of different ways and that reflecting on and accommodating to these differences can help each one of them not only to have a better attitude but to achieve more proficiency in maths. Potential limits to their learning can be removed.

Opportunities and encouragement to engage

Yahi recognizes that some students, either because of their previous experiences or because their strengths lie in other areas, need additional help and encouragement. This encouragement takes a variety of forms and is essential to the way Yahi sees his role in lifting the limits to his students' learning. As he sees it, all his students are entitled to equal access and it is an essential part of his role as a teacher to facilitate this access in as many ways as are needed.

In any class, including in a setted group, there are students who find some things easier or harder than others, and he makes accommodations for these variations. One accommodation Yahi consciously rejects, however, is grouping his students on the basis of such differences. To do so, he feels, does not further the interests of anyone. Instead he says that, 'for all the classes I teach, I encourage them to sit with their friends. My rationale is that it encourages them if they don't understand.' On other occasions, he deliberately moves the students around to work with others they do not know very well, because, as he says, 'I think it is quite important to go through a topic with someone you have never talked to before. I think they will understand it more.' Yahi has a clear idea of what he is working towards: 'Ideally, the stage I have to reach is where they are able to work in groups and feed from each other – it takes time and the group needs to look at the group dynamic.' If such groupings and pairings do not work out, though, he is ready to take action: 'I move them when I feel it's not becoming constructive.' The greater good is not served by prolonging such situations.

Charlene, one of the students who was interviewed, recognized that Yahi probably 'knows how people learn' and thought that this was certainly the case as far as she was concerned. 'He knows that I do need to be told more than once ... and I need to ask questions ... that I need to be given a bit more help.' Michaela, a student already mentioned, thought Yahi was one of the few teachers who 'did check that you've understood ... he knows that some people are quicker at getting stuff than the others and he's always checking, like, "Do you understand?"' She also appreciated the fact that in their reports Yahi pointed out the various things 'each of us needed to work on' and that he knew individual students well enough to be able to pinpoint very accurately what these things were.

Sometimes Yahi helps students in idiosyncratic ways that he has found to be effective in counteracting limits or obstructions to his students' learning. If, occasionally, he makes himself look amusing in the students' eyes he is unconcerned as long as he, their teacher, has managed to clarify their thinking. One student remarked that she appreciated the times when Yahi 'acted things out' in a fun way – not just because it helped her relax, but because it also helped her to recollect certain maths principles. 'Where he does some examples, like running fast from door to door, you know it then and you can imagine it ... and some stuff like that, you can remember what he's done because you think back and you think, oh that's the time when Sir did that!'

Building confidence and trust

In Yahi's opinion, such strategies help to increase his students' confidence: 'that is what I'm trying to do – boost their confidence'. It is not just confidence in thinking they can tackle the work; for Yahi it is important that his students have the confidence to say 'I don't understand'. He recognizes that confidence is a delicate plant and always has to be borne in mind when planning ahead: 'You need to build on something [the students] already know – just to make them feel confident they can handle this before we move on.' Yahi also recognizes that the increasing demands of continual testing are having a negative effect on his students' confidence, which could limit their potential achievement in both the short and long term.

As Yahi sees it, the greater the confidence his students are able to build up both in themselves and in him, the greater becomes the degree of mutual trust. This matter of trust is of particular importance to Yahi in his thinking about teaching, and he mentions it frequently. He knows it is not something he can achieve with his class though, unless he can demonstrate that he means it. Unlike a number of teachers, for example, he allows his students to leave the room to go to the toilet without asking. The onus is on them to mention where they are going, but they do not actually have to ask. Yahi hopes that by various means such as this he can 'raise the level of trust' that he sees as 'so very, very important'. He acknowledges that it is not something he can rely on from the start, but he consciously works at it because he sees it as 'so crucial, because if they trust me then everything should be all right'. That his students did come to trust him was evident from their observations about what it was like to be in Yahi's class and confirmed what he said, 'I think with this group we are now building more and more trust.' His use of the pronoun 'we' is unforced but significant: trust works in two directions in his class.

One way in which Yahi knows his class is generally becoming more confident and trusting is that more of them are prepared to ask questions. 'What I'm trying to do is boost their confidence and get them to systematically really explore questions.' Questions are another way of providing him with feedback, besides showing evidence of the students' real engagement with the subject. At the start of the year he made a point of telling the class that 'You must keep asking questions. Nobody should laugh at somebody who asks a question or gets something wrong and never take the mickey – it's too easy.' He saw that the best way of achieving this attitude to asking questions was 'to create a safe environment where they can make mistakes'. It took time to become part of the classroom culture, though; Yahi admitted at the end of the first term that he was still working on it with them and that 'they are not yet coming forward in terms of asking questions – I know some of them have weaknesses but they don't like to bring it out in the open. I'm still trying to create this environment where they can take risks with their knowledge and with their maths. It takes time.' Asking questions, he says, is all about this kind of risk-taking, and he was pleased with the progress of one student, Nicholas, who was now beginning to 'ask questions regularly'. Yahi said that he wrote in Nicholas's maths book: 'Please keep it up! Do bombard me with questions because that is how I'm going to do what I want to do.' By the middle of the following term, there were quite a number of students who seemed prepared to ask questions. Some were still rather tentative and would ask at the end of a lesson, but, even so, Yahi saw that as an improvement: 'now they sort of stay behind and try to sort out any doubts'.

Asking questions and more questions is part of what Yahi expects from his students. He also has expectations of them regarding behaviour and punctuality: that they will work as hard as they can, even if it is not their easiest subject, and that they will respect each other. He feels it is part of his job to let the students know quite clearly what his expectations are: 'I think my expectations for them are very high – and I think they need to know this.' These expectations apply to everyone in the class, not just a selected few. In Yahi's opinion, 'Once they know that the teacher has high expectations of every individual, not just a group of students, but every individual, I think they will do their best.' Yahi challenges his students, but he also gives them the kind of support and understanding that mean they are prepared to meet his expectations with increasing willingness, and, in so doing, experience the learning without limits that he aspires to on their behalf.

11 Julie's approach: access, security and success

Julie teaches history in a secondary school serving a predominantly white, rural community, 15 miles from the centre of a large Midlands town. She describes her Year 10 class as 'a very diverse group', who 'are all there because they want to be', having chosen history as an option. This, Julie feels, 'has created a different atmosphere, a positive atmosphere' within the group. Their attitude is also affected, Julie believes, by awareness that it is a mixed-ability group. 'The students can go to their lesson and feel totally equal because they are in a room with all sorts of different pupils. They are not in a group where they feel "I am in the top or bottom set". It is a complete mix, and I think they like that.'

Julie is deeply opposed to the practice of setting pupils because of the unfairnesses that it frequently embodies and the damage that she has seen it do to students' self-esteem, to their belief in potential as learners and to their attitudes to learning.

> Very often the type of pupils who end up in the bottom set, you look at their backgrounds, they are the ones who haven't had the help and support in the formative years, they haven't got resources at home, haven't got many books ... and on top of all that, they are placed in bottom sets, or they are told 'You can only do this.' And some pupils just accept that and they slip into this feeling of being worthless. Some fight against it and keep trying but it is very hard, isn't it, to keep trying when you are told 'Well, you are being entered for an exam where you can only get a D.'

When she was first appointed to her post in this school, she took over a 'bottom set' history group 'who greeted me with something like "We're the thickos, we don't do any work but we managed to give our last teacher a nervous breakdown." They had decided some time before my arrival, probably when placed in this group, that all they were good for was being pains and tried as hard as possible to fulfil that image.' Julie spent two years trying to help them to change their image of themselves, enabling them eventually to experience and achieve success.

At Julie's instigation, there is now no longer any setting in the human-ities department, a policy that receives full endorsement from the school's senior management, since exam results year on year compare very favourably with those of other departments in the school. Julie's antipathy to setting practices is linked to a deep moral and professional commitment to everyone she teaches. The learning of all students is of equal value, and is therefore equally deserving of careful consideration on the part of teachers. Students must never be made to feel second class or, worse, that they have been written off by their teachers as unlikely to achieve anything worth-while academically. If this happens, Julie believes, 'their work will become second class. It's a self-fulfilling prophecy.'

Three principles

Julie's teaching is guided by three central interdependent principles that describe what she believes needs to be done at a practical level if this 'ethic of everybody', her commitment to the learning of all students, is to be translated into practice in the classroom:

1   Accessibility: organizing teaching and learning in such a way that learning experiences are accessible to *everyone*.
2   Emotional well-being: ensuring that as far as possible *everyone* feels emotionally safe, comfortable and positive about their learning in history.
3   Worthwhile achievement: trying to ensure that *everyone* gains something from the lesson and leaves feeling good about themselves because something worthwhile has been achieved.

These principles operate together to create the optimum conditions for all students' learning. They embody Julie's understanding of the many barriers that can constrain and limit students' learning, and what can be done to overcome these, as well as her understanding of the conditions that foster learning.

Accessibility of learning opportunities

The first principle is to make sure that the learning activities and experi-ences provided for the group genuinely do offer everyone something that they can do. This may seem self-evident, but Julie is convinced that much challenging behaviour is attributable to students being given work that they cannot do. 'I think the majority of pupils, the only thing that makes them aggressive, or rude or uncooperative is because they are given a piece of work that they can't do, so they think "I can't do this, so I'll be a nuisance instead to hide the fact that I can't do it." [It's] just a reaction.'

Julie uses her knowledge of the range of attainments, learning styles and responses within the group to create a range of learning opportunities that are opened up to *everyone* in the group. It is crucial that they are offered to everyone, because of the negative messages that can be sent or received when tasks are differentiated for particular individuals and groups:

> I tend to do work that I think everybody can engage in at one level or another, which doesn't mean that I am not aware of their diffi-culties if they have any. It just means that I don't want to go round the room saying 'Well you're very clever, so you can do this but you're a bit thick so I'll give you that.' Because that's what you are doing isn't it really? And it's surprising how well students do perform at certain tasks ... if they are given the chance.

She prefers to set tasks that allow students themselves to choose how far to go (through a series of graded questions), or tasks that allow them to choose between a more demanding and a less demanding task.

> I don't like giving students different sheets. I'd much rather they choose what to do. We have some sheets that are double sided, they are the same tasks but they are worded in different ways, or they are using different sources ... I prefer to say to students, look at both sides and do the one that you can cope with best ... And what you often get is students who you would think will struggle who do both sides.

She also likes to include tasks that offer students complete freedom to respond in their own way. At the end of one unit of work, for example, on the history and culture of North American Indians, students undertook an assignment that involved using the knowledge and understandings gained to create an imagined interview with an Indian chief about Indian beliefs and way of life. 'The assignment is a very good example of letting pupils use their own imagination and knowledge ... I think it is an example of an activity that doesn't limit them ... they can just go about it in whatever way they want.' These approaches to task-setting help to create conditions for learning without limits because, while there is work that everyone can do, nobodys scope for learning is curtailed by decisions made in advance by the teacher about what might be 'appropriate' for them and what they might be expected to achieve.

In evolving her repertoire of approaches, Julie has developed a sophisticated understanding of the many ways in which tasks can present barriers to learning and of the scope available to teachers to help to make learning more accessible. She has achieved this understanding by systematically treating pupils' difficulties, for example, in following instructions, in sustaining attention or in understanding concepts, as a possible indication of difficulties inherent in the language, layout, phrasing, format or sequencing of classroom tasks. When lessons do not go as well as she anticipated, she treats this as a reason to look again at features of the tasks themselves and the associated classroom organization in order to see what might need to be changed. This is a necessary part of the process, she says, because it is inevitable that 'things will occur that you have not thought of'. The task of making lessons more accessible for all is 'an ongoing thing'.

When planning to use activities for the first time, she goes through a rigorous process of examining draft materials and ideas for potential sources of difficulty. Sometimes she involves colleagues, preferably non-specialists, to see if the wording of a task communicates clearly what is to be done. As a result, Julie says, 'Sometimes I will reset the task, reword it, or change it to try to avoid any possibility of confusion or ambiguities.' Sometimes it may involve changing features of classroom organization that might cause problems. With one activity on preventative medicine in Roman times, for example, she decided to make a very simple change to the materials when using the activity for the second time. By using different coloured card for different group activities, instead of all the activities being printed on white card, she helped to eliminate one possible source of confusion and frustration for students, and the group work was able to proceed much more smoothly.

What comes across as Julie describes what she does to ensure that learning experiences are accessible to all is a conviction that accessibility is a quality that is produced through teachers' judicious choices and actions – and the choices and actions that they enable and encourage on the part of young people – rather than an objective quality inherent in the relationship between particular learning objectives and the characteristics of particular students. The teacher's task is not a technical one of matching tasks and learners, but a creative one, involving careful design and sequencing of learning activities, taking into account not just the cognitive needs but also the likely emotional responses of learners to the experiences in which they are invited to participate, in order to make it possible for whatever knowledge, understanding and skills are intended be the focus of the lesson to be made accessible to everyone.

For example, during a topic on medicine, Julie wanted the group to use a passage from Chaucer as one of their central resources for learning about people's views of doctors and medicine in the middle ages. She considered it to be a very difficult text, but having used it before was confident that, with the right sort of support and lead-in, she could enable all pupils to engage with it productively and derive both understanding and satisfaction from working successfully with such demanding material.

Her strategy was to begin with some questions that helped the students to remind themselves what they already knew about medical practices and how people viewed doctors and medicine in other periods of history already studied. This was intended to build up points of reference that would assist them in interpreting the passage. She then provided some brief background to the *Canterbury Tales*, and used a short video extract to heighten interest and curiosity in the topic, to relax and reassure them that this was something that they were going to enjoy and be able to do, and to offer visual support as well as background information that would assist them in making sense of the source. Next she explained the purpose of the Chaucer passage, and read it aloud, to help students to hear the meaning and also to provide some initial explanations of difficult words and sections that might present barriers, before students worked on the ideas in the passage themselves with the support of a series of questions. Students were encouraged to work together and support one another in making sense of the passage, since students can often do with a partner what they would not have been able to do alone. Julie also closely monitored individuals' responses during the course of activities, and particularly their body language, for signs of frustration or confusion, so that she could judge when best to intervene to assist their learning.

In preparing this sequence of activities, Julie did more than just ensure that the students were adequately prepared cognitively to tackle the demands of the task; she was also anticipating and providing for their emotional needs. 'There are students in there who have difficulty with written sources, written anything really; the language of that particular source without a lot of guidance would have just thrown them and they would have gone into panic mode and wouldn't have been able to do anything.' She defined this reaction not simply as a problem for the less confident readers and learners, but as a natural reaction for any individual – adult or child – confronted by a complex text or task. 'You know that they are going to glance at it and think "What on earth is that about?" as you know sometimes we can, when you see a poem or something for the first time, it takes a few readings and you feel a little bit threatened by it.'

As well as providing the video introduction to prepare the ground and make them feel that what they were going to do was accessible, she made a point of acknowledging the difficulty of the source, 'So if they were feeling any sort of panic that was OK ... but it was all right because we were going to go through it together.' She attempted to make students feel comfortable and safe, by explicitly acknowledging how they might be feeling and not just legitimating their feelings, but reassuring them in advance that adequate support was going to be provided.

As this example illustrates, the task of making learning experiences accessible to all (Julie's first principle) is intimately bound up with and indissociable from the task of ensuring students' emotional well-being (Julie's second principle). Both need to be given equal attention, Julie believes, if the task of making learning accessible is to be achieved, as she felt it had been in this lesson.

> I don't think there was anybody in the room who was struggling with the work. Even if they were being prompted a little bit, they were still getting it done ... I think most of them seemed to enjoy it ... The source was difficult but they managed to cope with it after we went through it and they felt quite good about that.

Providing equal access to learning for all also, for Julie, means providing a variety of learning experiences that do not all depend upon skills in reading and writing. Julie is concerned about how the dominance of the written word tends to disadvantage students who can more readily engage and express their ideas in other forms: 'They have also got a wealth of different kinds of knowledge, orally, and experiences that they can talk about or things that they can do. We find this with model-making, that pupils are often very gifted in certain areas, even if they can't write it down.'

Julie's teaching includes use of role play, drama, model-making, video and collaborative group work, as well as activities involving listening, reading and writing. In order to record ideas in writing, a range of techniques is offered to students in addition to written notes: 'We try to use flow charts and spider diagrams, things in diagrammatic form, or get them to stick little cartoons in their books, because it is a more accessible format than loads of notes, which some pupils simply couldn't write down in the time they have got.'

Julie tries to ensure that the constraints of the exam syllabus do not close down opportunities for students to experience activities that encourage creativity:

> I am conscious that they need things to help them to get through the exam at the end of the day. But sometimes I think it's a bit of a shame because there is a lot of creativity there and a lot of inter-esting ideas which sometimes get lost in the pressure to complete the syllabus. I try to draw them out as much as I can ... It's amazing how creative students can be ... Sometimes, students are not allowed to be creative ... everything is too fixed; and occasionally, I like to do something like this [inviting open-ended responses to a poem] just to see what happens.

Emotional well-being

Just as close attention to students' emotional well-being plays an essential part in achieving accessibility for all, so accessibility plays an essential part in securing students' emotional well-being. 'I think if a student can't do something then, well they're going to react in one of two ways, they're either going to get quite aggressive as a defence mechanism ... or they are just going to withdraw into themselves and just not contribute at all because they feel scared or stupid.'

Julie believes that many of the less academically successful students have formed very negative perceptions of their own abilities, long before they arrive at secondary school. These can be very difficult to reverse, and it is only possible to begin to do so if students regularly find themselves in a position where they can participate and so are repeatedly provided with evidence of what they *can* do when given the chance. To participate, though, is risky and students will not take the risk unless they feel comfortable enough to do so. Julie's second principle, then, is to create conditions in which all learners feel emotionally safe, where they are encouraged to feel positive about themselves as learners and about learning history, and where none of them are embarrassed or have their self-esteem undermined.

The look and feel of the classroom learning environment has an important part to play in helping to create these conditions. To walk into Julie's teaching room is to be confronted by a lively and intriguing display of posters, models and artefacts, as well as students' work. The tables are arranged in groups rather than 'regimented rows' in order to give the classroom 'a friendlier feel', as well as providing a more effective environment for group work.

> Whenever I start at a new school, the first thing I do really is to make [the learning environment] look attractive, and it has an instantaneous effect on pupils. I think they have got to feel good about coming into the room ... and you've got to try and be cheerful and welcome them ... so that is the first thing really, coming into the room and feeling happy to be there and not feeling that they are in a really dismal place or feeling threatened in any way.

When she is planning lessons, as we have seen, Julie anticipates students' likely emotional reactions to the challenges presented by particular tasks and activities, and works out how to support and scaffold their learning so that they are able to rise to the challenges rather than be defeated by them. Different kinds of tasks may present a threat to different learners in the group, so it is important to know the students personally as well as academically. 'The worst thing that you could do would be to terrorize somebody by making them do something that they really feel embarrassed about. And for some of them that could be quite damaging.'

Julie empathizes with learners' feelings of vulnerability, and accepts them as an inevitable part of the process of learning, striving to take care of their feelings in all her interactions with them. She understands the point of view of learners who find it difficult to ask for help: 'It is quite a thing for children to do, actually to say "No, I don't understand that" ... we know ourselves sometimes as adults we don't always admit, if we are told to do something, that we don't understand, because we are exposing ourselves.'

She tries to reassure students that they are not being judged when they admit to difficulties, and is always prepared to explain again and again, until students are confident that they understand. 'You must try very hard not to make them feel stupid [by saying] something like "What do you mean you don't understand that, we went through it last lesson", and it's difficult sometimes when you've said something several times and some-body still says "I don't understand it".'

During lessons, she is alert to the shifting emotional states and reactions of learners, so that she can intervene when necessary to offset difficulties.

> There may be one or two students who ... when faced with a ques-tion, or faced with a source, may go into panic mode ... obviously I will be keeping my eye open for that and just directing them to the right part of the source, and hopefully once they have done one or two they will realize that it is accessible.

In every interaction, she pays attention to the possible emotional impact on learners. This can meaning treading a fine line between building and under-mining self-esteem:

> Sometimes ... I will direct a question at a specifically named person, either to wake them up or to make them feel good about answering again, the sort of pupil self-esteem thing. So I have to be very careful to make sure that they are going to get it right because if that backfires on me they will be really embarrassed.

These two principles of 'accessibility' and 'emotional well-being' work together in a mutually complementary way to help to lift limits to learning. In making work accessible, Julie is noticing and removing possible barriers to learning that might otherwise cause learners to fail, and so further damage their self-esteem. Attending to the emotional dimensions of learning helps learners to overcome psychological barriers that might otherwise limit their ability and willingness to engage with learning opportunities provided.

Gaining a sense of worthwhile achievement

Together these two principles are not sufficient, however. Tasks and activities have to be designed in such a way that not just participation but success, something that both they and their teacher recognize as worthwhile, is a genuine possibility for every student. What Julie does is to establish a 'baseline', the minimum worthwhile achievement to be expected of all students in the context of a particular set of aims and content.

> Make it realistic, so that you know that there is not going to be anyone in the room that doesn't achieve that, because that is worse in a way if they don't achieve the minimum if they have worked hard. Because they feel awful if they can't achieve the minimum.

On the other hand, if they can see for themselves that they have done the work, and feel good about what they have achieved, this helps to build confidence that they can be successful on further occasions. If there is the potential within every lesson for all students to be successful and to be recognized as successful, the teacher can begin with positive expectations of all students, and communicate this through her behaviour, support and feedback. There is a danger, Julie recognizes, that establishing and communicating the baseline to students will encourage them to settle for the minimum and do no more, but this was not how most students responded.

Julie believes that the current education system – and particularly the examination system – operates with a definition of achievement that is far too narrow and so fails to give sufficient scope for the development and recognition of the talents and abilities of many students. 'Success' tends to be reserved for those who have high levels of competence in literacy and recall, and who can function under highly stressful conditions. The rest 'fail' because there is no alternative means available – at least at examination level – for recognizing and valuing their particular strengths and talents.

She tries to widen the scope for achievement available to students by providing lots of different opportunities for learning, and demonstrating learning, that are not all reliant on facility with the written word. Although it is important, she acknowledges, for students to 'have something to show for their efforts' – and to have ideas recorded in their books for later revision purposes – there are many different strategies that can be used to 'make sure that they end up with something in their book', besides writing 'loads of notes'. She is also happy for classes, on occasions, to go 'for a few lessons' without writing anything in their books, if they are engaged in what she considers to be other equally or more fruitful forms of learning. With one Year 8 group, for example, she had 'abandoned all their RE lessons' for several weeks to work on an assembly on Ramu and Sita to present to the whole school. 'They could have written pages and pages about the story', she commented, 'but would they really understand it as much as when they are actually acting it out?'

By defining achievement more broadly, and making such opportunities for achievement routinely available for students in her classes, she helps to make it possible for all students to demonstrate their abilities and understandings more fully – and so gain a greater sense of achievement and satisfaction than would be available to them if formal recognition is given only to traditional, narrow forms of achievement.

What Julie accepts as worthwhile achievement varies for different individuals, based on prior knowledge and what she has identified as the current growth points and needs of different individuals. She is very aware, though, of the fine line that she has to tread between celebrating achievement in order to build self-esteem, and reinforcing low expectations by asking or accepting too little. 'And it *is* a fine line because you don't want to give somebody a piece of work that scares them, which could potentially happen with three or four. But at the same time you don't want to give them fixed limits yourself.' It is possible to lessen the pressure on learners, where appropriate, by adjusting tasks slightly – for example, the need to write out answers – without reducing the cognitive demand. It is important, Julie emphasizes, to ensure that students' achievement is not obscured by their difficulty in completing other extraneous aspects, such as drawing a table in which to record their thinking. In one of the lessons observed, one student produced very little written work, but Julie was nevertheless satisfied with what she had achieved and able to communicate this to her in a positive way.

> She's not actually written much ... but there was some discussion taking place and to be honest, today was really more about talking and thinking than necessarily writing and she was engaging. I would have been a lot more concerned if she had just been sitting there, looking glum and not doing anything ... She was talking, she was getting into it.

Julie has a collection of 'stamps', which she uses when marking to help reinforce a positive sense of achievement and to contribute to the written feedback provided about their work. The stamps convey a range of different messages about students' efforts and the quality of their work. These messages are conveyed by amusing cartoon characters, and the students look forward to seeing which ones she has used in their books. Julie finds that it is possible, with their help, to give critical feedback in a way that does not hurt or undermine students' self-esteem.

Teaching for learning without limits

Working in combination, these three principles are the means by which Julie seeks to ensure that everybody can participate, everybody can experience success and be recognized as successful and everybody can leave feeling good about themselves and with a sense that something worthwhile has been achieved. They also provide a set of rigorous criteria for evaluating teaching and learning.

> Sometimes you come out of the lesson and you think 'That didn't really work' Or 'I must change that next time' or 'So and so is sitting in the corner there and was very quiet and didn't seem to get anything out of that.' So that is what I am always looking for. I try to think beforehand but sometimes things happen that you don't allow for, or an activity just wasn't suitable for a certain student. So you have to try to change it.

The three principles provide the basis for a pedagogy for learning without limits, because they assume and extend the possibility of successful learning to every child. Since her own school days when students were divided at the age of 11, Julie has never considered it a sensible strategy to label young people as 'less able'. 'Less able to succeed in a rigidly structured testing system maybe, but not less able to develop into thoughtful, talented human beings with a great deal to offer society.' Julie's approach to teaching is informed by an understanding of the many barriers to learning that contribute to limited academic attainment that are inherent not in individuals but in the many external constraints that limit and hinder learning, including the damage done to self-belief and aspiration by prior and current school experience. As we have seen, Julie gives priority in her day-to-day teaching to the relationship between internal psychological and emotional barriers, and the immediate external conditions within which learning opportunities are provided. It is in this area, she believes, that as an individual teacher she has most power to make a difference.

12 Non's approach: the bridge between values and practice

Non's contribution to the research project followed a different pattern from the other eight teachers in that she agreed to develop her own account of her practice. She chose to do this through a reflective investigation in which she engaged her Year 11 GCSE English class as co-researchers. This chapter is the account of her practice produced through this cooperative venture.

On reading the flyer for *Learning without Limits*, I knew immediately that this was something I badly wanted to become involved in. It chimed with so many of my own deeply held beliefs about the potential of all students but also made me think carefully about my increasing anxieties about the impact on students' educational experience of a narrowed focus on standards rather than achievement in its broadest sense. Here was a chance to contribute to some research that might help to refocus our energies on education, rather than mere schooling.

I teach English in a 11–19 girls' comprehensive school in an outer London 'leafy' suburb. Students are taught, with the exception of maths and modern foreign languages, in mixed-ability classes from Years 7 to 11. This policy means I have seen for myself the clearly positive effects of such groupings on students' self-perceptions. It has also, however, opened my eyes to the dangers of thinking that mixed-ability grouping automatically leads to, or is even underpinned by, a widely shared belief, by both teachers and students, in the potential of all.

In July 1999, after some preliminary negotiation, the university team asked me if I would like to design and carry out an investigation of my own practice that would mirror the work of the partnership between the eight other members of the team and the university researchers. With some trepidation I agreed, by now concerned that in undertaking such research I might uncover the opposite of what I hoped! I knew that my intentions were to liberate students from the effects of negative labelling. I hoped I was teaching in ways that empowered their thinking and helped them to view themselves positively as successful learners – but is this what it feels like to the students in my class?

I felt that it was vital that this should not be a solitary journey; I was clear that both I and my students would be more likely to benefit and learn from the research if we engaged upon it together. Recruiting them as co-researchers would help me to make explicit the thinking that underpins what I do, to map the connections between my values and practices, and reconsider both in the light of the students' feedback about what helps and hinders their learning. As well as contributing to the wider aims of the project, I hoped that through the research I would come to understand more about the impact of my practice on each student in a class, and find ways of improving upon my current practice.

Getting started

The first decision I made was to invite the 25 students in my Year 11 GCSE class to research the reality of our classroom with me. An introduction to the research project, intended to take only 15 minutes, developed into an hour-long discussion of the issues raised. Their interest was infectiously encouraging; I was glad that I had decided to do the research with this class and felt that working together it would be possible to generate useful data.

I carried out a number of preliminary enquiries with them in order to investigate their current perceptions and concerns. These included questionnaires exploring their perceptions of their own abilities and external influences on these perceptions, including my own; I tried to find out more about their personal learning styles and preferences, and their sense of how they were progressing in English. I also began a journal in which I recorded my plans, hopes, expectations and observations, not just of each lesson with this class, but whenever I had some space for reflection, attempting to build a picture of my own developing thoughts and strategies.

I asked the students to contribute further to the research by keeping either a written or a video diary (recorded in private once a week). Fourteen students did one or the other. Three students volunteered to watch videos of a series of lessons and construct a written commentary on what was happening. I also held discussions with the whole class, during which they helped me to construct a list of teaching strategies regularly used in English lessons, and shared their views about which of these, individually, they found most enabling. By using this range of methods I was trying to triangulate my own interpretations, and gain fresh insights into my practice from the students' point of view.

The core values central to my practice

There are two concepts that are central to my philosophy as a teacher. These core values inform my approach towards teaching and students. The first is *equal value*: the conviction that every individual's contribution should be treasured and encouraged, that each student has the right to equality of access and opportunity, that all students possess talents and potential that can be unlocked and developed (Daunt 1975). The second is *empowering students*: the conviction that schools bear a responsibility to establish attitudes and patterns of behaviour and thinking which ensure that all students leave with a positive sense of how to continue to develop their own education throughout life; and an appreciation of how what they have learnt at school links with their adult life. Schools should not be content simply to transmit factual knowledge that can be tested, but must strive to give all students the power and motivation to shape their own lives and contribute effectively to society.

However, such core values are rarely expressed directly and openly within any teaching situation. One of the tasks of my research was to delve beneath the appearance and surface interactions to discover how my core values were manifest in planning and managing learning. How did the students in the class experience the impact of these values that are so precious to me? How wide is the gap between theoretical principle and active reality? Is a gap inevitable?

The bridge

Table 12.1 shows the list of key strategies that the students and I recognized to be characteristic of what I do and how they learn in English. Reflecting on the links between individual strategies and my core values helped me to identify the central bridge between my values and practices and connect these to the project's theme of fostering learning without limits. This central bridge is concerned with reaching out to all students, trying to make school learning meaningful for all students by connecting school knowledge with their world. The students' input to the research also turned out to be particularly crucial in identifying the cement that holds the whole structure together. They helped to make me more aware that the teaching strategies I use to connect school knowledge to the students' world would, in themselves, remain simply a series of teacher tricks without the cement of the personal interactions between us all.

Table 12.1 Key strategies

Type of activity/approach	Helpful	Unhelpful
Wide choice of tasks and assignments	23	1
Oral activities	17	5
Differentiation by grouping and type of task	12	6
Formative feedback on coursework drafts	24	1
Introducing exam techniques through classwork	13	
Scaffolding tasks	15	2
Scaffolding explanations	17	
Developing reusable study approaches	11	
Real life parallels and examples	25	

This bridge between my values and practices has two central planks. One is concerned with recognizing and allowing for variety in ways that are empowering, not limiting. The second is concerned with ensuring that teaching and learning proceed on the basis of common knowledge – a shared understanding between myself and the students. These two planks provide the basis and rationale for my selection of teaching strategies, as explained in the following sections.

Allowing for variety

One approach I use that received almost unanimous approval from the students is to provide a wide variety of tasks and activities, encouraging students to *choose* the types of tasks, questions or modes of working that they find most enabling. This avoids the need to make a precise forecast of possible achievement, which can lead to a reduction in challenge and opportunity, with students only being allowed to follow the routes through tasks predetermined by a teacher's judgement. Providing choices reflects both the principle of equal value, because everyone is offered the same opportunities, and the principle of empowerment, because students take the lead in selecting their own challenges.

I use my understanding of learning styles theory to check that there is a sufficient range of tasks and activities provided. The variety of different learning styles and preferences expressed by students in my Year 11 class (see Table 12.2) in response to the learning styles questionnaire is great, far greater than could be met by the approach to differentiation currently favoured by Ofsted, based on different levels of attainment. If practice is to reflect the principle of equal value, the range of learning opportunities provided should reflect equally those different styles and preferences. Otherwise some students will be seriously disadvantaged. I try to offer tasks, as illustrated in succeeding sections, that are different in type but equally challenging, and that give opportunity for everyone to access all levels of attainment.

Table 12.2 Preferred learning style

Preferred learning style or combination	No.
Visual	8
Auditory	2
Kinaesthetic	5
Visual and auditory	4
Auditory and kinaesthetic	3
Kinaesthetic and visual	1
Visual, auditory and kinaesthetic	2

I also use learning styles theory to talk with students about their learning, to help me communicate to them that I acknowledge, recognize and value differences, and that everyone's learning is of equal importance. By creating this shared language, encouraging dialogue around learning, I hope to enable students to feel more in control of their learning. The issue of variety goes hand in hand with choice. It is very important that students have the opportunity to make the *choice* of task or mode of working for themselves. While encouraging them to think about different learning styles and their own preferences, I try to ensure that students make their choices on the basis of what style of working they will find most enabling for a particular task or piece of work, rather than routinely channelling themselves or being guided into particular kinds of tasks.

Individual discussion to assist with choice of task, emphasizing guidance rather than instruction, leaving the final decision of which question or approach to use, is valued by students:

> I know I'll always get help when I have to decide on a question. But I like being able to make up my own mind. I'm glad my English teacher lets me do that, even if sometimes I choose something that doesn't quite work out as well as I hoped it would – I can always have another go at it.
>
> (Student G)

I do find getting this balance extremely difficult. It's so tempting to rush in with such firmly expressed 'advice' that the student is almost bulldozed into agreeing rather than thinking it through for herself. Students recognized that the opportunity to choose between different tasks allowed them to work from a position of strength.

There is always a large variety of questions to choose from. This means you can easily choose one which you feel confident on.

(Student L)

I can always choose one which I can answer well.

(Student S)

There are more creative essays and orals to very structured essays and orals which is good – people have something which suits their abilities to choose.

(Student M)

One student (F), however, felt that a wide choice made her feel inadequate simply because she found it so hard to choose which task to do. Her response prompted me to think about a more structured, supportive way of enabling them to make the most appropriate choice without them feeling overwhelmed by the act of having to choose. Student F was, I think, telling me that it is sometimes easy to let the principle of choice become a barrier to achievement.

Oral activities with multiple routes through

An alternative strategy is to set a broad question or task and allow students to construct their own ways through it. For example, working collaboratively in pairs or groups, students often design their own ways into a text, working from a set of assessment criteria that allow them into the secret of exactly what I am looking for in judging their knowledge and understanding. These are often oral tasks, including discussion, role play and dramatic interpretation. For example, one of the oral tasks used in our study of *Talking in Whispers*, a novel by James Watson (1983), asked students, in self-selecting groups, to present their final interpretation of the moral and message of the novel. The assessment criteria were provided and we had spent several weeks studying the text in detail in class.

The resulting presentations ranged from interviews in role with the author, hot-seating a range of characters, to a dramatized presentation of key moments from the novel. The level of understanding and response was universally high, matched only by the energy and commitment shown by the students. Each group was determined to meet the criteria to the very highest standard. Nobody uttered those dreaded words 'This is boring!' or 'I don't understand'; everyone felt they could achieve their goals. The value of predominantly oral tasks in helping with extended writing was acknowledged by some students:

> Because you have to really read the text, pick bits up, so it is more familiar, then it is easier to explain on paper as you know you can say it.
>
> (Student P)

> In oral tasks you have to look further into the texts and think of your own interpretations so this can help when you have to write about them.
>
> (Student L)

> It's like research in a way: find information, look things up, analyse information, present it to show how much you understand.
>
> (Student K)

Student B articulated her reservations but in so doing explored precisely why such tasks are so beneficial: 'I find it relatively easy to understand a text and sometimes I find it harder having to do an oral because I have to question my interpretation, but then that's probably a good thing.'

Four students would have preferred to respond in writing and would avoid oral activities if given the choice. This highlights one of the key problems in trying to open up as many different possibilities for learning as I can, while at the same time covering the demands of an externally set examination syllabus. Oral work is a compulsory element in the English GCSE (counting for 20 per cent of the final mark) and, for some students, is the most challenging aspect of the course because, quite simply, it is not what they enjoy or see themselves as being good at. Getting the balance right between extending the types of tasks that a student can tackle successfully and providing the variety required to maintain each individual's interest is an issue that I am still working on.

Establishing common knowledge

This second main plank of my bridge between school learning and the students' world is informed by the work of Edwards and Mercer, who underlined the need to seek to create shared knowledge and understanding between teacher and students as the basis for effective learning. They wrote: 'One of the points at which education commonly fails is when incorrect assumptions are made about shared knowledge, meanings and interpretations. In the achievement of shared understandings between teachers and pupils, failure is at least as common as success' (Edwards and Mercer 1987: 60). They explored how a teacher can try to establish an environment where the language used is transparent to all, where the conventional codes of classroom intercourse that all too often leave students grasping shadows in the dark are challenged.

Drawing on the work of these two authors, I try to remain constantly alert to the everpresent potential for misunderstanding arising from incorrect assumptions about shared knowledge and understandings. Misunderstandings can arise not just at the level of content, but at the level of what Edwards and Mercer call the 'implicit rules of interpretation', which affect how students make sense of what they are asked to do. I try to take account of this, for example, when I am introducing new topics, leading discussions, designing task sheets and assessing students' work. In all aspects of my teaching, I am seeking to create a language that is mutually comprehensible, that uses examples from the students' everyday or past experience, and functions upon a common knowledge base. The strategies I use are designed to support what Edwards and Mercer describe as the 'hand-over of control from teacher to learners', as explained in the following sections.

Scaffolding tasks and explanations

It is important to work at developing shared understandings by negotiating with students an awareness that there is no single correct interpretation of a text, so that they feel empowered to generate their own interpretations. A common strategy I use is to create a scaffold of tasks; for example, to uncover progressively the layers of meaning within a poem. Students' confidence rises as they feel themselves moving in a highly structured way through the initially difficult terrain of a poet's individual style to an understanding that allows them to interpret the work for themselves. One of the poems for which I used this approach was *To His Coy Mistress* by Andrew Marvell. After the poem had been divided into its 'natural' three parts, a worksheet was devised for each section, as in Figure 12.3.

In the first hour-long lesson the students initially worked in pairs discussing one-third of the poem with the help of the worksheet. They then joined together with all the other pairs working on the same part of the poem to share ideas and broaden discussion. In the second lesson these groups presented their ideas and interpretation to the other students so that each student had access to the composite of the views of all students. Each group began by explaining the overall meaning of their section, followed by an examination of Marvell's techniques. My intention was to make sure that, at each stage, all students felt secure in the knowledge that their explorations would be respectfully talked through and reprocessed within the whole group. At the end of the exercise they would have accurate factual knowledge but also the confidence to attempt individual and personally valid interpretations. These outcomes are reflected in the comments on the video recorded by the three students who reviewed these two lessons.

Had we but world enough, and time,
This coyness, lady, were no crime.
We would sit down and think which way
To walk, and pass our long love's day;
Thou by the Indian Ganges' side
Should'st rubies find: I by the tide
Of Humber would complain. I would
Love you ten years before the Flood;
And you should, if you please, refuse
Till the conversion of the Jews.
My vegetable love should grow
Vaster than empires and more slow.
An hundred years should go to praise
Thine eyes, and on thy forehead gaze;
Two hundred to adore each breast,
But thirty thousand to the rest;
An age at least to every part,
And the last age should show your heart.
For lady, you deserve this state,
Nor would I love at lower rate.

Summary of meaning and poet's desired impact on *To His Coy Mistress*

Things to do and questions to answer in your notes:

- Underline all references to places, noting the geographical range.

- Underline all references to time, either direct or implied. What do you notice about the lengths of time?

- Find all the references to love. What is the poet emphasizing and why is it important at the beginning of his argument?

- Identify the rhyme scheme. What effect does the rhythm and rhyme have on your response and understanding?

- Underline the imagery and explain the impact of each.

Figure 12.3 Worksheet on *To His Coy Mistress*

The videos of the lessons also bear very clear witness to the number of times and ways in which students need to ask, and hear answers to, questions about the details of a text before they can feel any kind of ownership of the whole. The repetition and struggle to find a clearer path through the text was irritating for me to review, but the students' comments on the lesson indicated that they recognized the value of the process and found it helpful. One said, 'It would be quicker if she told us, but we wouldn't think ... [she] forces us to think – no easy way out.'

Formative feedback on coursework drafts

Another strategy through which I attempt to build shared understandings between myself and students is offering detailed formative feedback on coursework. For example, for a coursework essay comparing *Pride and Prejudice* with a twentieth-century short story, I used the format shown in Figure 12.4.

Through the formative feedback that I provide, I am trying to help students to develop a clearer understanding of the criteria against which their work is evaluated, to strengthen their ability to evaluate their own work in terms of those criteria and to help them to appreciate at a very concrete level what they can do in order to improve their work. The strategy links to my core values in that it communicates my belief in all students' capacity to improve their work and, through dialogue, seeks to support them in developing the understandings that will empower them to make those improvements. It is a crucial part of my attempts to give the students access to how their work will be judged, to give them control over meeting the criteria as well as possible.

At the outset of the research, one student wrote in her questionnaire that she was learning to believe in herself as a result of the positive individual feedback she has received in English. Another wrote: 'Our teacher pushes us to our highest potential, is always willing to help outside of lessons and explains why she says the things she says to us in end of year statements and advice on drafts.' Although one student indicated that she needed her sister's help in interpreting some of the points made on her essay feedback sheet, all of the class were extremely positive about the amount and nature of the feedback they were given. One student commented:

> Mrs Worrall's numbering technique is really good! Because it helps to identify our mistakes easily and clearly. It also gives us a chance to change specific parts of the essay (Miss does not leave us clueless!). It also helps me to understand where I've gone wrong instead of just knowing that I have!
>
> (Student M)

Comments on first draft of essay comparing *Pride and Prejudice* and a twentieth-century short story

Name ....

Structure	
(1)	Strong introduction which launches straight into the essay.
(20)	Good sense of different styles of authors.
(23)	A rather brief conclusion. Try to expand it so it rounds the essay off rather than just coming to a halt.
Use of evidence	
(12)	Longer quote needed to illustrate your point.
(14)	Good choice of illustration.
(22)	Yes – perhaps contrast two more examples to illustrate your idea more fully?
Social, cultural and historical context	
(17)	This section needs to be expanded to show the differences between a novel and a short story in terms of potential for development of characters and plot.
(18)	Extend this section too, to show your understanding of the different social worlds of the two texts.
(21)	Note: 19th century
Style and SPAG	
(2)	What do you mean here?
(3)	Leave a line between paragraphs when word processing.
(6)	Elizabeth.
(7)	Full stop not comma.
(9)	have
(10)	No need to set out such a short quote.
(11)	Check sentence structure.
(13)	Spelling.
(15)	person
(16)	Check full stops.
Other comments	
(8)	No need to include title of book after quote.
(19)	Not quite the right expression. Can you re-write this sentence?

Figure 12.4 Feedback sheet for students

Apart from the need to ensure that I always modify my vocabulary to suit the individual student more immediately, this would seem to be a strategy that each student finds helpful and beneficial to learning.

Making learning relevant

A third way in which I try to build shared understandings and bridge the gap between school learning and students' worlds is to work to achieve a common understanding of the relevance of literature to students' everyday lives and the world around them. I know from experience how much more powerfully students engage and commit themselves to learning when they perceive the relevance of school learning to themselves and their lives. Obviously, their future success in examinations is an immediate incentive, but their investment is that much greater when learning links to issues that make sense to them personally and genuinely matter to them in their lives.

Trying to make relevant the content of an examination course can be problematic. Finding ways into helping them to grasp the importance of the social and cultural contexts of such writing is certainly challenging. A strategy I regularly use is to explore real-life and media parallels for texts we are reading together. This might include introductory references to stimulate interest in a text: for example, how Mel should behave towards Steve in *Eastenders* as an opening gambit in a lesson on *To His Coy Mistress*; or more serious explorations into the reality of the situation in Chile during the overthrow of the Allende regime. Following on from extensive factual research into the historical and current situation in Chile (aided by the publicity given to the arrest of General Pinochet while we were studying Watson's *Talking in Whispers*), I invited into school a victim of the Chilean junta's torture during the 1980s, to talk to the Year 11 class.

Dr Navarete's account of her imprisonment and treatment had a tremendous impact on all of the students and myself. Her explanation and description, not only of what happened to her but also the impact on her parents, made really clear the links between life and literature that are an intrinsic part of Watson's intention. Perhaps for the first time the 16-year-olds began to comprehend the power of literature to enable us all to experience emotions and reactions that only a few will actually live through. When asked what effect the visit had in relation to studying the book, student S seemed to sum up the class's reaction when she said:

> Even though we'd done all that research into Chile and watched the film[1] as well as reading the text in detail, the book only really came alive when Dr Navarete talked to us. Up until then I kept avoiding going through the torture scenes because they seemed too violent. Now I know why they're important. I expect to remember this book for a long time.

Such a powerful effect is obviously not an everyday event in my classroom, but it is an extreme illustration of a deliberate policy of trying to generate a sense of relevance and immediacy. Dramatically engaging the students' interest does make them feel more confident in their ability to deal with texts that can be difficult to decode, let alone truly engage with, such as *Talking in Whispers*.

Encouraging students to create their own parallels by relating the content of a poem to their own experiences, such as *One Flesh*, where a daughter contemplates the relationship of her parents, can generate a climate of greater familiarity with an apparently alien text. Encouraging them to make jokes about topics that are difficult to discuss openly, so that laughter defuses the embarrassment, is another strategy that frees the students to think fully about a text, to get underneath the surface difficulties of style and language. The evidence in the video diaries supports my conviction that these strategies help the students to extend their learning beyond the classroom door, beyond the school gate and into the outside world.

Ways of behaving: the cement of personal relations

A review of all of the students' video and written accounts helped me to grasp the importance of the dimension of personal relations between all participants. The students highlight particular 'ways of behaving' that seem to them to be highly significant. What the students picked up on was that the success of the strategies depended also, and very importantly, upon the classroom ethos built between us through the teaching and learning processes.

Because of my commitment to building common knowledge, I try to create an ethos in the classroom in which students feel safe to keep asking until they are confident that they do understand. The students' comments suggest that they do feel safe to ask, that their questions, no matter how repetitive or apparently minor, are always taken seriously:

> If there's something you don't understand in English you can always ask about it. Miss Worrall has a way of explaining that everyone can understand. She doesn't mind how many questions or if we repeat questions. She just keeps answering until we all understand. I really like that.
>
> (Student S, video diary)

> She makes the whole class understand that she's always prepared to answer our questions. You can really feel that she cares about our work, which motivates us.
>
> (Student M, video diary)

This sense of personal support is frequently referred to. For example, 'My English teacher makes me feel comfortable and explains the work really well. I have no problem going to ask her for help and she makes me realize I'm not alone.' Student P sounds a cautionary note, however: 'Sometimes I feel I'm being pushed too far and don't have time for other subjects as I spend a lot more time on English essays and other homework than what is recommended.' So finding a balance between the directly personal approach, which means 'doing your very best in this subject no matter what it costs' and a student's overall programme of study, needs to be considered. However, it is difficult to resist the rewarding enthusiasm of student M:

> I have been really encouraged since the beginning. The teacher's obvious interest in each individual (personally and academically) has motivated me to always do well in English. It feels like Miss really honestly *cares* about our work which I think is extremely important. Miss has not abandoned us!

Getting the mood right and judging how far to pressurize students to extend their thinking is another subtle part of classroom interactions independent of specific teaching and learning strategies. There are occasions when pushing a class too hard can impede students' capacity to think. As student Y said about the lesson on 'Rapunzstiltskin', 'Sometimes this makes my brain hurt – perhaps this poem's supposed to be just funny', and sharing jokey personal information about Amami Hair Lotion and bouffant hairstyles (when discussing *I Wanna Be Yours* by John Cooper Clark) can get a point across more effectively than a lot of serious talk or research. Trying to alternate the moods and always capture their sometimes capricious interests remains an ongoing challenge that the students are keen to expand on, particularly in terms of some of the constraints that limit learning.

The negative side of the importance of getting the mood right is emphasized in her video diary by Student M: 'She's always moody on Mondays. I think she doesn't like the room we're in. She always says it is stuffy and small. It's true, Miss, I'm sorry, but you are always moody on Mondays!' This insight, which I had to accept as accurate, has led to a revision of the ways in which rooms are allocated to all teaching groups for the new school year. The class had three different rooms for their English lessons: an ICT room, a geography room and an MFL room. The problems of ferrying books and having nowhere to display students' work or store resources compounded the issue of trying to teach a double GCSE course in a limited amount of time. Student M's comment helped me to grasp the potentially serious and constraining effects of this accommodation issue on my teaching.

Learning without limits

In writing this account, I was asked by the project team not just to describe what I do and why, but to try to explain what makes this teaching for learning without limits. In identifying the central planks upon which my practice is constructed, I have tried to explain how I believe they help to release students' learning from limits associated with particular aspects of classroom practice. These include limits associated with the range of tasks set, the degree of choice and control that students can exercise over their learning, the extent to which classroom interactions create shared understandings or misunderstandings and the question of whether classroom learning is meaningful to students in the sense of relating to what is important and interesting to them, to their lives beyond school. I have tried to show how the particular strategies I use reflect my core values and how they are intended, through the way that they work together, to enable all students to learn more powerfully and effectively.

Through the project, my awareness of the general and specific attitudes and factors that act to restrict our aspirations and constrain our students' achievements has become sharper. Inevitably, the social and economic forces that shape our personal lives and circumstances are strongly evident in the ways we see ourselves and our futures, but also act upon our perceptions of others and their potential. The influence of parents and other key adults in these young people's developing identities is critical and can perhaps only be tinkered with within the context of one subject's lessons. The teacher may well have to battle to establish a more open and positive attitude towards ability that will enable each student to 'delimit' her own perception of her potential.

I feel, too, that the pressures experienced by teachers, parents and students because of the emphasis on league tables, and the resulting perceived need to outperform other schools as well as our own previous results, are becoming increasingly intense. The time and space to encourage students to think, to explore their own interpretations and responses, to develop their sense of their own growing competence and potential will be further eroded as teachers are forced to play the tune demanded by the piper, and 'teach to the test' for predetermined outcomes, for a particular kind of learning.

Inevitably the most frustrating limit of all has proved to be human frailty, both mine and the students'. There were innumerable occasions when lack of energy or commitment, insufficient specific skill or emotional fallout in our private lives meant that what was achieved, within the classroom or beyond, simply did not match up to our aspirations. However, there was also the compensating sense of being together on a journey towards greater understanding and achievement. Coming to terms with having to keep on battling through towards the skyline was a critically important aspect of the research cycle.

Note

1 *Missing*, directed by Costa-Gavras (1982).

PART 3
The core idea of transformability

13 Transforming the capacity to learn

In the nine chapters that make up Part 2, we presented the work of the Learning without Limits project teachers, each operating in distinctively different situations and in particular ways, yet all committed to developing teaching and learning free from ability-based judgements. In Part 3, we draw on the nine accounts together to explain what the nine teachers have taught us about the core ideas and principles that inform their teaching, and about how they see their own role in creating learning without limits.

As we do so, however, we will not lose sight of characteristics that all teachers share, whether or not they consciously reject ability labelling. We are especially aware of all teachers' need to make their task manageable, to find ways of addressing the complexity of dealing with thirty or more individuals. We will argue that the nine project teachers are managing their complex task in ways that are distinctive, coherent, principled and thoroughly practical.

In this chapter, we consider what is common to the different practices that these teachers have developed in accordance with their rejection of the limits imposed by ability-based teaching. Does their shared commitment to the ideal of learning without limits lead them to approach their teaching in ways that have anything in common, and if so what? We explain that we do indeed find a great deal in common across their practices, and we outline some key principles that seem to inform the teaching of all of them. Then, since this chapter is couched in relatively abstract terms, in Chapter 14 we follow it up by more detailed examination of practice, showing how the common principles are reflected, in different ways, in the practice of members of the teacher team. In Chapter 15, we relate our analysis of the core ideas and principles that inform the nine teachers' work to what the young people in their classes had to say about their experiences of being taught by teachers who had consciously rejected ability-led practices. Chapter 16 examines ways in which the nine teachers were aware of being supported or constrained in their efforts to create conditions for learning without limits by the wider constraints in which they were working, in and beyond their schools. In the final chapter, we return to the wider concerns from which we started in the opening chapters, to reflect on the implications of our research findings for policy and practice more generally.

The core idea of transformability

Looking across the nine accounts, we gradually came to see that, in order to understand what replaces the concept of ability in these teachers' practice, we needed to focus first upon the different conception of the relation between present and future that guides their practice. When the nine teachers set aside the concept of ability, they did not just set aside a particular way of making sense of the complexity of their classrooms; they also, necessarily, set aside the assumed stable relation between present and future that is implied by ability judgements, the assumption that, in the future, things will remain much as they are at present, and therefore present patterns of attainment and response are reliable predictors of young people's future development. We found that the inspiration and driving force at the heart of the nine teachers' work is a fundamentally different sense of the relation between present and future that we have come to call 'transformability': a firm and unswerving conviction that there is the potential for change in current patterns of achievement and response, that things can change and be changed for the better, sometimes even dramatically, as a result of what happens and what people do in the present.

An alternative concept of learning capacity

This different sense of the power of the present to affect the future is sustained by a concept of learning capacity (see Figure 13.1), which differs in five key respects from the concept of fixed ability, as described in Chapter 2. First, it is constituted by external forces as well as by internal resources and states of mind. The range and quality of learning opportunities provided, and the relationships that support and shape learning opportunities, interact with internal subjective states to create and constrain capacity to learn. Second, it has a collective as well as an individual dimension. Capacity to learn is contained within and constituted by how a group of young people operate and work together as a group, and by the opportunities and resources made available to them as a group. Third, it includes internal resources and states of mind in addition to the purely cognitive-intellectual: the capacity to learn in any situation is affected, for example, by emotional states and feelings of social acceptance and belonging in the school or class group. Fourth, the cognitive elements are not mysterious inner entities, but are skills and understandings that can be, and have been, learned. Fifth, learning capacity is transformable because the forces that shape it, individually and collectively, are, to an extent, within teachers' control. The teachers recognize that they have the power to strengthen and, in time, transform learning capacity by acting systematically to lift limits on learning, to expand and enhance learning opportunities and to create conditions that encourage and empower young people to use the opportunities available to them more fully.

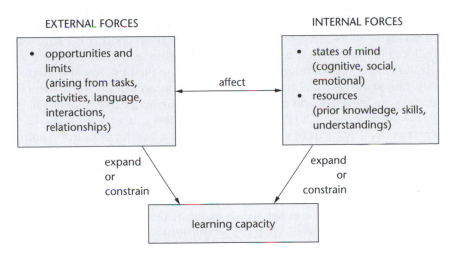

Figure 13.1 The forces constituting learning capacity

The nine accounts provide multiple examples of what the teachers believe they themselves can do to strengthen and enhance learning capacity. Julie, for example, feels passionately that young people's capacity to learn is constrained by the inflexibility of the current education system. She is deeply opposed to practices of setting and streaming. She feels that these practices damage self-esteem and contribute to the negative perceptions that many young people hold about their personal capabilities; rigid ability-based groupings curtail opportunities and place preset limits on what individuals in particular circumstances can achieve. 'It's hard to keep trying, isn't it,' she says, 'when you're told you can only get a D.' While she is clearly in no position to rebuild schools' structure, curriculum and pedagogy single-handedly, according to her vision of a better, fairer education system, she does what she can, within her own classroom and department, to lift limits such as these and free young people to learn in more open and flexible ways.

Non's sense of her own power to make a difference to young people's capacity for learning centres on her concerns about what Engestrom (1996) calls the 'encapsulation of school learning' – the idea that much of what happens in school often seems, from young people's point of view, to be cut off from what happens in the world outside school, and from what matters to them in their lives. Young people's capacity to learn in school is seriously impaired, Non believes, if they cannot see the point of what they are doing and what they are expected to learn. So Non's priority in her teaching is to find ways of making connections between school learning and the students' worlds, to find ways to make learning meaningful, relevant and important to them.

For Alison, emotional engagement is all-important. She understands that young people's capacity for learning in any given context is increased or reduced proportionately to the energy and enthusiasm that they bring to their learning. A central priority for her is to fire up their interest and excitement. She wants her children to see learning as an adventure in which everyone can take part, and where everyone has an active role to play. Their capacity for learning will be enhanced, she believes, if young people 'see themselves as being part of something rather than having something done to them'.

Narinder recognizes the important part that language plays in shaping thinking, that learning capacity can be increased by developing young people's understanding of and ability to reflect on their own thinking processes. She regularly uses key words from the domain of metacognition ('connect', 'explain', 'views', 'points', 'definitions'). Extending the idea of 'writing frames', she offers them 'speaking frames' to support their learning and the discussion of their learning.

Patrick laments the passive model of learners and learning, which, in his view, pervades national policy documents and curriculum guidelines. He believes that young people's learning capacity is ill-served by a narrow, delivery model of curriculum and pedagogy that emphasizes preset objectives, and where planning leaves little or no space for learning to be shaped by young people themselves. His bedrock belief is that young people are in charge of their own learning; the teacher's task is to know how to create conditions that will maximize their capacity for learning in any given situation by encouraging them to engage – and sustain effortful intellectual engagement – with worthwhile tasks and opportunities.

These examples illustrate the distinctive features of the concept of learning capacity shared by these teachers and help to explain the basis for their optimism relating to the transformability of learning capacity (see Figure 13.2). We can see that, among the external forces that impinge on learning capacity, the teachers consider the impact of prescribed curriculum content, styles of pedagogy, modes of grouping, expectations of teachers and peers and the nature, range and distribution of learning tasks and opportunities. Internal forces include states of mind, such as self-belief and the sense young people have of the meaningfulness and relevance of what they are learning, which teachers know have a profound impact on capacity and willingness to engage. The teachers' concept of learning capacity includes young people's emotional states, as well as aspects of cognitive and intellectual functioning; it includes their sense of identity and sense of identification with the values upheld by the school.

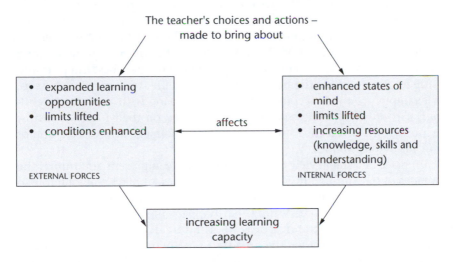

Figure 13.2 Transforming learning capacity: the teacher's part of the task

The examples also illustrate the *connection* between classroom conditions and subjective states: the teachers understand that external and internal forces operate together, each influencing the other, shaping each individual's capacity for learning contingently (but not unalterably) in the form in which it manifests itself at a given point in time. Learning capacity is transformable in principle, because its constitutive elements are themselves subject to change and variation; but learning capacity will only be strengthened and transformed if something happens to change the balance of forces, to make the conditions that sustain learning significantly more enabling. The teachers realize that, to the extent that they have control over the forces that impinge on learning capacity, they can work to enhance and transform it. Since their concept of learning capacity has a collective, as well as an individual, dimension, they can act on hypotheses about what will make a difference to learning capacity at a collective as well as at an individual level. Julie focuses particularly on increasing the flexibility of the curriculum; Non's priority is to strengthen connections between school learning and the students' world; Patrick's is to give students greater opportunity and encouragement to shape and control their own learning. By working out practical strategies, for instance, to increase flexibility, to make learning more pertinent to the world outside school or to increase control, the teachers act simultaneously in everybody's interests, to strengthen the learning capacity of everybody.

The core idea of transformability acts as an inspiration and driving force for these teachers' work, because the teachers recognize that whether this balance of forces shifts significantly is, at least in part, under their control. Since teachers have the power to make a difference to future development, they have a responsibility to use their power to maximum effect. Not to do so is not an option, because it would be contrary to their strong and deeply held commitment to acting in young people's best interests and trying to give everyone the best possible start in life. We have already seen, for example in Anne's account, how, even working with very young children, part of her awareness is constantly focused on their futures, on how the present will affect the future, on how what happens now can expand or limit future possibilities.

In place of a stable view of the relation between present and future, the core idea of transformability assumes that the present plays a pivotal role in determining the path of future development. The future is in the making in the present. Absolutely everything that happens in the present will have a formative effect, for better or worse, upon future development. Nothing is neutral. Either the effect will be broadly to maintain the learner's capacity as it currently manifests itself, because the balance of influences remains unchanged, or the effect will be to strengthen and progressively transform learning capacity. This will come about through the work of the teacher: by continually extending and enhancing learning opportunities, reducing and removing existing limits, progressively transforming the states of mind that condition young people's choices about whether to engage and how much to invest in the learning opportunities provided for them in school. So teachers exercise their power to make a difference by considering the choices available to them and systematically choosing the transforming options, those whose effects they have good reason to believe will be to increase young people's capacity to learn now and in the future.

Origins of the teachers' belief in transformability

The nine project teachers frequently referred, in their interviews, letters and our discussions together, to experiences that had influenced their thinking in their childhood and in their adult personal and professional lives. The teachers recalled injustices done to themselves or that they had witnessed done to others through the use of ability labels; they recalled the limiting of opportunities and other negative effects that they had seen for themselves when pupils were divided into streams and ability groups. They talked of unsupportive relationships, unhelpful teaching methods, humiliating or harsh treatment at the hands of teachers and other pupils that brought home to them the make-or-break effects on learning of these pow-erful external forces. They also recalled changes that they had seen take place in the lives of people they knew, in their personal aspirations and achievements, and the critical circumstances and turning points that had changed the course of their development.

These experiences helped them to understand the injustice inherent in treating differences in learners and their learning as a reflection of differ-ences in individual, intellectual endowment. They are the source of the teachers' commitment to working to create a better and fairer system of education, and of their belief in the transformability of learning capacity. Through these experiences they understood the limits that can be set on learning by the contexts, opportunities and pedagogical practices to which young people are exposed, and also saw ways in which these limits can be lifted and their effects negated. They realized that learning capacity could be significantly enhanced by lifting the limits imposed and disguised by ability labelling, and by working to create conditions that would build and strengthen the states of mind and personal resources that are so crucial to productive and purposeful learning. When they rejected ability labelling, however, and the practices that come in its train, these ideas did not simply vanish from their thinking and practice. The ideas continued to exert an influence in a very practical way by helping teachers to make increasingly informed choices about what to do and what not to do in order to build more enabling conditions for learning and exploit systematically the poten-tial available to them for enhancing learning capacity. In everything they do, in every choice they make, the teachers draw on this growing awareness to help them act in young people's interests, to ensure that the effects of their choices and actions, in both the immediate and longer term, will be optimally enabling.

Transformability as a joint enterprise

The teachers realize, however, that their power to make a difference to young people's future development also depends upon how young people themselves choose to exercise their power in relation to their own future lives. Just as with teachers, the choices young people make will *either* help to perpetuate the dynamics that permanently fix their capacity to learn in its current state *or* contribute to the progressive transformation of their capacity for learning. As active agents in their own right, young people can – and many currently do – use their power to resist and confound teachers' best efforts to engage them and enhance their capacity for learning. Teachers cannot make a difference to young people's future development unless the young people themselves choose to take up the invitations to learn that are extended to them in school, unless they choose to engage and sustain engagement with the learning opportunities provided. The teachers realize that if their own power is to be effective in working to strengthen and, in time, transform learning capacity, it must connect with and harness young people's own power to make a difference to their own future lives. The guiding principle of transformability can only be achieved through what teachers and young people do *together* in what is necessarily a joint enterprise.

The nine teachers are not incapacitated, however, by this awareness that their power is limited by how young people choose to exercise their own powers. They are convinced that they can positively influence young people's choices, because they know that how young people use their power is profoundly affected by every aspect of their school experiences. Part of the reason why they rejected ability labelling was because of the damage they had seen it do to young people's self-belief, sense of personal competence, attitudes, expectations and hopes for the future. They believe they can build and strengthen the states of mind that support learning, and enlarge the capacity to learn, by eliminating from their teaching the negative effects of ability labelling, and by systematically working to build, strengthen and restore the positive states of mind needed if young people are to choose to engage and sustain the effortful activity that worthwhile, personally meaningful learning requires. Their understanding of the connections between classroom conditions and the states of mind that affect young people's ability and willingness to invest in learning in school is what gives them confidence in their power to transform young people's capacity for learning. They put this understanding to work at the heart of their teaching, making choices for their classroom practice on the basis of what they believe will enhance the choices that young people themselves make in the exercise of their agency.

The core purposes of teaching for transformability

We can see, then, that teachers whose work is guided by belief in the transformability of learning capacity formulate purposes and intentions for young people's learning that go far beyond the acquisition of particular skills, knowledge or understanding. Through the tasks and activities they provide, the contexts they create, the classroom relationships and interactions they foster, they are seeking to improve learning conditions and to widen and enrich learning opportunities in such a way as to strengthen and build young people's desire to engage and their power to further their own learning through engagement with the opportunities and resources provided by the school. This broad conception of the teacher's task translates into a more explicit set of core purposes – specific things to do *and* undo –

that guide teachers' decision-making in all aspects of their practice. As the teachers talked about their work, and why they chose to do what they did, it became apparent that they continually referenced their decision-making to the internal states of mind and personal resources that they were seeking to develop and foster. For the sake of clarity, we have separated these into three categories: purposes in the affective, social and cognitive domains.

Teachers' purposes in the affective domain

One striking feature of the nine teachers' accounts is the importance that all of them give to the impact of their teaching on their pupils' emotions. Central to their professional thinking is the recognition that capacity to learn is affected by emotional states, and that the common classroom reality for many pupils is one of feeling unengaged, insecure and alienated. Previous experiences of schooling, other aspects of their lives, the seeming irrelevance of the tasks they are set and the threats to their self-esteem implicit in these tasks all contribute to this. A necessary ongoing task for teachers who want to increase young people's capacity to learn, now and in the future, is therefore the transformation of these emotional states. The nine teachers have a number of core purposes that they are every day seeking to attain associated with the emotional well-being of all the pupils in their classes.

Building confidence and emotional security

One central priority for teachers is to try to increase the extent to which young people feel emotionally safe, comfortable and positive about their participation in learning activities. Teachers aim to provide tasks that challenge young people and make sense to them but do not frighten any of them into non-engagement. This includes the demanding task of reversing negative preconceptions, possibly formed over many years, that some young people have of their own learning capacity. It includes recognizing the vulnerability of individual students and finding ways of building up their confidence and emotional security. 'Safety' and 'comfort' are recurring words in the teachers' accounts of what they aim for. Claire, for example, talks of the importance of the children's comfort, in terms of being happy with the teacher's expectations and understanding them. 'I would hate', she says, 'to think I was doing anything that made any child anxious.' Patrick formulates another aspect of this goal of student security in terms of students having their own 'space' both literally and metaphorically, 'where they can think and connect and make their own associations'.

Strengthening feelings of competence and control

Emotional security is intimately bound up with feelings of competence and control. A central purpose for all nine teachers is that classroom experiences should be explicitly designed to strengthen or restore young people's feelings of competence and control over their learning. This is especially important for young people whose experience of ability labelling has deprived them of feelings of competence and control over their own achievements and destinies; but, as Non's account illustrates, it is important and relevant to everybody, because even the most successful learners may be constrained in their learning if teaching and learning processes sustain and encourage relationships of dependency rather than the progressive handover of control from teacher to learner. The teachers work on the assumption that young people will develop or regain a sense of control to the extent that activities give them opportunities to make their own meanings, and offer them scope to make choices and shape the direction of their own learning. They aim to increase competence by creating conditions that routinely enable young people to experience themselves acting competently, and experience having their competence recognized and responded to by teacher and peers. These are key considerations in the construction of classroom tasks and experiences.

Increasing enjoyment and purposefulness

Learning capacity is also increased or reduced by young people's emotional investment in their work, and this is conditional upon activities being perceived as interesting, enjoyable and most of all purposeful from the perspective of the learners. The teachers know that there are many young people who rarely seem to be excited, or 'lit up' as Narinder puts it, by their classroom learning. Feelings of boredom, apathy and lethargy are, for some, long-established mental states that exert a corrosive effect upon individual learning capacity and upon the learning capacity of the group. The teachers interpret lack of enthusiasm and engagement as a compelling reason to keep looking for ways to rekindle young people's sense of excitement and thirst for learning. A central purpose for the teachers is therefore trying to make the classroom, increasingly, a place where young people want to come, because they find the activities in which they engage there interesting and purposeful. Anne says, 'They must do it for themselves, not just to please me.' For Alison, the goal is one of 'sharing the excitement of learning'. Narinder emphasizes both the importance and challenge of this purpose. 'Their whole lives are turmoil, and for them to come to school, they have got to see some purpose to it, and that purpose has really got to be built in very quickly because ... they have got to enjoy school to come in the next day.'

Enhancing young people's identities as learners: the experience of success

As the above quote suggests, interesting and purposeful as school activities may be, sustained engagement will only be achieved in so far as young people experience success. School activities not only have to be accessible and make sense to pupils, they have to be activities appropriate for them as they see themselves. Are they the kind of people for whom engagement in such learning activities makes sense? Sadly, there are many for whom that has not been the case. Sustained experience of successful learning, of achievement and of recognition of that achievement for all young people is therefore a crucial purpose for these teachers. In their decision-making, they try to ensure that every individual leaves every lesson feeling good about themselves because they recognize that they have achieved something worthwhile.

Increasing hope and confidence for the future

As we noted, the guiding idea of transformability has at its centre a view of young people's futures as open and in the making. A central part of the teachers' philosophy is that it is important for the young people themselves to recognize this openness, to recognize their own power to make a difference to their future development and to develop constantly expanding conceptions of what is possible. For Patrick, this means holding open 'a more than instrumental view of education' and leading them 'out of a delimited view of themselves and their possibilities'. Among teachers' purposes, therefore, are the development and sustenance especially of the important affective elements of this orientation, young people's hope and confidence for the future. The excitement, the purposefulness and the achievements of learning are not just for today, not just for the classroom: they are also for the future, for life, for the young people's lives, and the young people themselves must feel that to be the case.

Teachers' purposes in the social domain

Just as the daily achievement of these affective purposes is seen by the teachers as crucial to the aim of transforming learning capacity, so too is the achievement of social purposes. These teachers recognize the importance of social influences and especially the powerful influence young people exercise in relation to one another. They know that they as teachers cannot achieve their ambitious purposes on their own, but that instead they are dependent on the support that the pupils give each other. The struggle to transform learning conditions for their classes can succeed only if it is a struggle engaged in together, with solidarity. Across the accounts, we found two recurring themes in the purposes articulated by teachers relating to the social domain.

Increasing young people's sense of acceptance and belonging

Young people's capacity to learn in a particular classroom context is deeply affected by their sense of their rightful place in that classroom, that they are looked upon by others as an equal member of the community with a unique personal contribution to make that is recognized and valued by everyone else. Yet the teachers recognize that for many complex reasons, including how schools label, group and grade pupils, what comes across to many young people is that they are not valued equally, that they do not count as much as those who are more successful in the terms defined by the school. As Julie says, 'they feel second class', and when that happens 'they become second class, it's a self-fulfilling prophecy'. A key purpose for teachers, in the social domain, is to make everybody feel important, knowing that their contribution counts. This is not just about teacher praise and recognition. It is also is crucial for young people's contributions to be valued by their peers. Mutual respect is constantly emphasized and worked for, and time is allocated to fostering it. Patrick, for example, talks of the importance of achieving 'The feeling in the room that you don't do down what other people say; you might not contribute yourself, but you don't mock, cast aspersions, talk over, laugh; the awareness that actually that's serious and important.'

Learning to work as a learning community

Building mutual respect is important but it is not enough. The teachers describe how in addition they see learning to work constructively as a team as requiring such social skills as working with different people, actively listening, learning from each other, agreeing on shared goals and working relationships, resolving conflicts and playing mutually supportive roles, all skills that need to be developed. For Narinder, for example, learning the necessary skills and disciplines in order to act as a learning community, and to take responsibility for working effectively as a learning community, provides 'the foundations of learning on which acquiring academic knowledge takes place'.

Teachers' purposes in the cognitive domain

Reading the accounts of the nine teachers, it is surely impossible not to be impressed by their tough-minded and passionate commitment to the value of an intellectual life, and to the importance of making such a life available to all their pupils. In her comment 'It's best to leave them thinking and wanting to do it so we can pick it up tomorrow and work from there', Narinder exemplifies the way that all these teachers are seeking to induct young people into the life of the mind, with all its ongoing challenges and excitements. The teachers' concern with the emotional and the social aspects of young people's lives in school is in large measure instrumental in the development of young people's cognitive powers, which the teachers recognize clearly to be at the core of educational success. So they plan to ensure that all young people are helped to develop such powers. Within the framework of National Curriculum programmes of study, the teachers choose to emphasize a number of core cognitive elements.

Successful access by all young people

It is Julie who articulates this purpose most clearly, but it is a central concern of all the teachers. The teacher's success in any lesson is to be judged by the very demanding criteria that all members of the class should not only have understood and engaged with the content and learning intentions of the lesson, but also have engaged in whatever the teacher recognizes as worthwhile learning in relation to these intentions (whether knowledge, understanding or skills).

Increasing relevance, enhancing meaning

This is a constantly recurring theme in the teachers' accounts. They share a recognition that concepts and skills are useful and powerful only when they are seen to relate to other known things, most importantly through their relevance to the lives and concerns of the learners, but also to areas of the curriculum and the world other than those in which they were initially learned. For Narinder, 'learning doesn't happen if it doesn't mean anything in their lives'. For Claire, the learning of skills only makes sense if skills are 'transferable, relevant and interesting'. For Anne, the prime objective is 'making sense *of the world*'. For Patrick, 'the best lessons that I think I have ever taught have been lessons that work through creating intellectual connections with students, providing them with ways that they can make their own connections'.

Enhancing thinking, reasoning, explaining

The teachers put strong emphasis on the development of higher cognitive skills, and are less concerned about memory than about disciplined thinking. Narinder, for example, is concerned that her pupils should not only consciously engage in reasoning, but also be able to 'explain their thinking, their working, their insights, their conclusions'. She makes sure that they focus on the concepts, the big ideas, that will increase their capacity to make sense of the world. As with the other teachers, a priority is to help young people to develop a language for talking about their thinking, for reflecting on learning and what helps them to learn. Metacognition –

understanding how they learn and what they can do to improve their learning – can help young people to use their personal resources more fully and
effectively. Teachers' purposes in this respect echo the words of Bruner
(1996: 129), who argues that 'learning to think with what you've got lies at
the heart of every good curriculum, every teaching and learning encounter'.

These, then, are some of the recurring themes identified as the nine
teachers articulated the purposes that inform their practices on a day-to-day
basis. Although these purposes may, at first sight, appear to be ones that
most teachers would endorse, they are in fact, as we have seen, fundamentally incompatible with ability labelling. The teachers have turned their
awareness of the limits on learning imposed by ability labelling into understanding of what needs to be done – and undone – in order to free learning
from those limits. The core purposes could not be achieved in a learning
environment still permeated by ability judgements and practices.

None of the nine teachers would claim that they achieve these purposes
fully, every day, for all the young people in their classes. None the less, they
view these purposes as sensible and realistic; and all of them evaluate their
work in relation to these purposes. For our part, having observed these
teachers at work, and having talked at some length with them and their
pupils, we are deeply impressed not only by the ambitious nature of this
range of purposes, but also by the scale on which the teachers do indeed
achieve their purposes. But how is this done? In the next section we turn to
the fundamental question of how the aim of increasing and transforming
learning capacity is translated into a principled and practicable pedagogy.

Applying the core idea of transformability: practical pedagogical principles

This section is concerned with a set of practical pedagogical principles that
guide the nine teachers' work. All three words are important. These are *pedagogical* principles, in that they are concerned with the processes of teaching.
They are *practical* principles, in that they are not merely espoused ideals:
these are the ideas that in practice guide the ways teachers realize their purposes. Most importantly, they really are *principles*, not just instrumental
ideas for achieving the teachers' purposes, but also ethical ideas about the
right ways in which teachers ought to engage with young people.

As we shall explain, the practical principles do not function in isolation
from each other. Their power to contribute to the fundamental task of
progressively enhancing young people's learning capacity depends upon
the use of each of them in combination with the others. Figure 13.3
summarizes the interdependence of the principles. In the text, we must
perforce introduce them one by one.

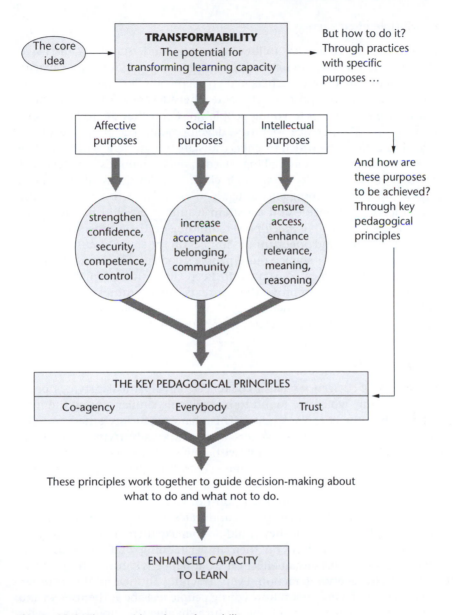

Figure 13.3 The core idea of transformability

The principle of co-agency

The principle of co-agency follows from the understanding, discussed earlier, that the task of strengthening and transforming learning capacity depends upon what both teachers *and* young people do, that it must necessarily be a joint enterprise. It reflects teachers' awareness that they must harness their own power to young people's power if they are to be successful in making a difference to future development. The principle of co-agency is the means by which teachers translate this awareness into practice in their classroom decision-making. It continually reminds teachers that what they must try to do, in all their classroom decision-making and in every teaching and learning encounter, is to use their own power (over the external forces that enable and constrain learning capacity) to affect how young people choose to use *their* power. Building on their understanding of how external forces and opportunities impact on the states of mind and the personal resources that shape young people's choices, the principle of co-agency reminds teachers constantly to keep this connection in view, to work systematically to improve the contexts, opportunities and external conditions for learning in such a way that young people are inspired and empowered to use their own agency more powerfully and effectively.

Making connections

The principle of co-agency seems to be reflected in a particular style of pedagogical thinking, which we found to be strikingly similar among the nine teachers whose practice we studied. This characteristic style had two distinctive elements. First, the teachers were continually trying to connect imaginatively and empathetically with their pupils' consciousness as people, to see and experience classroom events through young people's eyes as well as their own, to understand the states of mind that might underlie their actions and choices from their point of view. Second, they were continually connecting these perceptions and states of mind to classroom conditions, in order to see what they could do to make them more enabling. In order to do this they draw on their understanding that *everything* that happens in classrooms has an effect on what happens subsequently – every task or activity, every interaction, every teaching and learning encounter. Everything has an effect upon how young people feel about themselves and about what school has to offer them, in turn shaping the choices they make in the exercise of their agency.

Julie provided a powerful example of this style of thinking as she explained what she did to win round a group of disaffected students when she first arrived at her current school. 'They thought all they were good for was being pains', she says, 'and tried as hard as possible to fulfil that image.' Nevertheless, Julie was convinced that, in time, it would be possible to change their image of themselves, and that there were specific things she could do to enable that change to happen. As she described the steps she took, practically, in her own teaching, she emphasized the *connections* between these steps and the positive effects that she expected, and hoped, that they would have upon the self-image, attitudes and feelings of the young people she was working with. Interpreting the young people's comments as bravado concealing a deep-seated pessimism about their capabilities, she began by 'changing the whole image' of the room where they were working to create a more stimulating and relaxed environment, one that she hoped would give them the message that she took them seriously as learners. She changed the arrangement of desks to create a friendlier feel, and provided them with attractive new folders 'so that they could see that their work was going to be valued'. She carefully staged the demands she made on them, so that they would be able to experience success, using a lot of model-making initially, which they found they enjoyed. While they were working on the models, she had the opportunity to begin building relationships with them. Slowly things began to change. She found herself able to talk to them more as a group and eventually they were able to produce written assignments and achieve significant success in the examinations for which they were entered.

As we can see from this example, this reciprocal, interactive style of thinking takes the form of continuous hypothesizing about the states of mind lying behind young people's choices and actions, the classroom conditions that influence these and how classroom conditions can be changed in order to change the states of mind that influence how young people choose to exercise their agency. It is as if the teachers are saying to themselves, for example:

If I do this ... they may (feel more confident/ competent).

I mustn't do this because ... they might (feel embarrassed/singled out).

If I had done/hadn't done this, perhaps ... they would have (seen the point of what they were doing more clearly).

If I hadn't done this, maybe ... they wouldn't have (become confused).

Next time I'll try this so that ... they might (be more successful).

The teachers know that they are working from hypotheses, not certainties, about how classroom conditions have affected or will affect young people's subjective states, so they continuously review and revise their hypotheses in the light of experience. They also engage in dialogue with young people in order to check out their interpretations of behaviour, so that they are working from young people's own accounts of their experiences as well as from imaginative projection. Examples of this style of thinking permeate the nine accounts, suggesting that the teachers make use of it in all areas of classroom practice: in their design and selection of tasks and topics, in their classroom interactions, in their assessment and feedback on work and in the evaluation and development of their teaching.

Diversity through co-agency

In addition to influencing styles of thinking, the principle of co-agency informs how teachers conceptualize the task of ensuring diversity in learning opportunities. Unlike ability-based teaching, where the onus is essentially upon the teacher to plan for differentiation of tasks, resources and outcomes, teaching based around the core idea of transformability (understood as a joint enterprise between teachers and pupils) recognizes that diversity in learning is achieved by what both teachers and young people do and contribute to the learning process. Anne says, 'There is always more to the process than what I do.' What young people will learn from any particular set of tasks or activities cannot be tightly prespecified, because it will reflect not just what the teacher has prepared and anticipated for their learning but also what they put in, what they bring and what they make of the opportunities that the teacher provides. The teacher's task is to create activities and experiences that are attractive and meaningful to young people, that they perceive to be worthwhile and within their grasp; to create the classroom conditions that will encourage and inspire young people to take them up and exploit them as fully as possible; and then to respond respectfully to what they bring and offer, when they do engage, helping them to build on their existing understanding, and challenging them to extend and develop their thinking.

The planning task for teachers committed to the core idea of transformability is significantly different from the task of ability-focused teachers, who attempt to match tasks to what they see as salient differences between their students. This matching of task to student is an essentially external process, controlled by the teacher and conducted from the teacher's point of view. Judgements of what is appropriate for particular individuals or, more often, groups of individuals are made in advance by the teacher, and activities are designed accordingly. Tasks can be successfully 'matched' at an appropriate level of demand for young people of different abilities or levels of attainment without any genuine connection being achieved between young people's hearts and minds and the tasks that they are asked to undertake. Teaching that seeks to foster diversity through co-agency is concerned not with match, but with connection, achieving a genuine meeting of minds, purposes and concerns between teachers and young people – as Patrick says, 'them coming to meet you'. Tasks and outcomes are deliberately left open, or constructed in such a way as to offer choice of various kinds, so that young people have space to make their own connections, to make ideas meaningful in their own terms and to represent and express their thoughts, ideas and feelings in their own ways.

In creating tasks that everyone will find appealing and perceive to be within their grasp, the teachers project themselves empathetically into young people's minds and try to imagine, in relation to any particular set of curricular concerns and intentions, what will seem accessible, worthwhile and interesting from young people's point of view. This dual perspective on the learning process – their own and their projective identifications with young people's perspectives – informs all aspects of their planning, helping them to offset possible sources of difficulty and confusion, and helping them to anticipate the kinds of support and intervention that may be needed at particular points if all young people are to be encouraged to sustain purposeful engagement throughout the lesson or activity. It does not necessarily mean steering clear of tasks whose relevance may not be immediately evident to young people. There is a place, as Patrick emphasizes, for the strange, the unusual, the horizon-widening, as long as teachers recognize the need to help young people to make the necessary connections, and to reach outward, over the horizon.

The teachers acknowledge that the need to plan both from their own *and* from the young people's point of view means that they must get to know their pupils very well as individuals. We noted, for example, Nicky's detailed, critical and perceptive understandings of individual pupils, based on close observation of them. Nicky's commitment to understanding all her pupils as people, in all their complexity, exemplifies very well the teachers' recognition that any simple method of categorizing pupils, whether in terms of ability levels or in such other terms as learning styles, is dangerously inadequate: the aim of connection – meeting of minds – through relevant, meaningful and accessible learning tasks clearly depends upon a much more wide-ranging understanding of pupils as people. This includes, as Patrick notes in relation to working-class students, a need to understand their lives outside school:

> I try to learn from them, about the kind of situation they are coming from. What do they go home to? Are they likely to be able to sit and do this kind of homework? Are they likely to be able to go to the library? Are they likely to be able to bring stuff in? How would they feel about being asked about certain aspects of their life? I try to make decisions around that. Then you try to do what you can to alter the way the institution responds to those pupils.

We have seen too how Yahi and Nicky use categories of gender to help them to understand patterns of achievement and response among the students in their classes. They are aware how culturally specific ideas about masculinity influence young people's responses to school learning, encouraging many to hold back rather than engage wholeheartedly in learning experiences provided. They look for ways of working with rather than against these identities, knowing that young people will resist and subvert teachers' efforts to engage them if they do not feel accepted and affirmed in their identities in the school context. On the other hand, they also try to open up and encourage young people actively to consider alternative identity options so that they do not remain trapped in identities that unnecessarily limit their future life chances.

It should be noted, however, that this painstakingly acquired knowledge of individual students is not generally used to plan specific tasks for them. For teachers to do that would mean that they as teachers were trying to predict and control learning activities as if they were the sole decision-making agents. What happens instead is that the teachers tend to plan common learning opportunities for everyone in the class, ensure that tasks and activities are accessible to everyone and then extend an open invitation to everyone. A major consideration in the teachers' efforts to enhance learning capacity is their awareness that the narrow focus on ability labelling, an emphasis on perceived differences in so-called ability, and the consequent neglect of real differences of many kinds constitute a serious constraint on learning for many young people. The teachers recognize that one important way in which they can make a difference to future development is by organizing their teaching in a way that *does* make use of specific knowledge about individuals that is significant for learning, but uses it in a way that *does not* perpetuate or re-create the limiting and divisive effects that they associate with ability labelling. They use this knowledge to anticipate and lift limits that might hinder participation and learning, to create opportunities for all pupils to use. As Julie notes, 'I tend to do work that I think everyone can engage in at one level or another ... and it's surprising how well students do perform at certain tasks if they are given the chance.' Her immensely thorough preparation and structuring of tasks, as with the *Canterbury Tales* passage, is directed at ensuring that even the most challenging tasks are accessible to everyone.

Preparing one common set of opportunities for everyone helps the teachers to keep their task manageable; but if they are to be successful in enabling connection to happen, the opportunities have to be carefully conceived so that they genuinely do offer everyone the chance to connect, to exercise control, to make their own meanings. Examples drawn from the different accounts illustrate some of the common ways in which the teachers attempt to achieve this. The account of Claire's teaching, for example, shows how she allows for many different kinds of learning at any one time in her class of 8-year-olds, and that in every observed lesson such different activities as writing, drawing, making things, consulting reference books and examining pictures and artefacts were going on in parallel. The children themselves had to decide about which aspect of the work they would undertake, and it was noted that they tended to do so rather efficiently. Julie, in setting the same overall task for all her secondary-age students, always builds in choices; for example, encouraging them to choose for themselves the questions that they tackle, or to choose between more and less demanding versions of the task, or to interpret a very open task. Patrick, similarly, prefers where possible to start his English lessons with very open tasks:

> I think it is one of the things that should happen all the time in school, handing over to them and saying 'What can you make of it?' 'What you make of it is interesting and important' and 'How ingenious can you be?' and 'What things strike you?'

Such open tasks and opportunities for choice reflect the principle of co-agency, because part of their intention is not just to facilitate access and engagement but to reinforce young people's active sense of their powers and competence as thinkers and learners, that what they have to bring and contribute to their own learning is important, valued and welcomed in the classroom. All the teachers place emphasis upon providing opportunities for talk and collaborative learning in small groups, in addition to whole-class discussion, since they recognize that such activities and contexts often provide the greatest scope for making personal meaning, as well as extending and challenging the range of ideas to which individuals are exposed. A further dimension of openness and opportunity for young people to exercise control over their learning is the teachers' emphasis upon allowing time, wherever possible, for young people to complete a task to their satisfaction.

When connection is successfully achieved, it inevitably results in different experiences and outcomes, since everyone is unique and everyone brings and contributes something different, and makes his or her own meanings through active engagement with the learning opportunities provided. The teacher's task is to make the good choices, those that will enable and encourage everyone in the productive exercise of their agency; to extend an invitation to learn that can be accepted equally by everyone, and then to respond to the ideas and questions that result from their engagement in ways that validate, as well as challenge and extend, their thinking.

Enabling young people to take shared responsibility

Validating young people's ideas, and strengthening their sense of personal competence, is part of the process of educating young people into understanding their shared responsibility, their capacity as agents to take control, with the support of others, of their own learning. The principle of co-agency also implies active work on the part of teachers to encourage young people to share responsibility in many ways, and in relation to many different aspects of classroom life. Narinder says of the young people in her class: 'They are the ones that make the rules and the charters about what is acceptable. They are the ones that organize the classroom in the way they feel is best. They make the decisions, they decide on rules, rights and responsibilities.' Furthermore, the young people understand that their responsibility is significant. As one of them says, 'She always tries to help us, whatever the situation. But if we don't cooperate, then she can't help us.' Non tries to empower her students by giving them detailed feedback on their written work and suggestions about how to improve. She involves them in activities that help them to understand the meaning of the criteria against which the quality of their work is assessed, so that they can begin to take more responsibility for themselves for evaluating and improving their work. Yahi's main concern is to empower young people to ask more and better questions, as we shall see in more detail in the next chapter.

At its fullest, co-agency implies joint control by teacher and learners, with both parties operating as active agents, each with their different perspectives, but each none the less constantly ready to develop their understanding of the enterprise in response to the other. Patrick captures very well the complexity of the relationship. On the one hand, he asserts the importance of the students being in control: 'I think it's important for them to see that they are the experts ... they know stuff that I don't know ... I think it creates an atmosphere where people feel more able to contribute and more secure about contributing.' On the other hand, he says,

> The whole thing about being in charge is in a way paradoxical because I have a sense that I give direction, there's probably a lot of the time when I'm leading them places. So in a way they're not really in charge ... it's more about creating a communal space that yes we do want to go that way or we can get there ... And the way we're going isn't entirely the way I'd envisaged it or imagined it because they will bring and add stuff to it. So it becomes their space and they show me things I hadn't really seen.

This sharing of responsibility, through recognition of necessary co-agency, seems profoundly important for teachers committed to the ideal of learning without limits. It seems in practice to be important in three distinct ways. First, it is important *practically*, because by sharing responsibility with young people, teachers relieve themselves of the burden that comes with believing that good learning depends wholly on their own forethought, insight and expertise. The great and deceptive attractiveness of ability labelling is that it can be used to simplify the differences among young people, reducing many of these differences to one simple set of categories, within each of which pupils can for many purposes be treated as all very much the same. It is clear that these teachers do nothing of that sort: they not only go out of their way to understand individuals in all their complexity, but make their teaching decisions routinely in relation to a complex framework of affective, cognitive and social purposes. The sharing of responsibility seems to us to make classroom teaching more manageable in a quite different way, one that, far from attempting to simplify the task, accepts it in all its complexity. What these teachers do, faced with such complexity, is to give initial and ongoing priority to recruiting in their classrooms a whole team of some thirty active educators who will work with them to promote learning and to achieve the various purposes towards which the teachers are working.

Second, sharing responsibility is important *pedagogically*, because it reflects the inescapable truth that teachers *cannot* in fact do everything: young people are active agents in their own right; their active engagement is needed for any sort of learning to happen. The most the teacher can do is to transform the context, the curriculum, the conditions that sustain learning so that young people's powers are 'fired up', to use Narinder's arresting phrase. Moreover, everybody will benefit to the extent that young people come to see themselves as part of this team of thirty educators, all of whom have something to contribute to one another's learning.

Third, it is important and essential *ethically* because, as we have seen, the transformability of learning capacity depends upon it. As we saw above, working for transformability can only ever be a joint enterprise. Teachers cannot exercise their power, and fulfil their responsibility and commitment to making a difference to young people's future lives, except by working in partnership with young people, by using *their* power to strengthen and increase *young people's* learning powers and their desire to play their part in the joint enterprise.

The principle of 'everybody'

The principle of 'everybody' articulates teachers' fundamental responsibility and commitment to acting in the interests of everybody. It works hand in hand with the principle of co-agency to ensure that teachers' efforts to strengthen and transform learning capacity are applied fairly and equally to everyone. Decisions about what to do to enhance classroom conditions and the states of mind that support learning must be taken in the interests of everybody, and aim to benefit everybody equally. The principle of 'everybody' brings into play teachers' understanding that learning capacity has a collective as well as an individual dimension. As far as possible, teachers aim to act, simultaneously, in everybody's interests, by making one set of choices designed to enhance the learning capacity of everybody.

The principle of 'everybody' seems to have at least three different elements, all of them significant.

Teachers provide in the same terms for everybody

As we gathered evidence about the practice of the nine teachers, and as the whole team met and discussed what learning without limits teaching means, one of the very first principles that was identified and universally endorsed was the 'ethic of everybody'. It was noticeable how often in interviews, in discussions, in their letters and in their journals the nine teachers use the term 'everybody'. The teachers helped us to understand that they used it to emphasize their unshakeable belief in the learning capacity of all young people, their conviction that everybody can become a more powerful learner if the conditions are right; but it stands for more than a conviction. It also reflects their active rejection of the injustices and inequalities that they believe to be the consequence of ability labelling. For them, significantly, the polar opposite of 'everybody' is not 'nobody' but 'some people'. They reject out of hand 'some people' thinking, in which some people are fated to succeed and others fail, in which some people's achievements are valued more highly than others, in which some people are engaged and committed to learning and some people, through no fault of their teachers, are not. They use 'everybody' to express their determination that all pupils should be fully included in the teacher's goals and provision, in working for transformability. Julie's three principles, ensuring accessibility of learning experiences for *everybody*, the emotional well-being of *everybody* and worthwhile achievement for *everybody* perfectly articulate this concern for inclusive provision. Julie also articulates very well the principle that such inclusive provision is best made through planning common tasks for everyone, tasks designed to be accessible to everyone and to engage everyone, so that no one's scope for learning is curtailed by decisions made in advance about what might be appropriate for them. For Julie, that also includes realistic planning of minimum expectations, 'so that you know that there is not going to be anyone in the room that doesn't achieve that'.

Moreover, since the subjective conditions in which, according to these teachers, learning can most fully flourish are not yet achieved routinely, for everybody, on a daily basis, yet are achievable in principle, teachers approach their work in a developmental way, searching systematically for

ways of enhancing subjective experiences by enhancing classroom conditions. In this process, they give priority to collective strategies, ideas for
enhancing and transforming learning capacity, such as those expressed in
the examples drawn from the accounts at the beginning of the chapter. On
principle, they prefer collective strategies over individual adaptations,
wherever possible and feasible, because of their commitment to constructing learning as a collective experience. Working at a collective level helps to
expose and remove limits on learning at the level of general classroom pedagogy – for example, Julie's concerns about the exam-oriented bias towards
written outcomes – that prevent everyone from being fully included. Such
collective approaches are also preferable for practical reasons because they
make challenging, developmental purposes manageable. Where possible,
teachers prefer one set of choices designed to enhance learning capacity
and carefully selected so that they operate in the interests of everybody.

Valuing contributions from everybody

The principle of everybody is not just about equality of value as expressed
in the teacher's mind and actions. It is also about the value that young
people place on their own and one another's contributions. Everybody is
important not only in that they all must equally be included in the teachers'
provision for their learning; everybody is important too in that what they
bring to the classroom is valuable and must be valued. Ability labels and
ability-based grouping can prevent the development of community by reinforcing the idea that some people have very little to contribute to their own
learning or that of others. Learning without limits teachers recognize the
poverty of this approach, both in the narrowness of what it values and in
the simplistic individualistic interpretation of learning that it espouses.
They know that many different kinds of experience can contribute usefully
to learning in almost any sphere; they know too that it is not only or even
primarily the teacher who can contribute to learning, but that it is often the
thoughts, the questions, the actions or the talk of peers that can be crucial
for breakthroughs in any person's learning. The diversity of experiences and
understandings that young people bring to classrooms is, the teachers recognize, an asset as much to be valued as it has been widely neglected; and
they recognize too that the sharing of these experiences can contribute to
the learning of all, while at the same time enhancing the confidence and
self-esteem of contributors.

Such insights are evident in the practice of these teachers. Nicky
deplores the 'lack of recognition of how much the kids will learn from
each other' and frequently puts her students into situations where they can
capitalize on 'recognizing and making use of the importance of learning
from each other'. Alison ensures that her lessons are planned to give time

for the children to 'share each other's plans and value each other's contributions'. Patrick regularly chooses activities which he knows will place all students in a position of being equally expert, in the sense that everyone has relevant experience to contribute (e.g. a discussion of the pros and cons of McDonald's food) and no one's experience (including that of the teacher) can be considered superior or inferior in the ensuing discussion. Narinder's class comes together at the end of the lesson to review what has been learned: everybody is invited to contribute, everybody's learning is valued. Furthermore, the principle of valuing contributions to the well-being of the community does not stop at the classroom door. Narinder ends some tough talking about inappropriate behaviour in the playground with a 'big thank you to the people who helped to make the playtime a pleasant one, not just for themselves but for other people'.

Developing solidarity

The principle of 'everyone' informs the teachers' practice in a third way, which builds on and significantly extends the first two. In addition to ensuring that every individual is provided for, and helping young people to value and use one another's contributions, teachers invest considerable effort in developing the unity and solidarity in their classes, and they do so with considerable success. They recognize that there is immense potential, within the community of minds that constitutes the group, for enhancing and transforming learning capacity, if the resources of the group can be effectively harnessed and enabled to operate more purposefully and productively in support of everybody's learning. Claire talks of her class as working as a unit, with 'real shared goals'; Alison teaches her children to think of themselves a team, a 'learning community', as does Narinder, who emphasizes that she too is a member of the team, and with evident success models the idea of solidarity, 'all being on the same side', for her team.

Patrick's class expressed unanimous approval of 'working all together' and appreciation of the fact that their teacher 'always tries to set work where everyone can get involved'. Patrick is not satisfied, however, that all the students in his class are really pulling together as a group and gaining as much as they might from one another's contributions. He sees it as part of his continuing work, a major priority in the interests of the whole group, to build their capacity to listen attentively to and build upon one another's contributions, when they are working collaboratively and especially during whole-class discussion. Giving young people regular opportunities to develop their skills of working productively together is an important consideration for the teachers in planning learning opportunities for their classes.

The idea of working as an integrated learning community, with common goals, collaborative ways of working, an acceptance of mutual obligations and an appreciation of the benefits of learning from one another is very different from the individualistic thinking associated with ability labelling. It is also very different from an approach to teaching in which the teacher takes all the responsibility. In seeking to make their classes into 'learning communities' the teachers are indeed integrating the principle of 'everyone' with that of 'co-agency'. It is perhaps in this synthesis of these two principles that learning without limits teaching and commitment to the idea of transformability find their fullest expression.

The principle of trusting the learner

A third practical pedagogical principle for transforming learning capacity is that teachers make their choices, select the transforming alternative, from a basic position of trust; everything they do presupposes a trusting relationship between teacher and learner. These teachers all bring to their task an untouchable conviction that young people are to be trusted – trusted to make meaning of what they encounter in school and out of it, trusted to find relevance and purpose in relevant and purposeful activities, trusted to contribute to one another's learning, trusted to take up the teacher's invitation to co-agency and to participate in the worthwhile activity of learning. This basic position of trust means that, when learners choose not to engage or appear to be inhibited in their learning, teachers re-evaluate their choices and practices in order to try to understand what might be hindering their participation and learning. Trust sustains teachers' belief that young people will choose to engage if the conditions are right, and so sustains their effort to go on searching for ways to reach out and make connections that will free young people to learn more successfully. The accounts provide numbers of examples of teachers focusing on the learning of particular individuals, or groups of young people, and thinking about what might enhance their engagement and learning. We have seen how Nicky's work with Niall led to much more positive attitudes to learning on his part, a sense of enhanced competence and affirmation of identity. Alison relates Natalie's behaviour in school to things happening in her life at home. These experiences understandably make her 'a tough nut to crack', but Alison sees possibilities for change through building a stronger relationship bond. Narinder realizes that the behaviour of the child who hides behind the radiator is 'a symptom of something else' that requires close analysis if she is to take steps to 'bring him out' without risk of frightening him into further, and more resistant, styles of withdrawal. The teachers tread a fine line between on the one hand communicating acceptance and appreciation of young people as they currently are *and* creating the conditions that will enable them to change, to find themselves able to transcend existing limits. Indeed, they appreciate that communication of interest, and willingness to listen and try to understand how the world looks through the eyes of young people, can go a long way towards making such change possible.

Summarizing key ideas

So what have we learnt from the research about the distinctive features of teaching free from the concept of ability? We have found, across the group of project teachers, a common belief in the *transformability* of learning capacity that informs everything that teachers do. The core idea of transformability contrasts with the underlying fatalism associated with ability labels. It means that things always have the potential to change, and that people have the power to change things for the better by what they do in the present. *Classroom conditions* can change, and be changed, to enrich and enhance learning opportunities and free learning from some existing constraints. All young people can become better learners, if the *subjective conditions* needed to support and empower their learning are developed and consolidated through everyday experiences in the classroom.

Teachers understand that they must harness their own power to young people's power (*co-agency*) if they are to be successful in making a positive difference to future development. They do this by constantly making connections in their minds between classroom conditions and subjective states; they consider the positive and negative effects of their choices on the subjective states that influence the exercise of young people's agency, and systematically choose those options that they believe will encourage and empower young people to take up and exploit more fully the opportunities available to them in school.

Choices must be made in the interests of *everybody*, because an abiding belief in justice, in fairness, means that everybody counts and everybody's learning is equally important. What the teachers are working to achieve – at the level of subjective experience – is the same for everybody. So they do not have to start out each time from a perception of the class divided up in their minds into different groups of learners with significantly different needs. Teachers make their challenging task manageable by continually working to develop young people's ability to sustain and support their own and one another's learning. All of this depends on a fundamental *trust* which the teachers have in their students, trust in their powers as thinkers and learners, trust that they will engage if conditions are right, trust that they will find meaning and create their own personally relevant learning, if meaningful, worthwhile and accessible tasks are provided. Moreover, they trust that no matter what has gone before, there is always potential for growth and change as a result of what happens in the present.

These key ideas explain what we have learnt from the nine teachers about the processes through which they construct a principled and practicable pedagogy that is informed by their belief in the transformability of learning capacity, and by their passionate commitment to doing whatever is possible, through their work, to enhance learning capacity and so to bring about greater justice and fairness in the education provided for all young people. With the core idea of transformability, the alternative concept of learning capacity, the framework of purposes and the three guiding principles, we now have the means to articulate in a generalized form key aspects of the teacher's role in developing a pedagogy committed to learning without limits, as expressed in the practices of this group of nine teachers.

This alternative model of pedagogy is essentially inclusive in orientation because it is focused upon something that is perceived to be common to all young people. Everyone, without exception, has the capacity to learn. Everyone's capacity for learning can be increased, if the forces that constitute it – internal and external, individual and collective – can themselves be changed in ways experienced by young people as more enabling. In this chapter, we have seen how the core purposes and principles work together to help to ensure that the potential for transforming learning capacity is recognized and given equally serious consideration with respect to everybody.

14 Purposes and principles in practice

In Chapter 13, we saw how the teachers' confidence in their power to transform young people's learning capacity is rooted in their understanding of the connections between classroom conditions and the states of mind of engaged and purposeful learners. Their understanding of this relationship, which we represented in Figure 13.2, is translated, day by day, minute by minute, into practical choices. In this chapter we look more closely at these choices, in which we can plainly see the expression of the three pedagogical principles, and the rich variety of pedagogical purposes that we identified in Chapter 13. We illustrate the abstractions of the alternative pedagogical model we are constructing with particular and contextualized examples drawn from our original data: teacher observations, interviews, letters and discussions. This rich material allows us to describe what the nine teachers actually say and do, as well as illustrating the effects of their actions and interactions; we can trace the means by which the principled patterns of their choices in teaching have transforming significance for everybody's capacity to learn.

We should perhaps note the difficulty experienced in making our selection of examples, since it would have been possible to exemplify how the common purposes and principles were realized in practice by focusing on virtually any one of the nine teachers (an example of just such an account can be found in Hart 2003). Furthermore, that was a very attractive idea, because we should have liked to communicate something of the enormously rich combined repertoire of ways through which the different teachers, in their different contexts, pursued these purposes and realized these principles. Since space limitations clearly make that impossible, we have had to content ourselves in each case with giving only one or two examples, chosen because we consider them to be especially helpful.

Teachers' choices

The affective purposes of teachers' choices

We have already seen how much importance the teachers ascribed to their pupils' emotional states, and noted the centrality of their awareness that learners need to experience feelings of security, competence and control. This awareness is built into the choices they make in every aspect of their classroom practice. When Julie plans a history lesson, for instance, her purposes in curriculum terms are strictly historical, but she does not ignore the impact of the lesson on her students' emotions. So, to take a specific example, in planning a lesson on the Roman public health system for her Year 10 class, her curricular focus was on the use of historical sources to extract, interpret and synthesize information. But the overriding purpose of the work was to ensure that everybody should have a successful experience of using sources in this way. She was determined that this experience would result in the students feeling more competent and confident next time they tackle source work. Julie's planning illustrates the interactive, intersubjective thinking described in Chapter 13, referencing her decisions to the states of mind that she is seeking to foster in order for learning to flourish. She knows that many of her students find work with sources daunting, and could easily respond to work that they perceive as too difficult by 'going into panic mode' and switching off. She decides that encouraging students to work collaboratively will make the tasks more stimulating and enjoyable, and will make it more likely that they will feel confident enough to engage and rise to the challenge of a task that they are not sure is within their grasp. Working collaboratively allows students' own talk to become the central medium for learning, their own ideas and interpretations to become the focus of discussion. It also creates space for young people to exercise some control over their learning, allowing them to determine for themselves, within a common time frame, how long to spend on each source and what to discuss. There is space for personal understandings to be formulated and individual difficulties worked through.

Julie's choices are distinctively her own, but she is not alone in choosing ways of working that bring emotional benefits to all who take part. For example, Yahi works to establish particular classroom routines and rituals: the meditative silence at the start of a lesson, to be filled with private, positive thoughts; the five-minute break in the middle of each lesson, a chance to stretch, chat, relax; the deliberate introduction of what he explicitly calls 'fun', jokes, banter, a little rubber duck. These are not the superficial trappings of Yahi's practice, but the mechanisms by which he ensures his students' emotional engagement; they are part of his calculated opposition to the culture of cool. By surprising his students into enjoying themselves, he goes some way to breaking down the barriers they have erected against commitment and application. His choices as a teacher, to act in unexpected and unconventional ways, induce vibrancy and relaxed interaction in the student group. Almost without knowing how or why, they discover themselves having a good time in Yahi's classroom *and* taking mathematics seriously at one and the same time. In the same way, the exercise in concentration that starts the lesson affects the students' emotional well-being: it enables them to focus, to be present in the lesson, to be a willing participant. Then, when their attention starts to flag, the five-minute break stimulates the will to refocus, to regain concentration. Yahi has put these routines in place in the interests of motivation and engagement; they are equally part of the work of co-agency, in which Yahi and his students together create the totally supportive environment for learning.

Yahi's interactions with individuals have similar ends in view. By attending to the emotional state of individuals, 'giving them space', making 'a quiet suggestion in the right place', Yahi is playing his part in ensuring voluntary, not enforced, participation in the lesson. By giving very personal and specific feedback on individual achievements and setbacks, Yahi reassures his students of his understanding of their learning: the feeling of being understood by one's teacher is a deeply motivating one. Yahi deliberately spends time talking about himself, his life outside school, his feelings, his young son. When the teacher opens up as a person, he argues, we can all start to know each other. And in such an emotional climate, everyone can not only give their best but also expand their perception of what their best might be.

It is in ways like these that the teachers made actual and explicit their commitment to their students' well-being: to their feelings of confidence, competence and control, to their experiences of enjoyment, purposefulness and success, to their sense of security in the present and hope for the future.

Teachers' choices: the social dimension of learning

At the start of Chapter 13 we saw some examples of individual teachers' priorities in their work of transforming learning capacity. There is no doubt that one of Narinder's most distinctive characteristics as a learning without limits teacher is her emphasis on the concept of 'team' in the social world of the classroom, and the importance she ascribes to every pupil experiencing full membership of the team, a membership in which she includes herself. We can also see, as we re-examine her account through the lens of the necessary relationship between classroom conditions and students' internal states, that she finds a whole variety of ways of making a difference to the quality of the students' lives as social beings. One of the ways in which she does so is by involving her pupils in the process of establishing classroom rules and conventions, which work for the well-being of the whole class. The pupils are involved in the process not in a tokenistic way, but authentically, claiming 'authorship' for the code of behaviour they have drawn up. There are rules about listening, and others that protect the pupils from pain and violence: everybody knows what they are, because everybody took part in establishing them. The personal outcome for pupils of this particular aspect of their objective classroom conditions is a sense of harmony; Narinder's work guarantees that the classroom is a safe place, for everyone. The pupils care and are cared for. Everybody is listened to (with the heart, as the Chinese poster reminds them). Everybody feels safe. The social purposes of transformability that we described in Chapter 13 – the state of acceptance and belonging, the creation of a learning community – are a lived reality in Narinder's classroom: she and the pupils work together to create the conditions in which their community can grow, and she and the pupils experience together the sense of well-being that life in a harmonious community engenders.

As well as working to build the classroom community as a whole, Narinder organizes group experiences that contribute to her pupils' social and emotional well-being. Sometimes she groups her pupils on the basis of differences between them: their experiences in these groups, where, for example, one is a fluent and accomplished writer (but not all of them), teach them both how to give and how to receive support, a practical lesson in interdependence. Other groups are selected for tasks that can only be effectively carried out by working as a team, assigning roles and responsibilities. All the different groups that are formed and reformed in Narinder's classroom teach the pupils something about group membership and group working; and these experiences have other benefits too. Narinder's pupils feel a sense of belonging, of contributing, of participating, of solidarity. Each one of them can say to him- or herself: 'I am part of this; I have something to give and something to do. I am not alone. Other people are here to help me, and I can respond in kind. I am implicated in the work of all the learners in this room.' Narinder's methods of classroom organization, the choices she makes in assigning pupils to groups and group activities, are more than an expression of her efficiency and years of experience; her decisions bear fruit in her pupils' internal states, and their feelings of well-being.

The intellectual work of learning: teachers' choices in the cognitive domain

Narinder's account is also rich in examples of the choices she makes in organizing tasks and activities, and preparing materials and experiences for her class. She selects tasks that are relevant, that have meaning in pupils' lives, tasks with authentic purposes, tasks in which the pupils make decisions, tasks that require the application of learning, not just regurgitation, tasks involving the big ideas being studied, not just technical procedures, tasks that everyone can do. So, for example, a literacy task focused on speaking and listening took the form of an energetic classroom debate about animal rights, in which the pupils' talk was put to real life use in persuasion, argument and counter-argument. The history lesson described in Chapter 7 included the pupils' use of the terms period, dynasty, time-line; these terms were introduced through activities related to their own lives, their own time-lines and family trees, periods in their own life cycles.

What we can now see, as we look at these specific practices through the lens of the core idea of transformability, is that the young people in Narinder's class are not simply acquiring particular skills, knowledge or understanding. They experience more, and differently, because of the way she constructs the tasks they engage in. They come to feel the confidence engendered by acting as learners, making use of their learning; they come to know how it feels to make a difference; they discover that doing a worth-while task contributes to feelings of worthwhileness. They are engaged, with a personal purpose; they are fired up; they know success and mastery at first hand. The supportive environment that Narinder builds for them as learners and meaning-makers today creates what we have called the 'promise of tomorrow', the knowledge that they can go on with the intellectual work of learning. It is interesting to note how often Narinder identifies and draws attention to particular aspects of this work. Her pupils know what it is to be asked to explain, connect, put it together, reason it out: they are at home with their own acts of mind and can identify their growing powers as learners. The outcomes of this distinctive intellectual environment are distinctly worthwhile. Narinder's pupils are gaining a sense of respect for themselves as people and learners: they gain in self-respect, in self-awareness and in self-esteem. Their capacity to learn is unmistakably increasing, day after day.

Because Yahi is a teacher of mathematics, some of his pedagogical choices have a specific subject focus. He chooses, for example, to make explicit the historical context of the mathematical concepts he teaches; he selects problems that have relevance and meaning for the students, using examples from outside the classroom; his teaching emphasizes an awareness of how to tackle a problem, rather than speed in arriving at a solution. In all this, as in Narinder's careful construction and selection of tasks, Yahi is deliberately setting out to affect his students' states of mind. He is determined that they should feel for themselves the relevance and power of mathematics, not just hear about it from their teacher. He is committed to boosting their confidence as problem-solvers, not just their facility in finding solutions. His students' full-hearted engagement is crucial to their mathematical learning: 'If your mind is elsewhere, I can't teach you', he tells them. He is working towards a community of minds at work, a collaborative enterprise in thinking and questioning, especially in questioning.

A close scrutiny of the language interactions that characterize Yahi's classroom makes it clear that he attaches considerable importance to his students' questions, which he sees in a very particular way. When Yahi encourages his students to ask questions, he is doing more than finding a way to patch up gaps in their understanding: he is teaching them that help is always available, and that no question is valueless. The teacher's priority is for all the students to understand; an individual's question can help the whole class to move on in their thinking. In Yahi's ideal school, which he discussed in one interview, he described how 'healthy questioning would be permanent'. Healthy questioning is at the heart of Yahi's working approach; access to worthwhile learning for all, a central concern we identified in Chapter 13, is achieved in Yahi's classroom through the mechanism of the students' questions. It is as if Yahi is saying 'I can do anything if you ask me questions. When you show me your thinking, through your questions, I can come alongside you. I can put the scaffolding in place for your next bit of learning. Individual questions benefit the whole community: I can open up your problem and disclose its workings for everyone.' Furthermore, Yahi sees 'healthy questioning' as a critical way of thinking that can be transferred, that is applicable to any subject, that lifts limits, regardless of context or content. In the community of learners that Yahi is working to create, the students' power and willingness to question play a crucial role: for Yahi, their questions are not signs of weakness, ignorance or lack of understanding, but conscious acts of participation in learning; he welcomes them as invitations to respond, and does so, every time, with generosity and patience. Their willingness to participate in this way is daily being transformed by Yahi's work in building a questioning classroom, where 'questioning is permanent' and successful access to learning is ensured.

Practical pedagogical principles: the work of application

In making their transforming choices, teachers are not governed *either* by purposes (of whatever kind: affective, social or cognitive) *or* by the principles we elucidated in Chapter 13. Purposes and principles always work together. It is for the sake of clarity and completion that in the following sections we separate out for detailed scrutiny the ways in which the teachers apply the three interdependent, practical, pedagogical principles in their own classrooms, with their own students.

The principle of co-agency

As we saw above, the task of transforming learning capacity is a joint enterprise, depending upon both teachers and learners. The power to create and transform conditions for learning is shared between the teachers and the learning community of young people. They play out this state of interdependence, these acts of power-sharing, in a variety of ways: here we illustrate their work in ensuring diversity in learning and in establishing a sense of shared responsibility.

Diversity in learning

We saw in some detail in Chapter 13 how the principle of co-agency informs the way in which teachers understand the task of ensuring diversity in learning opportunities. We saw, for example, how Nicky used her sensitive understanding of individual students to anticipate the different kinds of support and attention they might need, if all of them are to be purposefully engaged in a lesson. We also saw how Patrick's capacity to see things as his students might see them, to add their perceptions to his own, to treat them as co-opted partners in the process of planning and provision, enables him to dispense with the limited concept of match (in which teachers match their demands to the perceived attainments of their students). In its place, because of his broader view of what his students bring to the classroom, Patrick fosters diversity, by offering choices and open-ended tasks; to these opportunities young people can respond on their own terms, in ways that make personal sense of them, expressing their own thinking, in their own ways.

We also noted, very briefly, how some teachers, especially Yahi and Nicky, take account of gender issues. They acknowledge the need to find ways of working with, rather than against, their students' gender identities, permanently keeping the door open for learning and being alert to alternative approaches that may seem more relevant and worthwhile for their students. Here we return to an example from Julie's classroom that we have already started to analyse in considering students' emotional well-being. The history lesson about the Roman public health system was, as we have seen, highly effective in increasing the students' sense of competency, security and control. It was equally effective in the contribution it made to the theme of diversity. Julie designed an activity that modelled for her students the process of interpreting sources, and extracting and synthesizing key ideas. The activity involved matching sources relating to preventative medicine in Roman times with cards, each containing a brief summary of key ideas relating to one source. Some of the pairings were straightforward, and could be accomplished by scanning and matching key words. Others required students to read carefully and make inferences. The activity

was carefully constructed to achieve a balance between support and challenge. Julie took care to alert students in advance to the presence of some
quite tricky pairings, and to suggest that they look for the ones that are easy
to do first, to help to reduce the choices by the time they reached the ones
that required more complex thinking. She remembered that, the last time
she tried a similar task, some students experienced frustration because all
the cards were printed on the same colour paper. This time, to make the
task more manageable and less confusing, she provided the sources and
matching cards in different colours. The matching cards doubled up as
(optional) support material. Students could choose to stick the sentences
into their books rather than write the information out if they preferred,
since Julie wanted them to concentrate their efforts on thinking, rather
than consuming lesson time with mundane (but necessary) recording tasks.
Julie made this choice of modes of recording available to everyone, so that
no one could be embarrassed or singled out – and knowing that only a few
students would choose to take it up. The activity was followed up by the
construction of a spider diagram, using brief notes and pictorial represen-
tations of the key information. This provided an opportunity for students
to record and represent their thinking visually, as well as through the
medium of words. It helped them to move towards a summary and synthesis of key ideas, and served both as an aid for recall and as a preliminary
to writing a paragraph, drawing on the evidence in the sources. In Julie's
plan, it was essential that this final activity should be offered to everybody,
but not that it should be completed by everybody.

Within a common activity, then, there is scope for diversity in experience, content, activity, modes of recording and outcome, through the
choices young people make, the personal meanings they construct and the
understandings they develop. 'Success' will be judged by the extent to
which the activity does succeed in connecting with students' hearts and
minds, enabling everyone not just to learn something about preventative
medicine in Roman times but also to have experiences that build and
strengthen the states of mind needed to transform learning capacity.

Sense of shared responsibility

Another aspect of co-agency that we discussed in Chapter 13 was the work
of establishing a sense of shared responsibility; the discussion included an
analysis of its practical, pedagogical and ethical significance. Here we consider further aspects of shared responsibility: the interactions between
teachers and young people, their responsiveness to one another, the messages of recognition that pass between them and the way in which these
elements of classroom life contribute to the continuous process of transforming learning capacity.

The theme of responsiveness runs through many of the details of classroom interactions that are given in the nine accounts. Patrick emphasizes the possibility of negotiation, welcoming his students' suggestions about pace, classroom layout, specific tasks and ways of forming groups. After one exciting and rewarding lesson (a Radio Verona phone-in, debating the plight of Romeo and Juliet) in which there had been numerous adjustments, suggested by different groups as they selected their own direction, their own learning pathways, Patrick reflected that this lesson came particularly close to what he was trying to achieve. The shaping and pacing of the lesson, selecting specific content and ways of representing the students' thinking, had been undertaken, as they should be, in the effective application of the principle of co-agency.

The theme of responsiveness is also clearly to be seen in Narinder's classroom, though expressed in a different way. There is a deliberate use, by both Narinder and her pupils, of the language of respect. Requests are framed politely, as requests, not orders; there are expressions of gratitude and acceptance; verbal acts of kindness, gentleness and sensitivity are recognized and praised; Narinder articulates her pleasure at being together with her class and identifies the sources of her pleasure and her pride in them.

These public expressions of value and recognition are also a theme in Alison's classroom, where, at the start of each day, there is an unstructured, unplanned period, which she calls the 'independent learning' session; this is a strategy she has adopted to convey the message of recognition. During this time, the pupils are free to select their own pursuits, which they do with great seriousness and a sense of responsibility. Some practise their spellings or catch up with unfinished written work. Others devote themselves to reading, or an ongoing practical project: one pupil commented, 'You can do it every morning, when you're really into something.' Alison's deliberate gift to the children of unplanned time for their own interests and concerns, her recognition of their individual priorities, engenders a sense of control and the secure knowledge that they are capable of making thoughtful decisions for themselves, as their part of the work of shared responsibility.

There is a striking example of how young people take up the offer of shared responsibility, and actively contribute to the work of co-agency, in Non's discussion of the way she engages her students in dialogue of various kinds about their learning. She discovers that the opportunity to select from a range of tasks offered is experienced by one student as intimidating rather than enabling. This information prompts her to think about what she can do to provide more effective support and structure for students who are not sure how best to respond to the invitation to choose for themselves. Her response is a transforming one, because she chooses *not* to reduce choice but to alleviate the student's sense of being intimidated by choice. She seeks to lift the limit in the student's mind, by influencing how the student sees the opportunity to choose, and supporting her in making good use of it. This example of the workings of co-agency is a useful one because it illustrates the interdependency and responsiveness of teacher and learner, in the process of transformability. Non assumes that offering her students a choice of assignments is generally enabling (as most of them confirm), and she only finds out about this student's feelings of intimidation because the student is prepared to be honest about her feelings. This willingness to be honest could be risky, but in Non's classroom the evidence suggests that the student's relationship with the teacher is one where she feels safe and empowered to speak her mind. Her honesty is rewarded not only by having her feelings taken seriously but also by the teacher taking steps to address the problem she is experiencing. Non treats the 'problem' as indicative that something needs changing in her teaching: this particular student is making a valuable contribution to her teacher's capacity to enhance learning for everybody. The ensuing thought that Non puts into how to adjust and additionally support the process of choice for that particular student can help her to refine her strategies in ways that are likely to be beneficial and enabling for all students.

This example also illustrates how teachers' power to intervene effectively in students' learning relies on their understanding of the connection between classroom conditions and subjective states. Non automatically connects this student's expressed feelings about choice to aspects of her classroom practice, the conditions for learning that she has created. She is convinced that she can find ways to empower the student to choose more confidently. How the student feels and responds is not fixed; it is open to change if Non can respond to her discovery with a strategy that the student will find more enabling. They are working together to improve both external conditions and subjective states: they are co-agents in enhancing learning capacity.

The principle of everybody

In the application of this principle, we have already seen how teachers' choices are made in the interests of everybody, in order to benefit everybody equally. There is no room, in a classroom dedicated to learning without limits, for learning opportunities that only benefit 'some people', the fastest readers, or the most accurate writers, or the highest achievers. The classroom conditions that teachers create to enhance learning capacity must be evaluated against this very strict criterion: the conditions must positively affect everybody, must positively shape everybody's state of mind, both as an individual learner and as a member of the learning community. Alison structured the provision she made for everybody around an emphasis on her pupils' capacity to make informed choices. After a whole-class session in a maths lesson, for example, Alison gives the children a wide range of possible tasks to do. Some tasks are easier, some harder (like Julie's cards for matching original sources with key ideas), but it is left to the pupils to decide where their starting point will be. No child is assigned a particular task; no task is deemed too straightforward or too challenging for particular children. The emphasis is on the starting point, not on the stopping place or ceiling. Alison assumes that every child having started, having taken up her invitation to engage, will have the opportunity, the capacity and the desire to go further, to continue the learning journey. Emphasizing the starting point, Alison argues, can lift the limits on learning that often go unrecognized, the limits imposed by the tacit assumption that some pupils are simply not capable of going very far. As a result they are not given sufficient opportunities to disprove their teachers' damaging judgements. Alison works from the opposite assumption: she provides in the same terms for everybody and, at the same time, makes sure this provision guarantees success for everybody. She insists on 'ceaselessly having opportunities there [so] that children can show you what they can really do. I want to give them as much opportunity for success as I can.' For Alison, providing opportunities for success is a powerful strategy for lifting limits, and engaging every pupil with the same sense of capacity to go 'always a little further'.

The principle of everybody also requires the teachers, and the pupils, to demonstrate the value they attach to everybody's contributions, not just those of 'some people'. The individual accounts in Part 2 of this book show how in all nine classrooms, the teachers made it a priority to recognize and thank young people genuinely for all their contributions. As we shall see when we examine young people's perspectives in detail in Chapter 15, in all nine classrooms the young people knew that their teachers wanted to hear their ideas, and really listened to them when they offered them. Getting that message across, however, in a system more typically characterized by teachers telling and students being expected to listen, is not easy. The teachers therefore work hard to ensure that their students know that their choices, initiatives and contributions have been noticed, recognized, valued and appreciated, that their activities as active learners are taken seriously. They comment on the detail of the initiatives taken by young people. They show that they understand and value the initiative and how the young people have met the challenge that they, the teachers, had offered. They applaud the work done, they respond to the young people's ideas with relevant information of their own, they sensitively but seriously push the young people to take their ideas further or challenge them to justify their ideas.

In all this we see a third element of the principle of everybody at work: the development of solidarity, the maintenance of a learning community. We saw some strengths of this aspect of the teachers' work earlier in this chapter, when we considered their purposes in the social domain. In preceding chapters too, the themes of community and solidarity are supported by a wealth of evidence. In Patrick's classroom, for example, we saw how even the way he circulates around the room, moving among and between the students, does more than create a particular kind of warm, informal space: it is a very effective way of establishing, as Patrick puts it, 'a whole group sense ... where everyone is basically on board, and going the same way ... They're all in the same boat, all got something to do. They're all part of it.'

The principle of trusting the learner

The third practical pedagogical principle we identified in Chapter 13 is that everything that teachers do in the interests of transforming learning capacity presupposes a position of trust. The teachers start from an assumption that all young people can safely be trusted as learners. They can be trusted to engage, to connect, to commit themselves to the work of learning and to the solidarity of the community when conditions are right. If they do not, if they disengage, or fail to connect, or absent themselves, physically or metaphorically, from classroom life, then teachers can start to enquire whether something is wrong, and apply themselves to working out what they can do to put matters right. In these circumstances, teachers are obliged to reconsider choices and decisions they have already made, in order to see what is setting limits on their students' engagement and their capacity to learn.

In Patrick's classroom, for example, we met a group of students who were actively withdrawing from their class activities, exercising their capacity to opt out, to stay silent, not to participate. Patrick is, naturally, concerned about these students, but far from writing them off, dismissing them from his mind or responding punitively to their lack of engagement, he considers strategy after strategy that might re-engage them. His 'first instinct is to try to vary the menu and look for things they might find more involving ...' But he is not content to stop there. He considers copious possibilities, and concludes: 'it needs energy and invention'. The students' apparent lack of energy stimulates Patrick to greater inventiveness in calling forth the energy that he continues to trust these students are temporarily holding in reserve. He does not deny their continuing capacity to learn, despite the determination with which they seem to be spurning his advances; instead he continues to experiment and innovate, to change routines and dynamics. His persistence, his obstinacy even, in not giving up on these students is a telling example of how the principle of trust works in the interests of every student. Patrick continues to offer this group of students choices, even when they appear to be choosing the dysfunctional option for their learning; the other option open to him, to withdraw his trust, close down on their choices, become the 'scary' teacher, might have even more regrettable consequences in the future.

Patrick's commitment to his students' capacity to make choices for themselves, an expression of his trust in their capacity to learn, is paralleled in other accounts. In Chapter 5 we looked at a music lesson of Claire's, analysing the effect of the choices she made in organizing the children into groups. Here we emphasize the choices the children made in the course of that same lesson.

The starting point for the children was Claire's provision of an eclectic range of percussion instruments and a variety of other inviting materials, including tissue paper and aluminium foil. Claire emphasized to them that although the lesson had a clear and specific purpose (they were asked to create an accompaniment to a song they had heard the week before), all the other decisions to be made in their working groups were theirs. In this way, all the children were given opportunities to take part in authentically engaging ways. As a music specialist, Claire is eloquent about the significance of music in offering these authentic opportunities: 'There's such a lot in music that every child can get something *from* it and every child can bring something *to* it.' In this particular lesson, the choices she offered, of what to bring and what to take, were planned to engender a feeling of confidence in the children. In addition, she wanted them to feel proud of her trust and confidence in them, of her assumption, made open and explicit, that they were capable of making worthwhile choices and tackling the task successfully.

As the lesson progressed, it was clear that Claire's trust was well placed. Claire herself was particularly encouraged by the way Jessica, 'the shyest girl in the class', had responded, devising a delicate and original response to the task and being willing and eager to share her achievement with the rest of the class. She was equally delighted with Stephen's contribution, which showed an unexpectedly high level of physical coordination. Unexpectedly, because Stephen had been labelled 'dyspraxic', and had been assessed as having 'poor' skills of coordination. Claire's trust, however, and the reiterated expression of that trust, seemed to lift those limits on Stephen's perceived capacity to learn, and proved to everybody that his contribution, too, was to be valued and recognized.

The provision of an abundance of materials is another interesting feature of this lesson. Some children were observed carefully selecting one or two instruments; others picked an entire handful. The choice was theirs, unforced by lack of availability. No one had to make do with what was left over at the end. They were trusted to make good use of this munificence. We may also speculate about the feelings of well-being that may have been induced by this generous provision; plentiful materials may reinforce feelings of being both trusted and well cared for, just as insufficient resources may suggest to children that they are undeserving, or not quite trustworthy enough to be properly provided for. More simply, the children's capacity to make decisions was enhanced by there being plenty of instruments and other materials to make decisions about. And their confidence was still further increased by Claire's expressions of trust in their competence and her continued assurances that they were going to succeed at their open-ended task.

Acting on principle

The longer we studied the approaches to teaching and learning described in the nine accounts, the more coherent became the patterns of the teachers' choices. They are all made on the basis of the teachers' understanding of what limits young people's capacity to learn, and what will lift those limits, freeing them to become more powerful and committed learners. The more familiar we became with the constructs at the heart of their teaching, the more clearly we understood why it is so important to identify not just what teachers *do* and why, but also what they *do not do* and why, in order to see the full significance of their practices and underlying choices. The positive choices gain in meaning and significance by virtue of what they are negating, the limits to learning that they are trying to prevent or overcome, the damage that they are trying to undo in order to strengthen and transform learning capacity. For each of the principles we have identified that guide the practice of transforming learning capacity we can see the nine teachers acting on their hypotheses about what limits and what enhances the capacity to learn, at a collective level, acting on behalf of everybody, in the interests of everybody. Some of the choices they make in this process are given in Table 14.1 (pp.208–9).

In this chapter and the previous one, we have moved on from our starting point, which was an exposition of our reasons for rejecting ability labelling in all its guises. But our analysis of the damage that ability thinking and ability-focused classrooms can do to young people, to teachers and to curriculum was never intended to be a sufficient response to the problem we had identified. The task that we set out to accomplish in our research was to identify one or more models of teaching capable of providing a theoretically sound and practically feasible alternative to ability-led teaching and learning. Using the accounts of the project teachers, which make up Part 2 of this book, we have explained and illustrated how the concept of learning capacity and the core idea of transformability provide the basis for an alternative model, while the core purposes and guiding principles provide the means by which the transformation of learning capacity can be brought about. In articulating our alternative, we have made a move similar to the shift in thinking to which the American sociologist Henri Giroux refers, when he writes that the struggle for greater justice in education and in society needs 'to move away from being the language of critique and redefine itself as part of the language of transformation and hope' (Giroux 1997: 227). Just as we align ourselves with Giroux's recognition of the struggle against injustice, so we aspire to articulate the language of transformation and hope, drawing, as we do so, on the thoughts and actions of the nine teachers who have worked with us to construct this alternative approach.

Table 14.1 Teachers' choices

Teachers committed to transformability don't	*Teachers committed to transformability do*
Acting on the principle of co-agency	
Manage classroom activities through the imposition of authority.	Actively encourage and enable young people to share responsibility for achieving a purposeful, productive and harmonious working atmosphere.
Respond to individuals on the basis of categories of perceived ability.	Respond to individuals by trying to understand classroom experience through their eyes, by using that understanding to ensure meaningful diversity and openness in learning opportunities.
Write off anybody, ever, no matter how intractable the situation seems.	Draw on all the information available to them, through observation and dialogue with young people, to try to understand what is blocking their learning.
Conduct classroom interaction on the basis that teaching and learning require the passing of knowledge from teacher to the learner.	Construct classroom interaction on the basis that teaching and learning involve a meeting of minds – depending as much on what young people bring and offer as on what teachers contribute.
Acting on the principle of everybody	
Overtly differentiate between young people in tasks or activities.	Construct learning activities as a common endeavour in which everybody can take part on an equal footing.
Routinely use ability-based grouping or grouping by similar attainment.	Encourage diverse groupings and negotiate patterns of grouping and seating with young people.
Keep peer interaction to a minimum to avoid interference with learning.	Work to develop the peer group as a community of learners who support and increase one another's learning capacity

cont.

Table 14.1 Teachers' choices *cont*

Teachers committed to transformability don't	*Teachers committed to transformability do*
Acting on the principle of trust	
Match tasks to perceived attainment/ability.	Construct a range of attractive opportunities accessible to everybody, with space for learner input to shape experiences and outcomes.
Attribute the problem to the learners when they are unresponsive to the tasks and experiences provided for them.	Constantly seek for better kinds of opportunities through which initially unresponsive learners might be encouraged to engage effectively with classroom activities.
Take for granted the value, relevance and worthwhileness of curriculum content.	Choose content and devise tasks that encourage young people to draw on diverse experiences and make connections with what is worthwhile and important to them.

15 Young people's perspectives on learning without limits

As we explained in Chapter 3, it was an essential part of the research to find out how the young people viewed the experience of being taught over a certain period of time by teachers who had quite determinedly put aside the notion of fixed ability, and the use of ability labels. The young people to whom we spoke were as varied as the school contexts in which they were to be found. Some were refugees from Somalia, Sierra Leone and Eritrea; others knew that their great grandparents had lived in the same village as they lived in now. Some were inner-city children; others lived in the suburbs of small county towns. We used the various individual, group and whole-class activities described in Chapter 3 to find out how they saw themselves as learners in these classrooms. How did they view their teachers and think their teachers saw them? Were there aspects of their classroom experience that they considered especially helpful, or that presented them with difficulties? To what extent was there a match between what the teachers said they were trying to do and the perceptions of the young people?

As the core ideas and principles explored in Chapters 13 and 14 began to emerge, these ideas began also to shape our ways of making sense of and learning from the material gathered from the young people about their experiences. Once we had established the core idea of the transformability of learning capacity as a joint enterprise, we realized that it would be necessary to develop our understanding of this task, and what it entails, from the perspective of the young people, as well as from the teachers' perspective.

Making choices

When we looked again at the young people's contributions to the research, we noticed many instances where they explicitly recognized their own power to make choices: to engage or disengage, to accept or refuse the invitations to learn extended to them by their teachers. Their awareness often went deeper, too. Studying these instances, we could see that, like their teachers, the young people were making connections between their choices, their states of mind and classroom conditions. They were not simply drawing attention to what they liked or did not like about particular teachers' classroom practices. They were articulating their understanding of the classroom conditions that they found enabling; they were expressing their understanding of how what the teacher was doing was empowering them to make choices they might not otherwise have made, and as a result they were prepared to engage and play an active role in classroom learning.

In this chapter, we examine the kinds of choices that young people acknowledged themselves to be making, what they said that they felt empowered to do, as learners, in these classrooms because of the conditions that prevailed there. It is important to emphasize that the kinds of choices that we discuss below do not reflect categories that were already there in the questions we asked the young people, nor categories derived from our analysis of the teachers' thinking. In pursuing this focus on young people's choices – and what makes a difference to their choices – we have sought to be responsive to the issues that they themselves identified as important. In deciding to focus on choices, though, we have inevitably left out other issues that the young people raised in discussion. As a result of our choice of focus, too, the discussion in this chapter draws more on the views expressed by the secondary students than on the views of young people in primary schools. This is because more secondary students articulated their experiences in sufficient detail for us to trace the links they were making between their choices, states of mind and classroom conditions. Although references to the primary pupils' experiences are more limited, they do provide some of the richest insights into young people's experience of co-agency and community.

Asking questions

In the early stages of the research, one striking feature of our discussion with different groups of young people was the frequency with which their teachers' willingness to explain was identified by young people as an important enabling condition. Those interviewed expressed over and over again their appreciation of teachers who welcomed and actively encouraged them to ask questions, who explained things well and who, they knew for certain, would always be prepared to explain things as many times as necessary until understanding was achieved. For example, one 15-year-old girl commented: 'If there's something you don't understand, you can always ask about it. ... [Our teacher] doesn't mind how many questions or if we repeat questions. She just keeps answering until we all understand. I really like that.' Her comment reflects an awareness that whether or not people achieve understanding is greatly dependent upon students' willingness to ask questions. She knows that hers is a classroom where 'you can always ask' and 'the teacher doesn't mind', and so people are empowered to keep asking until they do understand. There is a matter-of-factness about the statement 'she just keeps answering until we all understand' that implies a normal state of affairs where understanding is the entitlement of everybody. It seems that, through her patient responses to questions, the teacher has succeeded in communicating to this student both her care for everybody's learning – that nobody should be left in a state of 'not understanding' – and her faith that everybody can and will understand in time, with appropriate support. It is also notable that this student formulates her appreciation not just from her own perspective, but from the perspective of '*we all*', the class community, who benefit collectively from the teacher's attitudes and practices.

This was by no means the ethos of other classrooms in their experience. While the young people readily acknowledged that there were many distractions that could and did interfere with their concentration, nevertheless they felt that some teachers did not seem to appreciate that careful listening does not automatically lead to understanding. The young people's comments indicate their awareness that understanding is an active process, something that they as learners have to do, not something that arrives ready-made in their heads, by virtue of listening to the teacher's words. It takes time to make sense of ideas and, as one boy stated, 'people understand at their own pace'. So they felt very indignant when their requests for help were treated as a failure on their part to attend to the teacher. One Year 9 girl commented: 'If you don't understand it, then you don't understand, and then they start shouting at you "Oh why weren't you listening at the beginning of the lesson?" and you just say "Well I was listening but I just don't understand".' The young people said that if they were made to feel uncomfortable about asking questions, they stopped asking altogether. As one person put it, 'If the teacher speaks to me like that I don't bother.' They appreciated teachers who made it clear that they did not 'expect you to get it the first time'. Then 'not understanding' could be accepted as just a normal part of the process people go through in moving towards understanding, and there would be no embarrassment about asking questions or requesting further help.

From the young people's comments, it was evident that they were very aware that the choice to engage or disengage was theirs, and that the choices they made to engage and to persist with work in the face of difficulties were intimately bound up with 'understanding' or 'not understanding' the work they were doing. One 13-year-old said bluntly, in the context of a discussion about what makes people switch off, 'If I get the work, I work', whereas another said, 'I might stare at the board and then like just think "What the hell is that?"' These comments and others like them show the students' awareness that there are many alternatives to persisting with the effort of trying to understand – not just switching off, but copying from the person next to them or simply going through the motions of getting the task done. One person made a clear differentiation between simply 'getting the answer' and 'understanding how to get the answer, working it out for yourself'. If the young people were to make the choice to go through the sweat of 'working it out', and to persist even when feeling confused, they had to trust that understanding would eventually be achieved, and that they could count on the teacher's support.

In the early stages of the research, although we noted this recurring theme about the importance of teachers' willingness to explain and capacity to explain well, at the time we did not consider it to be particularly significant for the research. We took these traits to be characteristic of all good teachers, not just those who have set aside ideas of fixed ability. Nevertheless, reconsidering them in the light of the emerging principles of co-agency, trust and community, we were able to gain a new perspective on their significance for our understanding of teaching free from ability labelling. We began to see that, while the active encouragement of questioning, on the part of the teacher, cannot be considered a distinctive characteristic of teachers committed to transformability, it does follow logically from the idea of transformability and from the core pedagogical principles. The teachers' willingness to go on explaining – and if necessary to look for other routes to understanding – reflects their commitment to co-agency, to empowering young people to act more fully and productively as agents in their own learning. It also reflects their trust in all young people's power to understand and to learn, given the right conditions. We can now see the reciprocal form that this trust, when effectively communicated, takes in the minds of students, who trust that their learning is in safe hands, who are prepared to sustain their efforts even when they do not understand, who trust that appropriate help will be forthcoming, that their difficulties will be given sympathetic attention and that the teacher will organize things so that, in the end, they will understand.

Contributing ideas

A second recurring theme was to do with the circumstances under which young people said they were prepared to express their ideas and actively contribute to class and small group discussion, as opposed to opting out, keeping quiet or just playing a minimal role in class activities and interactions. There was general agreement that 'feeling confident' was an important precondition for contributing their ideas, but there was by no means unanimity about where 'confidence' comes from, and whether it can be increased. Feelings of confidence on a day-to-day basis were influenced, for some young people, by a global sense of being good, or not good, at particular subjects or areas of learning. As one Year 5 boy commented, 'Some people are good at maths, and some people are good at robots.' A secondary student admitted that because she saw herself as no good at maths, she was prone to give up before she even tried: 'I'm just like, "Oh well, I can't do it so I'm not going to be able to do it".' For some young people, 'being good' at a particular subject was not something they could do anything about because it depended upon the 'kind of brain' they had. Some subjects, and especially maths, were considered by some young people to be inherently difficult and daunting, especially 'if you have got a brain that is not good at maths'. Other young people agreed that there are subjects that you are 'naturally into' and others that you are not.

Nevertheless, there was recognition that feelings of self-confidence and capability could be influenced by experience with a particular teacher. As one secondary student commented, 'I feel confident in his class, I think I can do things, and it's just a matter of concentrating, sitting there and learning it.' This comment clearly expresses a feeling of empowerment ('I think I can do things'); the student's confidence inspires him with a sense of capability not just to engage but to pursue his learning, independently, through his own efforts ('It's just a matter of *concentrating* ...'). Teachers helped to generate confidence, and make people feel good at their subject, some other students acknowledged, by personal encouragement, by their feedback on work and by the way that they responded to people's ideas. One student said, 'I don't feel I am that good [at the subject] but he makes me feel that I am good at what I am doing. And makes me feel more confident.'

A number of young people mentioned 'feeling relaxed' as helping to heighten their sense of confidence and capability, and linked this to a classroom atmosphere that was 'friendly' and 'relaxed'. If the teacher is relaxed, 'it makes it seem easier', according to one person. There was agreement (though not unanimity) that, in a relaxed environment, talking was not only permitted but actively encouraged, that people had some choice over where they sat and were encouraged to share ideas together and support each other's learning. This perception of how confidence can be increased by the class working together as a group seemed to echo closely the teachers' understanding of the power of the community to enhance everybody's capacity for learning. One Year 10 student commented that where a rule of silence or near silence was enforced, 'we don't learn much'. A Year 9 girl offered a more detailed commentary on the importance of learning by talking and working together. She said:

I tend to find if you work on your own you don't have as much confidence as what you do when you are working in a group. In some classrooms, you have to work in silence and I personally don't think that's right because you want to share your ideas with people, you want someone to back you up with your ideas and say, 'Yeah, that's really good, write it down.' But when you're working on your own, you want to talk and say 'Oh is that good?' but then you can't.

It was widely agreed that sharing one's own ideas with others, and hearing theirs, helps to build confidence, because people do not feel on their own, they are exposed to more viewpoints and can learn from each other. One secondary student made an analogy with sharing personal choices and preferences in music, saying 'It's like, if I listen to other people's music and I learn to like it, I add it to my collection.' However, many of those interviewed also acknowledged that interaction with peers could destroy their concentration, and that individuals could impede effective group work by their behaviour. Like their teachers, they were conscious that if working together and sharing ideas are to build confidence and support learning, there needs to be an acceptance of the principle that (as one student said) 'everyone listens to each other and respects each other'. Before they contribute their ideas, people need to know that they will be given a sympathetic hearing and will not be subject to put-downs, even if their ideas are wrong or misconceived.

Across all the classrooms, there was recognition that feelings of confidence were bound up with feelings of safety. In some classrooms, sharing ideas with others could have the opposite effect. 'It puts down your self-esteem', one Year 10 student said, 'if your ideas are not taken seriously or are rejected by others.' 'If that happens', she continued, 'I won't say anything.' Another agreed: 'If other students are giving you a hard time, you won't put your hand up or give your ideas.' From their comments it was clear that the young people were acutely aware that identity is continually at risk in the public arena of classroom interaction.

Feeling confident was also linked by some young people with the opportunity to choose tasks and styles of learning that they found most comfortable, or that they thought would enhance their achievements. One 16-year-old appreciated how, with a particular teacher, 'there is always a large variety of questions to choose from. This means you can easily choose one which you feel confident on.' Having conversations with the teacher about learning and being consulted about your own needs and preferences as a learner also helped to contribute to a sense of competence and capability.

A recurring theme, then, in many of the students' comments is that feeling confident enables them to do things and take risks that they would not otherwise feel able to do. One Year 10 student made explicit her under-standing of the connections between her choices, her states of mind and classroom conditions when she commented that 'I can express my ideas because I feel comfortable with the teacher, and the environment and the atmosphere.' Her comment reveals her understanding that expressing her ideas is a choice that she can make or withhold, depending upon prevail-ing conditions. Confidence, bred by classroom conditions, is the precondi-tion for this student to take up her role as an active learner and to take the risks (beginning with a willingness to express her ideas) that are a necessary part of it.

Getting into a learning mood, concentrating

The young people also demonstrated awareness that their choices to engage or disengage, and their ability to sustain concentration, were powerfully affected by their mood. Among some of the young people, there was also evidence that they saw their mood as something over which they could exercise some control. Mood was not something that simply happened to them, the result of external events, good or bad, which put them in a frame of mind that helped or hindered their learning. There were things they could do to change their mood and get themselves into the right frame of mind for learning. This idea was most powerfully expressed by one group of 9- and 10-year-olds in a discussion about the value of having time for 'independent learning' at the start of every day, which was to be used in any way the children chose. The teacher had introduced this independent time at the start of the day at the children's own request and, as we saw in Chapter 14, they were convinced that it was helpful. They reported that 'it gets you going at the beginning of each day', and 'gets you into a working mood'. It was time to 'organize yourself' and also to talk over any 'trouble at home'.

From their comments, we can see that having the experience of this independent learning time helped these young people to appreciate that degrees of concentration, motivation and distractedness are not stable features of their personalities or their attitude to learning. Starting the day in this way, they have observed, makes a difference to their powers of con-centration and to their motivation. They recognize that their teacher enabled this to happen by offering them their own time, but they also rec-ognize that getting into 'a working mood' and 'organizing yourself' is work that they do for themselves. Their comments acknowledge their perception of themselves as active learners – people whose minds need to be alert and active, and whose learning will consequently be impaired if they do not take steps to ready their minds for it. It is striking how these 9- and 10-year-olds recognize each other as people, with lives outside school and who sometimes have troubles which need to be talked through, before they can be freed up from external preoccupations to concentrate on the tasks and activities intended to promote their learning.

Making suggestions

The young people's accounts of their experience also revealed an awareness of being empowered to make suggestions to the teacher about what they and/or the teacher could do to make learning conditions more enabling. A secondary student said that she felt she could approach her English teacher and make suggestions about the balance of activities she would find helpful. She said:

> [Our teacher's] one of the people, like, if I say I didn't like something, I'd probably go up to her and tell her and say, 'I didn't like that much' or 'It's a bit boring – could we do this?' and I think she takes it on board. She doesn't do it straight away because I used to complain a lot that we didn't do a lot of oral work, and then this year she's taken it on board and we do a lot more stuff like that.

The student's comment suggests that she trusts this particular teacher to take her suggestions in a positive way, but she would not necessarily feel empowered to make this choice with other teachers. It seems, as well, that she is implying that she feels more committed to learning with this teacher, as a result of knowing that she can not merely make suggestions but actually have her ideas taken on board.

The importance of encouraging young people to make suggestions and communicate honestly to their teachers about their learning was underlined by some of the information that came to light as a result of the activities carried out for the purposes of the research. Clearly, there were some young people in these nine classrooms who took the opportunity provided by the research to express thoughts and feelings that they had not previously communicated to their teachers, and that came as a (sometimes uncomfortable) surprise to them. One of the primary teachers was taken aback to be told by a number of her pupils in an anonymous 'comments' box that they felt there was very little time in the day when they could actually talk to her. She consequently set some time apart for children who felt they needed to discuss anything with her.

It was salutary for these teachers to discover just how different young people's self-reported feelings and experiences were, in a few cases, from how they themselves perceived those young people. It reinforced for those teachers the importance of continuing to work at building channels of communication that actively encourage young people to express their honest feelings, and of inviting them to make suggestions, to take a greater share in the task of building optimally enabling learning conditions.

Increasing commitment

In their contributions, the young people also demonstrated their awareness of the link between classroom conditions and the degree to which they were prepared to invest of themselves in classroom tasks and activities. One Year 10 girl said that it made a difference to her to feel respected by the teacher, as it made her feel like 'giving more to the lesson'. The opportunity to choose between different tasks and activities was also identified as being important in generating greater feelings of commitment. As one person commented, 'Since I chose what I wanted to do, I had to work harder on that.' Although the young people did not use the word commitment, they seemed to imply it as they spoke about the importance of the feeling of being known, cared for and responded to as an individual. One person appreciated the fact that her teacher 'knows I'm not very confident about asking questions, so he always comes round the class and checks that you understand, and he goes through the stuff with you'. Another was touched by her teacher's sensitivity when she had problems at home.

The importance of the teacher genuinely listening and paying attention to young people's ideas was a recurring theme across the interviews. The young people contrasted genuine listening with pseudo-listening; as one student put it, 'You have got something to say and the teacher is going "yep, yep" and they are not listening to you. It's like you are in your own little world and no one can see you.' When they felt that teachers were genuinely listening, and using their ideas to contribute to the lesson, this reinforced their commitment to the learning of the whole group and their sense of the value of what they had to offer.

Closely linked to this sense of being known, respected and listened to attentively was a sense that the teacher cares. Care breeds trust, as one Year 10 student commented: 'You need to know he cares about your work … we trust him.' This sense of care is noteworthy precisely because young people know only too well that it cannot be taken for granted. They know classrooms where it is absent, and that its absence generates fear and inhibits engagement. In such classrooms, they maintain distance and try to avoid notice, rather than actively seeking interaction with the teacher to exchange ideas, ask questions and have their thinking challenged and extended.

Identifying with the community

A further striking feature of the young people's accounts of their experience was the extent to which their comments revealed both a sense of themselves as part of a community and a sense of responsibility for the other members of the community. They were, it seemed, willing to identify themselves with the class as a learning community, and in doing so to take on some responsibility for the needs and well-being of others as well as themselves A group of Year 9 students, for example, were asked in an open way, following a particular lesson, what most helped their learning. Their unanimous response was that it was 'learning all together' that helped most. Learning in solidarity, learning as a community, has become the preferred and deliberate choice for them, as well as for their teacher. Working in pairs, in groups or as a whole class, but, in any case, collaboratively, has changed them as learners; they are more confident, they are exposed to different points of view. The resources of these individual learners have been pooled, in the interests of the collective, in support of everybody's learning.

Their sense of shared responsibility includes a strongly held conviction that, for the good of the collective, it is important that opportunities to be involved are equally distributed. The students appreciated that their teacher made 'lessons really fair'. 'He evens it up', they added, and makes 'you feel like you are a part of it.' Moreover, this group clearly experienced their teacher as an integral *member* of the community, not simply as a sensitive orchestrator of *their* community. They commented favourably on the quantity as well as the quality of his involvement in their learning:

P1: He gets involved more.

P2: He doesn't just sit there at his desk and start writing like most teachers do.

P3: He walks round the classroom ...

P4: He will come round and make sure you are doing your work, make sure you understand it.

P5: He checks it. He will come round, look at your work, and tell you it's good, gives you ideas, gives you clues.

With this group, as with the other young people we spoke to, the teacher's commitment to co-agency seemed to be reflected in a sense of solidarity, on the part of young people, in their relationships with the teacher. They felt that they and the teacher were on the same side. A heated debate arose in one mixed Year 5/6 primary class about whether it was right and proper for a teacher *always* to be 'on your side'. The debate was triggered by a discussion card that read 'My teacher is on my side'. One boy disagreed with the statement, saying 'She's not, she's not on *your* side, is she?' His friend replied, 'She is! She is!' The first boy explained his thoughts more fully:

P1: Say if you bullied Tony. [Our teacher] isn't going to be on your side saying you ain't done nothing.

P2: Not that way. Like when a teacher shouts at us she is trying to say something.

P1: If you've bullied Tony, and Tony's got bruises all over his face, and [the teacher's] got evidence that you've bullied him, [the teacher] can't stay on your side saying you ain't done nothing.

P2: No, not that way. She's trying to get you not to do it.

The subtleties of what is meant by the teacher being 'on your side' were also focused on in a second discussion group drawn from the same class. The issue, it seemed, arose from the use of the word 'my' on the card. One boy insisted that his teacher did not side with individuals but with *everybody*, the class as a whole. He said, 'She's on *our* side, not my side.' In another exchange with the same group, a pupil commented, 'All my best friends, they know I will trust them any day.' His comment provides persuasive evidence of the mutuality and reciprocity of this trust. He is not just saying 'I trust them' or 'they trust me' but, in so many words, *we know we trust one another*.

Choosing to be an active learner

In this analysis of young people's accounts of their experiences, we have explored some of the recurring themes of the previous two chapters and identified the choices that young people felt that they were being empowered to make because of the conditions that prevailed in the project teachers' classrooms. We have explored the states of mind that, according to the young people, support those choices and how they felt their states of mind were affected by particular classroom conditions. The analysis has enabled us to understand, from the young people's perspective, why most of them, most of the time, choose to take up an active rather than a passive or resistant role in these classrooms, why they choose to use their power to work with rather than against the teacher's intentions and aspirations for their learning. It has also begun to clarify what 'being an active learner' means to them, what an active learner *does* that a disengaged, uncommitted or passive learner chooses *not* to do. Their comments recognize and express their awareness of the power, the drive and the desire to engage and learn that comes from within themselves, and without which a teacher's own power to make a difference cannot come into play, and so is effectively incapacitated.

We have seen that there is a close correspondence between the teachers' theories of the conditions that young people will find more enabling and these young people's own accounts. Interpreting what the young people said about their experiences in the light of the principles of co-agency, trust and community helped us to appreciate the significance of what they were saying, and to use these insights to further our understanding of the conditions – and the connections – that enable young people to become more powerful and committed learners. In this way, we have added to our understanding of how teachers make their choices, a new understanding, built from young people's contributions, of the bases upon which young people make *their* choices in the joint enterprise of lifting the limits on their learning.

Transforming learning capacity

When the young people talked about their classroom experience, it was evident that some of them were still using conventional notions of fixed ability to account for the difficulties they experienced, or to explain differences in learning and achievement. Some of the comments, however, reveal a developing awareness that the encouragement and belief of a teacher, effectively communicated to them but carefully judged not to push them too far, can be critical in enabling them to take risks and surprise themselves. Describing her experience, one secondary student said, 'I always used to let myself down. I didn't think I could do well in things. But the teacher always told me I could achieve more. And when I got into this class, I thought I couldn't do what she asked but she made me.' Asked to elaborate on what the teacher actually did, she continued, 'I don't know one special thing, but *all* she did … well, because she was always giving us a fair try. She's very good at that. Unlike other teachers – they say "Oh, you can be in that set, you will not get above that". But she is always helping us to achieve.'

Other comments similarly suggested an awareness that when they were empowered to make choices they might not otherwise have made, the young people often surprised themselves by doing things that they had not thought they could do. One secondary student recognized, for example, that 'If you do your best and believe in yourself, you can do more than you think.' A Year 5 girl had changed her self-perceptions dramatically, as a result of being prepared to have a go at an activity, when she had initially felt reluctant to get involved. She said, 'When I started rock and roll in the school hall, I didn't want to do it and I didn't think I was any good at it, but now I'm doing the rock and roll concerts!'

In the comments of at least some of the young people to whom we spoke, there is recognition, then, that their perceptions of their capacity to learn can change. Indeed, we believe that the evidence presented in this chapter shows that implicit in young people's understandings of what

empowers their choices is a concept of learning capacity that is very similar
to the concept that the teachers themselves are using. Those students who
made explicit connections between their choices, states of mind and classroom conditions seemed to understand very well that their capacity to
learn in any given situation is in part within their control. If they choose to
take an active role, and do all the things that active learning entails, as outlined above, then their capacity to learn will be very much greater than if
they choose the passive alternative or resist altogether the invitations to
learn extended to them by their teachers.

As well as recognizing that they have choices, and that only *they* can
make these choices, they also acknowledge that they do not or will not
make a particular choice unless the conditions are right. Since the responsibility to create and transform learning conditions is shared between the
teacher and the learning community of young people, there is a state of
interdependence between them. The teacher's power to create and transform the conditions that empower and engage students itself depends on
the students' power to recognize, welcome and actively respond to these
conditions. The students' choices to engage can transform learning conditions, just as their teachers' choices do.

There are many comments quoted in this chapter that suggest an
awareness on the part of young people that they and their teachers can
work together in such a way that their capacity for learning is increased.
One Year 9 girl perhaps came closest to expressing belief in the transformability of learning capacity, through the joint efforts of learner and teacher,
in her contribution to a discussion of what it means to be 'clever'. She
summed up how her work with one of the nine teachers had changed her
perception of her own learning capacity, as follows.

> I must admit that when I first started at [the school], I wasn't doing
> very well, but since then, I look back at my books, and now I have
> realized that I can be clever if I want to and [the teacher] really
> encourages me and tells me that I have been doing well ... If you
> see yourself improving, then it makes you feel to yourself, 'Yeah, I
> am clever, I can do it.' It makes you push yourself, it gives you so
> much self-confidence.

Our efforts to understand young people's experience of learning in the nine
teachers' classrooms have clearly been limited by the fact that when we
were carrying out the activities and interviews, we did not know exactly
how we would want to use the material we collected. There is a need to
explore in more depth other dimensions of young people's concepts of
active learning and their understanding of the conditions that empower
them to take up this role. Further work in this area is urgently needed if our

model of pedagogy free from ability labelling is to encompass as full an account of the learner's role as it does of the teacher's role. The transformability of learning capacity as a joint enterprise requires an understanding of pedagogy as an interdependent relationship between teachers and young people, giving equal consideration to the role of both as co-educators, as Michael Fielding recognizes in a powerful article on student voice. He writes:

> Teachers cannot create new roles and realities without the support and encouragement of their students; students cannot construct more imaginative and fulfilling realities of learning without a reciprocal engagement with their teachers. We need each other to be and become ourselves, to be and become both learners and teachers of each other together.
>
> (Fielding 2001: 108)

16 Framing learning without limits teaching: contexts and retrospectives

Introduction

Chapters 13 to 15 have focused on the classroom practices of the nine teachers and on the students' experiences in these classrooms. In this chapter, we try to stand back a little and to see these practices from a wider perspective. We do that in two ways.

First, we were interested from the beginning in how teaching for learning without limits might be constrained or facilitated by the contexts within which teachers were working. Is it only in certain contexts that such teaching is possible? Or is it at least made easier or more difficult by identifiable contextual factors? What kinds of things are happening in English schools today that support and facilitate such teaching? And what things are making it more difficult for teachers? These are the questions with which we shall be concerned in the first part of this chapter.

Second, in accordance with the agreed division of labour within the team, it was the university members who wrote this book, so that (with the exception of Non) the voices of the teacher members of the team were represented only at second hand. It seemed desirable, therefore, that the teacher members of the team should each, if they wished, write a brief commentary on the research, their engagement in it or any aspects of the project they might choose. Most of the teachers decided that they did indeed want to do this, and their commentaries are presented in the second half of this chapter.

The significance of context

A diversity of settings

The nine teacher members of the team worked in very diverse settings. To some extent this was deliberate, in that such diversity was sought when the teachers were recruited to the project. We were pleased at that stage to find teachers attempting to engage in teaching for learning without limits in such apparently different contexts, but we still had to investigate the possibility that these contexts might have important things in common. It was also necessary to ask whether or not differences in contexts might either influence teachers' pedagogical aspirations or make it differentially possible for teachers to engage effectively in the kind of teaching to which they aspired.

The types of school in which the teachers worked included infant, primary, grammar, mixed comprehensive and girls' comprehensive; the classes involved in the research varied from Year 1 to Year 11. The communities served by the schools were equally diverse, varying from traditional rural villages to areas of major cities, from the relatively affluent to the severely disadvantaged, from those that were relatively homogeneous in socio-economic terms to those that were internally very diverse, and from communities where almost everyone was white to others with ethnically quite diverse communities, including one school in which there were students from forty nationalities and where English was the first language for only a minority of students.

School buildings were equally varied. Some did not appear to impose constraints on what the teachers wanted to do. Most, however, presented one or more serious problems, including general neglect and dilapidation, severely overcrowded classrooms, unwelcome open-plan arrangements and the staffroom having to double as the school's computer room.

The professional contexts within which teachers had to work were also very varied. As we shall discuss later, some of the teachers experienced strong support from senior managements and/or colleagues who shared their values, while others found it necessary to pursue their ideas and practices in isolation, sometimes even in quite hostile environments.

The settings, then, were genuinely very diverse. They seem to us broadly to represent a fair cross-section of English schools in the early part of the twenty-first century. In particular, there do not seem to have been any *common* factors in the contexts in which the teachers worked that led them to espouse learning without limits values or that facilitated the development of their capacity-transforming practices. On the contrary, the experience and findings of this project suggest that it has been the values, determination, reflection and insights of the individual teachers, rather than anything special about their contexts, that have led them to develop practices based around the core idea of transformability. That is not to say, however, that contextual factors are unimportant. We shall seek to explain, in the following sections, just how important they can be.

The policy environment

The nine teachers are in no doubt that the kind of teaching necessary to lift limits on learning is made a great deal more difficult by current government policies. As a sympathetic member of one senior management team said:

> I think we're very constrained in what we can do by ... the government prescribing how one sets one's targets, and one target has to be about raising achievement in a completely measurable way... it's a very limited view of achievement ... enough to turn children off being lifelong learners, rather than inspiring them to become that.

The nine teachers were equally outspoken. The major problem, the teachers seem to agree, is the enveloping prescriptiveness, which seems to leave no room for public debate about alternatives or for teachers to learn from each other's innovative practice and reflection. The value of this project, in contrast, was the opportunity it gave teachers to come together to articulate, share and compare their developing practice, outside the context of the specific demands of the system. As one of them said, 'Teachers often get trapped into a very restrictive work situation.' They wanted more opportunities to work with others to develop their own practice, and they also felt a strong need to challenge the government's damaging policies and its pervasive prescriptiveness.

In part, this overwhelming prescriptiveness is resented because of its stultifying influence on teachers and students. As one said, 'My prime concern is the nature of the educational experience. And I do feel that it is increasingly impoverished and that the space to enrich it is increasingly denied.' Teachers are encouraged to do what is prescribed without reflection, thus constraining the development of practices that enhance learning capacity. The problem, however, is not just the prescriptiveness itself, but also that so many things are prescribed that run contrary to the teachers' own professional understandings of what good teaching involves.

Most obviously, the teachers' work is made more difficult by official enthusiasm for ability labelling. The teachers find themselves having to try to undo the damage that official policies have already had on children: 'the powerful impact that the present climate of equating ability to attainment has on the child'. This labelling is most apparent in the officially endorsed practices of setting and ability grouping, differentiated target setting and tiered examinations. 'It's very hard', one teacher says, to break away from students' low self-estimation, 'what they think they can't do', because their negative self-perceptions are continually reinforced when they are in lower sets for several subjects.

Almost equally damaging is 'the narrowed focus on "standards" rather than achievement in its widest sense'. The teachers experience a severe tension between this very narrow official agenda and their own efforts to enhance their students' learning capacities by pursuing both much broader cognitive agendas and their equally important and demanding social and affective purposes. They are frustrated, for example, by the GCSE syllabus:

> My efforts to create conditions where school learning is experienced as meaningful, important and empowering by students are inevitably constrained by examination syllabus requirements ... the lack of real quality in the set selection of poems ... the sheer volume of texts to be covered ... the time limitations ... plus the workload of other subjects on the students, mean that expanding what is taught would probably be unrealistic. And yet the current diet is frustratingly 'thin'.

This sense of constraint, and a strong feeling of injustice, relate also to the narrowness of the attainments that are valued:

> The majority of students are quite able to discuss things orally and they have quite a sophisticated understanding orally ... The problem is that they have to learn to write that down in some sort of acceptable form for the exam board and that is harder ... pupils are often very gifted in certain areas (model-making, cartoons, diagrams as well as orally) even if they can't write it down. It just seems a shame that we can't judge that more.

Most of the teachers similarly find the amount of material to be covered in the National Curriculum constraining, in that it makes it more difficult for them to be responsive to their students' interests, enthusiasms and needs, and because of particular issues of principle. One teacher, for example, believes that the scope to develop his teaching according to his principles has been constantly eroded by the National Curriculum reforms, which 'have all been, it seems to me, based on reducing teacher autonomy'. He sees specific battles as needing to be fought in relation to the neglect of spoken English and the place assigned to Standard English. His deputy head comments that the 'huge prescription' of the National Curriculum 'stifles intelligent creative people like him'. Further constraints are imposed by the Numeracy and Literacy Strategies on the teachers' capacity to use time fruitfully: the primary teachers had already experienced these constraints and the secondary teachers were apprehensive about their introduction.

Perhaps the most exasperating feature of the policy environment for the teachers is the amount of paperwork generated for them by government policies. 'There is so much paperwork in this job', one commented, 'that I fear for the world's forests.' This work is unwelcome because it is mainly directed not towards teachers' greater effectiveness, but towards their fuller accountability, and is therefore not seen as a productive use of time. Moreover, much of it is concerned with more detailed planning than is sensible for teachers who aim to be responsive to their students, and much of that planning is concerned anyway with the kinds of target-setting that depend on inappropriate predictions about their students' achievements.

What is the impact of all these policy constraints on the teachers? Our evidence suggests that the teachers consistently and directly resist ability labelling practices, wherever possible, and do so quite effectively. We shall consider that more closely in relation to the differing school environments. With regard to syllabus and assessment constraints, however, and even imposed teaching strategies, their response is different. Our account of one of the teachers highlighted her 'binocularity', through which she concerned herself equally with the externally imposed structures, respecting their emphasis on coverage and outcomes, and with her own priority, the processes of learning. This willingness and ability to accept official agendas, to treat them flexibly and to integrate them into their teaching is true of all the teachers. Quite consistently, it seems, they accept official demands, but feel professionally obliged and entitled to interpret these demands in ways that they believe to be in their students' interests. Of course this can be difficult and the teachers need to work hard and to be creative in order to meet both the official criteria and their own broader criteria. Often compromise is necessary, but the far greater sophistication of their own practices in comparison to those that are officially prescribed means that the narrow official requirements can often be contained within their own broader and more educationally ambitious agendas. And they have the confidence to *use* what is officially prescribed as they think best. One teacher, for example, explains that:

> We use the QCA guidelines as a basis for our curriculum planning – one of the criticisms of them is that they are quite prescriptive and restrictive in some ways ... So you have always got to consider the children whom these guidelines don't fit. You don't want to disadvantage children because they can't write at all. So it's case of focusing on the real objectives.

For another, a central part of his task is that of re-engaging disaffected students, especially boys, and 'this isn't easy given the need to work through the set Shakespeare play'. But he does hunt for ways of squaring that circle, such as taking the class out of the classroom to the school hall, which 'immediately gave people space to do what they wanted in their groups, or by themselves, and at least took pressure off those who aren't at ease in the classroom'.

Another teacher defends the creative deviations she plans from the narrow way, in terms of the students' learning:

> The fact is that they do need something in their books because they have got to come back and revise this in a year's time … I think we can get lost in assessing and exams, but a bit of fun, even in Year 10, why not? If you want to do a bit of role play, why not, because it does actually help them to learn.

Asked about external constraints, one of the teachers responded:

> Yes, but I try not to worry about it. I try to look at what is wanted from the National Literacy Strategy and think 'Right, what can I do with that?' What I tend to do is think 'What are the areas they are supposed to be learning? What sort of skills do they need? What is the better way and the most exciting way we can get into it?' … We have always needed a structure to what we are doing, we have always needed to ensure that we are covering a breadth of learning. So what I am trying to do is use the work that other people have done as a sort of tool for me … so that I don't have to waste my time worrying about that.

From the perspective of the teachers, the policy environment is certainly a negative one. It not only fosters ability labelling, which they reject, but also makes many demands that constrain and complicate their professional work. It does not prevent them teaching as they believe they should, but it tends to make their work more difficult and more demanding. These are teachers who are clear about their professional values; they are both confident in themselves and deeply committed; they have had to learn to be highly skilled and imaginative. In the face of all the policy constraints and in the absence of practical structures to support them in the development of practices that go beyond what is prescribed, it is on their own values, commitment, skills and imagination that they have to depend.

School environments

In many respects, of course, individual teachers are not exposed directly to the demands of government policy. Instead, these demands are mediated through the schools in which they work. Headteachers, governors and senior managers can do anything between accepting the demands of government, uncritically passing these demands on for them to be met by teachers, and at the other extreme having a clear consensual vision for the school, and considering carefully how to respond to each government demand in the interests of the students and their teachers. In addition, of course, schools in England vary widely in their histories, traditions and cultures. So the school itself is probably the most important part of the context in which a teacher works.

No common patterns are apparent in the extent to which the teachers were able to count on their schools' support for their capacity-enhancing practices. Each teacher seems to have been in a different situation. We know more about those teachers who were well supported than about those who were not, since those in the latter category tended to be very professional and guarded in what they said. It was clear, however, that for this latter group of teachers there was not only little recognition of the special quality of their teaching but also little encouragement of reflection on the merits or implications of government policies. Teaching to transform learning capacity was something in which they engaged in relative isolation and against the grain of their schools' overall policies and priorities. To do that, they needed to be tough, as well as deeply committed, to cope with what were very stressful as well as demanding professional lives. One teacher, for example, was concerned that her students 'were coming to be judged by data ... management only sees the numbers'. She was not totally isolated, having the support of her departmental colleagues in implementing only a minimal version of the school's general policy of setting based on test scores. However, she was constantly frustrated by what she saw as the unreasonable target demands of the government, school governors and senior management – 'setting us up to fail' – and her lack of freedom to teach with an emphasis on student input and engagement.

Being well established in a school, and in tune with its ethos and, in secondary schools, especially in tune with with the ethos of one's own department, seemed to be important: colleagues and students not only knew what to expect, but also might share in large measure the teacher's values. Senior status too, as head of department or deputy head, meant that one's views counted for more, and in several cases led to some modification of school policies in relation to the areas for which the teacher had particular responsibility. In addition, some of the teachers had very strong support from senior figures in the school.

It was, however, clear that even for teachers who were well established, had seniority themselves or had support from senior figures, the scope to pursue their capacity-transforming practices was conditional upon demonstrating relatively impressive performance on various standard accountability measures. One head of department in a secondary school, for example, was acutely aware that, despite being described by her headteacher as 'probably the outstanding practitioner in the school', she was allowed the freedom to opt for mixed ability grouping in the department because, 'fortunately, exam results have backed up what I have been saying we should do'. The deputy head of another teacher said of him that 'He's just the sort of teacher that we want when we talk about advanced skills teachers. You're never going to get a better teacher than him', but admitted that this teacher was 'left alone because he always gets fantastic results'. The headteacher of another team member, despite expressing the view that 'I think that what she's doing is absolutely brilliant', seemed to need to reassure herself that 'There's been no parent who has come in and said what on earth is she doing? She enjoys good relationships with the children but also with the parents.'

Apart from policy issues, the teachers were of course conscious of other constraints upon their practice, relating to the resources available, to school buildings and space, to furniture and to the organization of the school day. Constraints of time, timetabling and space were the most frequently mentioned, and the desire for greater flexibility than these constraints allowed was certainly consistent with these teachers' values and practices.

The evidence of our study suggests that in the present political climate teachers who pursue capacity-enhancing strategies can find themselves in vulnerable positions. Attempting such teaching and succeeding in isolation and without support are demonstrably quite possible, but it can be a demanding and stressful thing to attempt in such circumstances. Even if the teacher's work is genuinely admired by senior management, even if he or she is a well-established member of a sympathetic school or department, and holds a position of some seniority, support for such teaching is likely to depend on regular 'hard' evidence that his or her teaching is meeting all the external accountability criteria.

Community environments

As noted previously, the community contexts of the nine teachers' schools were very diverse. Did these contexts have an impact on their practice?

All the teachers were aware that, as one put it, 'The influence of parents and other key adults on these young people's developing identities is crucial.' We have commented on the teachers' careful study and knowledge of their students and this extended, especially with the younger students, to a considerable knowledge of their homes, based primarily on frequent conversations with their parents. For teachers with older students too, there was a full recognition of the importance of the home. One secondary school teacher, for example, commented about her students, many of whose parents had immigrated quite recently to England, that 'the ethos among the students is that they want to learn. I think that comes from home partly'.

All the teachers were very concerned about educating their students for the world beyond the classroom. It was noted of one teacher's practice, for example, that 'learning must not be limited to the classroom, however meaningful and active that classroom may be', that 'the essentially rural setting was unmistakably observable [in her practices] on every visit to the school', but that 'only the world is big enough for children's learning'. Similarly, the teachers used a range of strategies to ensure both that school learning should make sense in terms of children's lives outside school and that their horizons were constantly widened.

All the teachers were very aware that limits on learning resulting from ability labelling are systematically related to disadvantages for many students stemming from their families' socio-economic position. Removing limits arising from ability labelling also meant helping students to overcome the disadvantages that a stratified society and its schooling system imposes on them. One of the teachers articulated his thinking about this as follows:

> Perhaps I haven't been able fully enough to articulate a macro account, not just working in a large comprehensive school in the London suburbs, but working within the state education system in a particular social and economic system ... it does have an impact, it seems to me, on why I choose certain kinds of curriculum content and why I might pursue certain kinds of activity or lines of questioning ... schools remain middle class in a number of areas, particularly in the nature of the curriculum offering, the nature of what's valued ... The issue surely has to do with how successful the school is in reaching out to those [parents] whose own school experiences were not positive.

And again:

> As a working notion, class has to be there in terms of how you read individual kids. The class background, the kinds of likely life experiences, the difference between the culture of this institution – at least its formally presented culture which would be middle class – and how that rubs up against what they bring ... I think, if I recognize students who I believe come from particularly hard working-class backgrounds ... I think I'm more likely to attempt in some way to value these students, kind of as clearly and explicitly as possible ... but they will be categorized, they will be pigeon-holed, they will be written off, and understanding of class can prevent me from doing that.

The teacher expresses here the struggle in which he and the others were engaged both to understand the educational disadvantages at which their working-class students were put by the educational system and by the wider socio-economic system, and to use that understanding to help their students to overcome these disadvantages. They sought to protect their students by making at least their classrooms safe places within which they could learn meaningfully and constructively, and they sought to collaborate with their students to empower them for learning in their future lives. Beyond their classrooms, they sought to influence the ways in which the school, through its curriculum, organization and methods of teaching and assessment, communicated acceptance and value to those students. Yet they were also conscious that at best they and their students were working together against enormously powerful social forces.

Conclusion

Ultimately, individual classroom teachers can only do what they can do within the boundaries of their responsibilities for their classes. However aware they are of the influence that socio-economic structures, national education policies, their own schools' policies and practices and their students' parents and communities exert on the young people's development, they do not as individuals have the power to change the structures within which they work or to break out of them. What they have the power to do is to create, within the boundaries of their own classrooms, learning communities that, under their leadership, can transform the capacity for learning of all their members. It is clear that the nine teachers have worked very effectively to do just that.

They were not, however, content with just that. Joining together in this project reflected, for all of them, a commitment to the pursuit of their values and ideals on a wider front, seeking to change the balance of forces supporting and constraining the work of teachers like themselves. As one of them suggested:

> So much work stands to be disregarded if again it depends only upon individual teachers – that is where it comes from, but it needs to move to a bigger platform to create a climate whereby teachers can be freed to make choices ... the project has taken something that was confined to individual teachers ... and made it accessible to a wider audience ... providing choices in teacher behaviour and rationale.

The teachers' intention for the project – an intention that we hope and believe has been realized – has been that it should give other teachers both conceptual and moral support of a kind that they as isolated individual teachers often found themselves lacking.

Teacher afterwords

Six of the eight teachers whose ideas and practices have been represented up to this point only by the university-based members of the team accepted the invitation to add some final words of their own. Their six afterwords are presented here, in alphabetical order.

Alison's afterword

I learnt a tremendous amount about my approaches to teaching and learning through the process of being part of the *Learning without Limits* team. During an interview I described my work as being similar to going 'on a kind of journey' together. I believe this to be a very important aspect of my work. The metaphor of a journey implies movement forward but not necessarily to a predetermined destination. One of the challenges, I suspect, of working in a partnership with children is that the teacher has to be prepared to explore ideas and new ways of working as part of the process. Preconceived ideas and outcomes need to be tempered with the art of possibility and surprise. This is what makes my work with children so rewarding.

During the period of research my role within my school has changed. I became deputy head and am now preparing for headship. In preparation for my contribution to this book, I revisited the descriptions of the key constructs that underpin my work in the classroom. It became immediately apparent to me that these key beliefs are the ones that I see as crucially important in leading a school. In my work as deputy, I aim to provide opportunities and establish relationships with staff members that are very similar to the way in which I have tried to build a learning team with any group of children I have taught. My vision is to build a staff team that can provide a *Learning without Limits* school: a listening school where a learning culture is developed for teachers in order that they can have the confidence they need to avoid prejudging outcomes and develop independence among the children.

When preparing a scheme of work or planning lessons, I aim to provide as many open-ended tasks as possible. I monitor the children's progress carefully and assess their learning through a range of qualitative and quantitative methods, including SATs tests. However, I also aim to provide a learning environment where children have the capacity to surprise me. Children in my classes are not grouped by ability but work together in learning teams where the aim is that everyone recognizes the importance of building on individual strengths. I provide a range of tasks and the children rapidly become skilled at selecting the activity that will help them towards the next step in their learning. It has been my experience that, far from taking the easy option, children prefer to extend their knowledge and accept a challenge. We work hard together to achieve a supportive approach where success is celebrated in relation to effort, rather than ease of accomplishment.

It is wonderful when a child takes a huge leap forward in his understanding and is able to demonstrate this through undertaking a task in a way that gives him the freedom to explore his capacity to learn. Bill was in my class last year. He was a small, quiet boy who had needed a lot of support in class, particularly with maths. He disliked reading and writing, but loved art. He liked making models and always enjoyed responding to tasks in a practical way. On one particular afternoon, I set the class a maths investigation, which was to engage in a problem-solving activity based on the amount of popcorn that could be contained in different sized bags. The majority of children in the class set about this task using pencil and paper and calculators, and in some cases drew diagrams. Bill, however, began straight away to make a popcorn bag from the dimensions that had been given. He then filled the bag with unifix blocks. Having noted this result, he went on to make the larger bag, once again filling it with blocks and using these as standard units; he was thus able to understand how the volume of the bag increased once the dimensions were increased. Bill went on to solve the investigation before anyone else in the class.

I encourage the children to reflect on their learning and to take a collaborative approach with me in the classroom so that we work in partnership. Children meet in mixed-aged circle groups throughout the school each week and are beginning to recognize the interactive role that they can take as learners. Recently my Year 6 class planned and taught lessons on shape to children in Key Stage 1. This was a particularly exciting development because the older children were subsequently able to empathize with the role of teacher and reflect on the importance of helping everybody to achieve success. Laura commented, 'It wasn't as easy as I thought. I told everyone what to do and thought they were listening ... but then they were confused and I had to start again.'

My school has recently been undertaking research into 'pupil voice' and, as part of this work, the children identified the most crucial aspects of a 'good' teacher. Children suggested qualities such as 'kindness', 'fairness' and 'sense of humour', and these ideas were displayed around the school in order that votes could be given to the most important. The results of this work were fascinating. The most important quality that children decided they wanted from their teacher was *trust*. They needed to feel they could trust their teacher, but, most importantly, they wanted their teachers to trust them.

Establishing a climate of trust in the classroom implies allowing children the freedom to respond in the way that makes the most sense to them. In many ways this aspect of my work with children has often provided the most joy. It is wonderful to see youngsters take on challenges, tackle problems creatively and achieve success, knowing that you have provided the opportunities and framework but have allowed for the unexpected. The potential for memorable, meaningful learning is much greater when all parties have been engaged in the process. Every teacher knows of the satisfaction achieved when children show enthusiasm for learning and want to take the lesson further. This is the satisfaction of 'learning without limits': a way of working together that takes us on a journey together, leaving no one behind, and with hope and ambition for what the next steps will hold.

Anne's afterword

The period of time during which I have been involved with the project has also been a period of dramatic change in school and in education generally. I don't think I have changed how I work, but I am determined not only to teach the children specific skills but more importantly to teach them how to learn. My involvement in their lives will be very small, but there are endless opportunities for learning things during the whole of their lives. I want the children I teach to know how to take advantage of those opportunities.

I started work at my present infant school 15 years ago. The school had a magical feel, which immediately attracted me. The children were all in mixed-age classes and stayed with the same teacher for all the three years they were at the school. There was not a hint of a syllabus or a target but there was a great emphasis on exploration and learning to learn.

Things have changed in the school over the years. For several years we were able to make the changes fit our style, not our style fit the changes, but now I sometimes feel that I am trying single-handed to keep alive the flame of education. Too much of what happens today is instruction and rote learning; there is little opportunity for children to take the lead.

I don't use the word pupil because that seems to be a very tightly defined position: pupils receive instruction from a teacher. I try to involve the children in their own education as much as possible. Unless the children interact with me and the activity, all the instruction in the world will teach them nothing. I can relate to the Dewey quote in Chapter 4; he reflects my feelings about children and their learning. I am concerned with what the children do with their education in the future.

Education does not just 'happen' and activities need to be planned so that skills are taught in a realistic order. There is no point in asking children to spell 'cat' if they are not aware of letter sounds. However, I feel planning has reached new and dizzy heights. In some classes, if children bring a shell or a postcard from their holiday to school they are not allowed to show the items to the class 'because it is not in that day's plans' and then the items are just sent home again. There is not a spare moment, it seems, to look at something a child has brought in with the class and to look for the holiday venue on the map.

As a teenager I was an avid reader of books about Roman Britain by Rosemary Sutcliff. The characters in her books were struggling to guard their country from the invading Saxons. Eventually the Saxons win but the defeated troops know they have held out long enough for some remnants of civilization to remain and to be carried on by others. I feel just like that: I can't alter the whole of the education system, but I hope some of the children I teach will have been sufficiently motivated and that they will carry on the flame of education.

Claire's afterword

The day I submitted my application to join the *Learning without Limits* project marked the starting point of a developmental journey. This journey has been marked by constant challenges to scrutinize my own practice and to consider how it reflects my teaching and learning philosophy. Aspects of my practice that I considered to be good and effective have been, and will continue to be, reconsidered, redeveloped and remodelled as I have reflected, read, debated and listened both to myself and to colleagues within the project. The remodelling has not happened overnight, but has emerged almost by stealth and will develop further as I continue on the Learning without Limits journey throughout my time in education.

Since the project began I have moved from a medium-sized village primary school to becoming a headteacher with significant teaching responsibility in a very small, two-class school, and then to my current role as a lecturer in higher education, specializing in teacher training – three significantly contrasting settings, all with their own challenges and agendas yet all in the business of teaching and learning, are all capable of embracing the principles that underpin learning without limits.

My own thinking about the significance of preferred learning styles has continued to develop, alongside a growing awareness (and, perhaps, suspicion) of the development of preferred teaching styles in our primary classrooms. I am sure that a review of classroom practice could show that many schools encourage preferred teaching styles among staff, in line with national strategies. Thankfully, however, an increasing number of schools are becoming more confident in developing a more autonomous approach to the use of national strategies and frameworks, recognizing that preferred teaching styles do not always match preferred learning styles. It is a reconsideration of the needs of individual learners that is exciting to see, both in schools and across all learning 'institutions', and this is essential for learning without limits to take place.

In addition, I fully expect that a redefinition of the roles of teachers and learners may soon become necessary in order for effective teaching and learning to continue to develop. This would involve an element of role reversal for teachers and learners. In my view, there is a continued need for the teacher to become a learner in the classroom. As a learner, he or she would know, understand and respond to pupils' attitudes, aptitudes, learning needs and learning styles. Consequently, the learner would take on a teaching role in the classroom – communicating 'how and why I learn', not just 'what I learn' in order to enable teachers to be learners.

To facilitate this move towards role reversal, or at least towards true teaching–learning partnerships, further developmental work could be done on creating a 'thinking classroom'. The teacher would constantly look for ways of evaluating the effectiveness of his or her own practice and would encourage reflection and evaluation from pupils. Evaluation would be done truly collaboratively: a 'We're all in this together' approach. Therefore, teachers and learners would ask, together, questions such as 'What are we learning? How are we learning? Why are we learning?' And the essential question when looking for links and connections in our learning is: 'How could this help us to learn other things?' The establishment of organizational strategies and frameworks in order to achieve this high level of collaborative reflection and evaluation, and to give value to the process within a busy school day, would be a useful practical step forward.

In my view, learning without limits is not concerned with winning formulas, perfect solutions or cut and dried answers. Instead, the project acknowledges that educational establishments are full of individuals and *that is a good thing*. The journey we embark on as teachers and learners must not be limited by false assumptions and perceptions about capability and achievement, but should be a celebration of the unlimited contributions all can make to the learning partnership.

Julie's afterword

Since the culmination of the *Learning without Limits* project, my own ideas and principles as to what equates to good classroom practice and egalitarianism in the classroom have been reinforced by a number of factors.

I have recently been awarded Advanced Skills Teacher (AST) status, which has not only helped to confirm in my own mind that my own beliefs are justified, but also given me a great deal of faith in the much maligned inspection service.

Like all committed colleagues, since I began teaching in 1982 I have constantly analysed what I do, looked for ways to improve the learning taking place and questioned my own strategies regarding individual students. Although on good days I had unquestioned faith in my own beliefs regarding education, there have been times when the constant opposition from some colleagues regarding the issue of setting has been very wearing. There are very few colleagues, other than staff in my own department, who share my repugnance for setting and imposing rigid limits on learning potential. The common argument, that a fixed setting structure from the age of 12 is better, is based on the belief that the 'more able' will be suitably challenged, while the 'less able' will be given easy work that they feel comfortable with. This approach, in my view, can only succeed in creating some individuals who feel worthless and embarrassed about their academic achievements. However, there have been times when, because of the huge numbers of colleagues who adhere to the benefits of these academic divisions, I have reconsidered the appropriateness of my own approach.

The *Learning without Limits* project therefore came at a crucial time in my career. It allowed for careful analysis of my own teaching philosophies and practices in a much more structured way. It also provided invaluable feedback from students who were articulating to a member of the university team just the sorts of feelings and fears that I had always assumed students to have. This gave full justification to my enduring belief that the current system of rigid setting in our education system can do immense harm to developing individuals already suffering from a shortage of confidence.

Apart from confirming some of my existing beliefs and giving me greater confidence in my own principles, one particular task taught me that to assume that all students feel comfortable within lessons is misguided. The activity was designed to get anonymous responses from students regarding the level of enthusiasm, happiness and comfort they felt when participating in one of my history lessons. While the majority of responses were favourable, there were a small number of students who occasionally felt uninterested or even unhappy in the lessons.

This was a complete revelation to me and my initial reaction was one of incredulous indignation: how could students possibly feel like that in my lesson? However, after this initial reaction, I began to understand that for some students the whole experience of school was uncomfortable; given a choice, they would rather not be there. This made me more aware that as a teacher one should never become complacent. It is necessary to try to empathize with all students and strive to find new strategies to help them to cope with the emotional nightmare of being compelled to come to school and participate in lessons.

Confirmation of my beliefs and principles concerning education also came from what I would have considered to be an unlikely source. Like many of my fellow colleagues I have often viewed the Ofsted system with mistrust. It was therefore like a breath of fresh air to have an AST inspector endorsing my teaching philosophies, strategies and lessons as good practice. The fact that this person took great interest in the Learning without

Limits project was also heartening, as one must assume that he agrees with the basic premise of the project and my attempts to bring these principles into practice within my classroom. I hope that his views are representative of many within the inspectorate. The AST status that I have been awarded will, I hope, allow for greater dissemination of some of the project's guiding principles among colleagues. This gives me great hope that in some way I can help in the development of a system of education that is truly an environment where there are no limits placed on the development of individual children.

Nicky's afterword

Since this research was carried out, I have had more managerial experience and now feel far more sympathetic to the managers I accused of just 'seeing the data'. Given the pressures that they are under (from the DfES etc.) to justify the school's position and even its existence, it is now inevitable that they will draw on data and use them to prove and document 'progress'. Data in isolation are really the problem; used in the wider context, they can provide good, initial, baseline information for teachers.

The student identified in the account as 'Yahni' continued to flourish in this mixed-ability environment. He was not given any explicit teaching in English and absorbed his language skills from those around him, learning from the positive role models within the class. He is now taking on whole-school responsibilities and winning prizes for achievement.

Having moved to a school with a completely different intake and profile (still comprehensive but more middle class and in a suburban area of London), I still notice frequent (negative) comments from some staff about 'the bottom set' and how unteachable they are. A couple of departments still operate a setting system and, too often, it seems, the students with behavioural difficulties are immediately labelled less able and put in the lower sets, creating demoralized and difficult to manage classes. I still feel that many teachers regard bi- or multilingualism as a limit to learning. On two occasions, teachers have asked 'where is she from *originally*?' about a new student, a Muslim child, recently arrived from another London borough, whose parents were born in England. Having said this, I do feel that colleagues are keen to hear about the concepts behind learning without limits and I now work with a team of English teachers who are very keen to avoid any limits or ceilings to achievement.

Patrick's afterword

I left my post in a London comprehensive and have since taught at two different Norfolk schools. Both, called high schools after the local custom, are non-selective, with my current school taking especial pride in the inclusiveness of its intake. The overwhelming majority of students in both schools are white. The nature of these student populations and the backgrounds from which they come provided a huge contrast to the situation in which I had been teaching for the previous decade. Moreover, the English departments in both Norfolk schools set students in all years, as the department I left in the capital would shortly find itself forced to do. Whatever else might happen in my classroom, I at least would have much to learn and quickly. The Norfolk students, I trusted, would teach me and I would find myself altering and at times abandoning approaches and methods I had developed during my teaching in London in an attempt better to meet what I perceived to be the needs of my new classes. I would also find proven once more some of the core beliefs that I think inform the work of the project.

Yet there is no utterly fresh beginning: we make our own history but not in conditions of our own choosing. Students arrive at a classroom, they and their teacher meet and a lesson commences recognizably like yet distinct from the lesson next door. I began to learn what it means to teach a group who had been 'set according to ability', and who knew their place in the rankings. I began to learn again what the students brought with them and to confront how much of that I could incorporate, work with, build on. In certain sets of students, I encountered large numbers of young people the school had organized together who believed they did not work well in school; nor did they often seem to want to. Talk for them all too often seemed to mean the opposite of work, and the chance to sit in self-chosen groups rather than alphabetically in rows signalled for many not so much an opportunity to develop ideas together as an abandonment of any constraint upon them to focus on the given tasks. Many of these students seemed to me to have no expectation that there might be small-group talk that sprang from and explored in a sustained way the issue or task to hand.

Attempting to make sense of why this should be the case, and looking to work to better the situation and establish the kind of classroom within which talk of many different kinds, and careful listening, were the norm seems to me to have been among the most challenging tasks I have faced as a teacher. It has raised in stark terms some key issues. The obstacles put in the way of students by the labels the school (and previous schools) have given them (based primarily on SATs and CATs scores) have been made clearer by work in setted environments. Within mixed-ability classes unexamined notions of 'ability' remain current, but the overt ability labelling that is the system of setting constitutes in my view an even greater barrier to learning without limits. It denies students the benefit of each other as models of alternative and perhaps more fruitful ways of being in school. It confirms for those students likely to have been already unsuccessful inside school their sense of themselves as 'not good at … ', and, more insidiously, it can bolster their sense of *themselves* as not any good. Hence there are anger, frustration, rejection, confirmation of failure, antagonism towards the teacher, self-fulfilling limits. Worst of all, justification for the system of setting rests on a belief in fixed innate ability, however much its advocates sometimes attempt to cloak it as benign, commonly claiming that students in the lower sets are able to get more help, or have work better tailored to their needs. Silence attends the view that setting replicates and helps to reproduce social and class stratification, that it deliberately enables the more middle class children to be kept from those more working class.

Students in all the sets I taught belied every now and then, or as a matter of course, the labels accorded them. If staffroom comments are anything to go by, the same was true in other colleagues' experience. *'That's not what I'd have expected of a top set … A real star, but only a level 3 for English … '* But setting makes this harder, partly by constructing students as passive and voiceless in the setting process. Many students I have discussed this with resent being separated from friends in other sets, for example, and can articulate how being with friends improves their work. But they have no powerful say; they are set by other people, and their own activity in class works against them in true alienating fashion to ensure they are channelled into lower sets, placement in which is perceived by many as a slight or an abandonment.

Yet every class, setted or otherwise, might be able, could be enabled. The issues confronting teachers looking to follow a 'transformability' model are not solved bureaucratically, by merely producing an alternative way of grouping students. They require a radically different way of seeing those students and of talking about them. Yet the discourse of fixed ability remains a *lingua franca* in staffrooms, a two-faced, fork-tongued language that may introduce itself as provisional, soft-edged, not to be taken too seriously (*'bright, a bit slow, good at English'*) or as self-consciously and even apologetically inadequate (*'you know what I mean … you know the kind of kid'*), but that hardens in a moment's summative judgement to define and fix a student as *'gifted, underachieving, average'*. Trying not to speak this language (whose dialects are CATs and SATs scores, predicted grades, target grades, test results, National Curriculum levels, even unguarded gender generalizations) can make communication difficult with colleagues.

In my current school a debate of sorts is under way to do with teaching and learning. There is a genuine desire for the learning experience to be as good as possible, to be interesting, inspiring, effective in terms beyond the narrowly instrumental. The ideas and approaches encouraged by 'transformability' have met with some positive responses by some staff, while others have called such perspectives 'very naive'. Each teaching day I ask the question: does this work? Am I doing what's best for this child, this group? I find I can let classes take more charge in some circumstances and shape more of what happens, as the space opened up by being able to talk in groups or as a whole class exercises its influence. I am conscious of more frequently asking ahead of a possible intervention: 'Just what is the student or the group doing? Is learning happening there, then? Do I need to be there or not, and if I do, how do I need to be there?' This may just be a sign of settling in, of reading the road, having learned again the basics of how to drive. I try to gauge the extent to which I have made any beneficial difference, particularly to my set 4 classes, by working as I do, for I am very conscious that I have no pedigree out here. The exams of course will give one riposte, but teaching is deep roots and a slow bloom.

I recall some good moments. A 'bottom set' Year 9 class making and playing their individual *Macbeth* board games: coming into my room, getting out their trays of materials and putting together the character pieces to play their game, its board tracking their chosen events from the text, and the Fate cards (both felicitous and doom-filled) that would help to decide the outcome. For several lessons, they were entirely self-directed and very fully engrossed. I remember the focus and attention to detail my set 4 Year 11 group gave to analysing the credit sequence of their favourite show *Friends* for half an hour, their ready perceptions and ability to link specific insights into the use of shot, colour, sound and lyrics to a growing sense of what the credits might be made to mean. And a contrast was apparent when we did a similar task on the opening of *The Sopranos*, a programme only one of them watched. *Friends* was in their lives and was important to them. But the comparison task was to be done for GCSE English, which for many diverse and no doubt very complex reasons meant much less to them, for all that I might strive to alter that view.

I was invited back to London to the 'graduation' event for the cohort of students we focused on when they were in Year 9. I was moved to be asked (and particularly to receive a letter along with my invitation from one of the group) and very happy indeed to see them all dressed in their finery and celebrated in the presence of their parents, carers and friends. I spoke briefly to some of them, they asked about the project, I told them of the book and at parting we wished each other well. May the schools their children go to help them to learn without limits.

17 Towards an alternative improvement agenda

In Part 1 of the book, we elaborated in detail our critique of the concept of fixed ability and its effects on young people's learning. From this critique, we drew the conclusion that it is not possible for educators to fulfil their professional commitment to treating all young people fairly, and to giving them all the best possible start in life, as long as school organization, curriculum and pedagogy continue to be permeated by ability labelling. It is a matter of profound concern, we argued, that the idea of fixed ability is being given renewed strength and legitimacy within the current standards agenda, and as part of officially sponsored definitions of good practice. We made a case for replacing the agenda for school improvement as currently conceived with an alternative improvement agenda focused on freeing learning from the limits imposed by ability labelling and ability-led practices. We recognized, however, that in order for this alternative agenda to be put forward as a serious and practicable possibility, we needed to be able to articulate clearly and convincingly how the values and understandings that lead to a rejection of ability labelling translate into a coherent, principled and practicable pedagogy.

The task, as we saw it, was not to invent a new pedagogy. It was to articulate, in a public and generalized way, approaches to teaching free from ability labelling, drawing on the classroom practices already being developed by teachers committed to fostering this different kind of learning, learning without limits. However, while we were convinced that we would find teachers who shared the aims and values of the project, we were not sure how far it was actually possible, given the constraints of teaching large classes and the pressures and requirements of the current context, for such teachers to develop and sustain classroom practices congruent with their values and understandings.

In Part 2 of the book we have described the practices of nine such teachers. In collaboration with them, we have identified the core ideas, purposes and principles that guide their work, and we have shown how these different elements of their pedagogy relate coherently to one another, and reflect the teachers' commitment to learning without limits. In the preceding chapters of Part 3, we have looked across the nine individual accounts to construct a generalized account of how the values and understandings that lead to a rejection of ability labelling translate into a radically different pedagogy. We have examined the core ideas and principles of this alternative model of teaching and learning from young people's perspectives, and have also considered how the potential for working in this way is affected by the contexts in which teachers work.

In this final chapter, we take stock of what we have learnt overall from the nine teachers about teaching free from ability labelling, and consider how our new understanding can contribute to the construction of an alternative improvement agenda. In the first part of the chapter, we consider how the core idea of transformable learning capacity, which lies at the heart of our alternative model of pedagogy, can be understood as an 'alternative template', capable of challenging and displacing the template of fixed ability at the level of thinking and practice. We then move on to consider some connections and points of comparison between the model we have developed and the ideas and theories of other educators and researchers who share similar values and ideals or who have been working in related areas. Finally, we explore the implications of this alternative model of pedagogy for teachers, managers, government and researchers.

An alternative template

In Chapter 2, we argued that the idea of fixed, inherent ability can be thought of as a particular template that we place on our experience to make sense of the vast differences in the attainments and responses to tasks and activities seen in young people of the same age. Our expectation was that, by studying the practice of teachers who have rejected ability labelling, we would be able to identify other, more just and empowering ways of making sense of such differences. From these, we hoped to be able to construct one or more alternative templates and describe how these provide the basis for alternative models of teaching.

However, we gradually came to understand that the task of replacing one template with another involves a more profound shift in thinking than we had anticipated. Setting aside the ability template does not just mean setting aside a particular explanation for differences and replacing it with a more adequate and empowering one. It means adopting a radically different mind-set, a different way of making sense of what happens in classrooms, based on a radically different orientation towards the future. When teachers meet a class of young people, they can engage with present patterns of attainment and render them meaningful so as to act upon them in one of these two contrasting ways. Taking differences in ability as the natural order of things, they can compare young people's attainments, infer differences of future potential and differentiate their teaching accordingly. Or they can treat present patterns of achievement and response in a spirit of transformability: seeking to discover what it is possible to do to enhance young people's capacity to learn, and intervening to create conditions in which their learning can more fully and effectively flourish.

We believe that, if presented with these alternatives in such a stark way, most educators would identify themselves with the second of them. All teachers approach their task in a spirit of intervention, wanting to make a difference to their students' lives. Some of the greatest satisfactions for teachers come from evidence that their work has indeed been effective in this way. Yet, as we argued in Chapter 2, the ability template actively impedes these efforts, suggesting that there is only very limited room for manoeuvre, since the principal determinant of learning is something outside teachers' control. We can now see more clearly how the transformability mind-set frees teachers from that uncomfortable paradox, restoring their full power as educators, their power to use their knowledge, expertise and creativity to make a significant difference, and not just a small difference, to young people's future lives.

As we have seen, the teachers we studied base their choices on a firm conviction that things can change and be changed for the better, sometimes dramatically, as a result of what happens in the present. They construe classroom diversity primarily in terms of the forces impinging on learning capacity, and the potential for taking action to enhance and transform learning capacity now and in the future (see Figure 17.1). Their priority is always to work out what they themselves can do to enable young people to become more and more powerful and committed learners. Whatever young people's present attainments and characteristics in performing classroom tasks, the teachers maintain an unshakeable belief in everybody's capacity to learn, and are convinced that, given the right conditions, everybody's capacity for learning can be increased and enhanced.

Approaching their task with this mind-set, on a day-to-day basis, the teachers use their classroom experience to evaluate the extent to which the core purposes of teaching (as described in Chapter 13) are being achieved for each and every child. They notice where there are clear gaps between their aspirations and what is actually happening; they analyse the connections between internal resources and states of mind and external classroom conditions; and they work out how they can intervene in order to shift the balance of forces so that they can come closer to achieving the core purposes for each individual, and for the group as a whole. As they do so, they draw selectively on all their knowledge of the group, and the individuals within it, including their awareness of differences of many kinds, in order to expose limits on learning capacity and identify opportunities for enhancing learning capacity. The limits and opportunities identified as a result of this analysis may be different for particular individuals, or for groups of individuals, but, as we have seen in the accounts, they may equally be applicable to all learners. Interventions can be made with a view to enhancing the learning capacity of everybody.

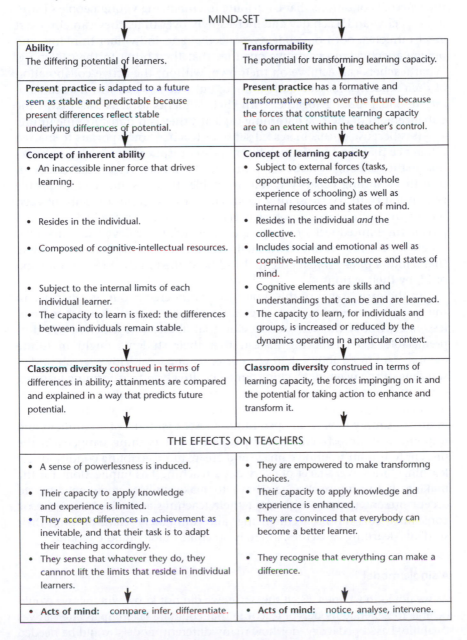

Figure 17.1 The mind-sets of ability and transformability

The concept of learning capacity, as we have described it in Chapter 13, is a genuinely educational idea, because the forces that shape it are in large measure within teachers' control. Teachers can most immediately control the external conditions that contribute to enhancing young people's learning capacity; and, each day and increasingly over time, they can also exert great influence both on students' collective and individual thinking, and on the affective and cognitive qualities that they bring to their learning. What teachers can achieve on their own, without the active collaboration of their students, may be quite limited; but teachers can win that collaboration, and, working together with their students as active agents in the enhancement of their own learning capacity, they can transform the future.

It is because of this increased sense of teachers' own powers to make a difference that the transformability mind-set inspires as well as gives direction to the teaching of those committed to this model. When teachers recognize that learning capacity is transformable, they assume an inescapable responsibility to try constantly to enhance the learning capacity of each one of their students, and of each class as a group. Instead of having to pursue the limited task of enabling all students to achieve their predicted potential, teachers embrace the challenge and the excitement of knowing that a future of unlimited potential will be shaped in the present, for good or ill, by their actions.

In the early stages of this project, we wondered about its relevance to the many teachers who, it was suggested, viewed their students as more or less able without themselves believing that ability was inherent, fixed or predictable, even believing instead that their students might in future demonstrate more ability than was currently apparent. However, an understanding of the need for teaching aimed positively at transforming learning capacity shows that there is no room for compromise: the present carries too many implications for the future for teachers to be able to enjoy the luxury of simply having an open mind. Present patterns of attainment and response will almost certainly be perpetuated if nothing happens in the present to lift limits, undo damage and create more enabling conditions for learning. Since every facet of every day's teaching has implications for the making of the future, teachers have to make choices about whether to accept present patterns and adapt their teaching accordingly, or to look constantly for ways of enhancing and ultimately transforming their students' learning capacities. There is no comfortable middle ground.

A single model

As we noted in Chapter 13, at the outset we did not know whether we would be able to generate models of teaching that could be taken up as alternatives to ability-based pedagogy, nor how many different models would be needed to reflect the thinking and practice of the nine teachers. We did not choose to have a single model: the evidence seemed to impose that outcome. Minimally, what we have found is that it is possible for classroom teachers to pursue teaching of this kind, and to do so in a wide variety of settings. It may also be, we more tentatively suggest, that this kind of teaching is necessary if teachers are to avoid and counter ability labelling in their teaching.

That this may be so seems to us the more likely because of the coherence and logic of the model that is implicit in all the teachers' practice. In articulating this model, we are not merely claiming that the thinking and the practice of the nine teachers were similar in several different ways. We are also claiming that there is a clear and powerful logic that connects the several different elements of the model. In Chapter 13, we identified four of its five interconnected elements: the core idea of transformability, the particular concept of learning capacity, the practical purposes of teaching and the principles of co-agency, trust and community. The fifth concerns the many teaching strategies and skills that teachers use in the transformation of learning capacity. Some members of the team, both from the university and from the schools, had hoped that we might generate a full prescription of such strategies and skills, a precise specification of how to do teaching for transforming learning capacity, offering an alternative to Hay McBer's prescriptions (DfEE 2000). However, the majority were against this in principle, and in practice our research findings made it clear that any such prescription would be quite inappropriate.

We do not want to suggest that each teacher's situation is unique to the extent that teachers cannot learn from one another. We do very firmly conclude, however, that there can be no standardized procedures for transforming learning capacity. Since teaching with this aim is always concerned with what is happening in the minds of individual students, and since it is concerned with the mind of every student, such teaching has to be highly sensitive to the particular needs and strengths of the students in each class on each occasion. Teachers' knowledge, and their expertise in applying their knowledge, enable them to act effectively as educators and to recruit their students to join with them as co-agents in making schooling an effective, inclusive, educational enterprise. We have had the privilege of studying at close quarters nine examples of this being done.

Connections with other theoretical ideas

We explained in Part 1 of the book why we chose to study the practice and practical thinking of experienced teachers rather than turn to the abundance of theoretical writing about school, teaching and learning from which we could have chosen or constructed our own preferred model of how learning without limits might be pursued. Having taken this path, and developed our model, when we now return to the published work of other educators and researchers we are able to read them with a new understanding of their significance for our work. In some cases, we find in their ideas early formulations of aspects of the model at which we have gradually arrived. We also notice connections with the work of contemporaries whose values, ideals and developing practices have much in common with our pedagogical model. In a sense, this project is a member of a much larger community of ideas spanning a century or more, and it is fitting, in this final chapter of the book, to trace some of these echoes and connections.

Benjamin Bloom and mastery learning

A proper place for us to start is with the thinking of Benjamin Bloom (1976), which is distinctive in its direct confrontation of the ability labelling problem, both in showing how ability-based thinking is theoretically misguided and in trying to provide a clear, radical but practical solution to it. In many respects, we see ourselves as having tried again to do what Bloom made an excellent attempt at doing, thirty years ahead of us. As we shall explain, our understanding of the problem is very similar to his, but our solution is very different.

As we noted in Chapter 2, Bloom argued that all differences between students' attainments could be satisfactorily accounted for in terms of alterable factors. The three main alterable factors that Bloom identified were very similar to elements of our model. The first key factor for Bloom (corresponding to the cognitive criteria used by teachers in our model for judging their day-by-day success, and especially the criterion that the curriculum should be successfully accessed by all students) was that all students should have mastered in advance whatever prerequisite skills and understandings are needed for the learning task they are asked to undertake ('cognitive entry behaviours'). Bloom's second factor (corresponding to the affective criteria used by teachers in our model) was that all students should be sufficiently motivated to make the necessary effort to complete the learning task successfully ('affective entry behaviours'). The third factor for Bloom (corresponding to the emphasis in our model on the whole classroom environment being capacity-enhancing for all students) was the quality of instruction and, in particular, teachers' day-by-day attention to the success of each individual student's learning. Thus Bloom's analysis has much in common with our own.

While Bloom's analysis of the problem seems to us valid and helpful, his solution, mastery learning, seems to us – especially now in the light of our own research findings – deeply flawed. Its flaws stem in part from a concern for tight control over classroom teaching and learning to avoid 'errors', and a consequent narrowness and rigidity. This dependence on tight control is reflected both in the substantial evidence for the effectiveness, under experimental conditions, of 'mastery learning procedures done systematically and well' (Bloom 1984: 7) and also in criticisms that these impressive claims are based primarily 'on brief, small, artificial studies' (Slavin 1996: 210).

There are striking differences between our model of teaching to transform learning capacity and Bloom's mastery learning model. The most fundamental differences are as follows:

1   Mastery learning requires that each learning task should be unambiguously aimed at the 'mastery' of a clearly specified skill or concept by all students. Our model in contrast allows for much more diversity in learning. This in turn allows teachers to be much more responsive to students' own concerns and allows learning and teaching to be both more rewarding and more practicable.

2   In mastery learning, it is of key importance that the prerequisite knowledge for engaging in the necessary learning should first have been developed by all the students. It depends heavily, therefore, on the curriculum being structured so that each learning task builds on what has been learned previously, and so, after the earliest stages, depends exclusively on school-based learning. In contrast, our model emphasizes the diversity of prior knowledge on which students can usefully build and the diversity of sources from which that knowledge may have been learned; it thus allows value to be placed on students' personal knowledge and on the home cultures of all students.

3   Mastery learning quite rightly places central importance on ensuring success for all students, however long it takes, as a basis not only for the next learning task but also for students' self-belief and motivation. However, it tends to rely exclusively on this success to provide the 'affective prerequisites' for learning. Our model recognizes the importance not only of success but also of students' much wider range of affective needs (e.g. for respect, acceptance, emotional safety, interest and curiosity) and therefore of affective purposes in teaching.

4   Mastery learning is focused on the learning and achievements of all individuals and in general shows little concern for classroom social processes. In contrast, the concept of 'everybody' in our model includes not only the success of everybody but also the importance of learning from each other, of social solidarity, of collaboration among students, of social justice and of

mutual respect in the classroom as both necessary conditions for learning and valuable teaching purposes.

5   Whereas mastery learning is a model of 'instruction', which is entirely about the ways in which teachers can ensure effective learning by students, at the core of our model is the practical principle of co-agency, acknowledging that teachers can be effective only if they can first recruit their students as active co-educators.

6   Whereas the mastery learning model offers instructional procedures, with its effectiveness depending on these specific 'mastery learning procedures (being) done systematically and well' (Bloom 1984: 7), our model recognizes the need for each teacher to develop and use procedures appropriate to their contexts, to their students and to specific situations; it offers pedagogical purposes and principles to guide teachers' choice of 'procedures'.

Valuable as Bloom's analysis is, we can be confident not only that our model incorporates a number of key theoretical concerns neglected in the mastery learning model but also that it makes sense in relation to the realities of classroom teaching in English primary and secondary schools, since that is where it came from. There is good reason to believe that this is an important advantage.

Lev Vygotsky, Jerome Bruner and the cultural nature of learning

As the concept of learning capacity implicit in the nine teachers' work began to take shape, as outlined in Chapter 13, we began to see links between some of the distinguishing characteristics we identified and Lev Vygotsky's theories of learning and the development of mental functioning (Vygotsky 1962, 1978; Daniels 2001). Vygotsky's view is that external influences play an important constitutive role in the development of internal mental functioning, and that the development of cognitive functions is mediated by the psychic tools (language, dialogue with others, other means of symbolic expression) to which young people gain access through participation in social activity in the external world. As the higher cognitive functions develop, what Vygotsky refers to as the 'biological line of development' is transformed into a 'cultural line of development'. The central task of education is to promote this development and transformation of young people's mental functioning.

In the concept of learning capacity at the heart of our model, external forces (range of opportunities, tasks, interactions), in interaction with internal forces (states of mind, prior knowledge, experience, skills), are considered to be constitutive of young people's capacity to learn in any given situation. However, Vygotsky does not generally focus on the institutions of schooling or the complex social forces that come into play in school contexts. He is mainly concerned with establishing his theory that mental development occurs through a process of internalization of externally mediated experiences. He focuses predominantly on the individual in order to establish the priority of social and 'intermental' processes over 'intramental' processes in the development of individual consciousness. He does not address the question of how external influences may curtail development, except by implication.

Jerome Bruner, whose own seminal work has been influenced by the ideas of Vygotsky, confronts more directly the issue of external influences and constraints on learning. In *The Culture of Education*, Bruner acknowledges that his own earlier work was overly concerned with what goes on 'inside the head', with 'solo, intrapsychic processes of knowing and how these might be assisted by appropriate pedagogies'. His thesis now is that 'culture shapes the mind, providing us with the tool kit by which we construct not only our worlds but our very conception of ourselves and our powers' (Bruner 1996: 1). He considers that a theory of mind is 'inside out' and of limited applicability if it is concerned only with mental tools and resources, rather than also with the 'settings and conditions required for effective operations'.

As we do, in our account of learning capacity, Bruner accords great significance to the impact on learning of states of mind and personal resources other than the cognitive-intellectual, and explores how these are affected by external influences, and in particular by success and failure in school. He argues that educators must 'constantly reassess what school does to the young student's concept of his own powers (his sense of agency) and his sense of being able to cope with the world both in school and after (self-esteem)', and mirrors the teachers' purposes reflected in our model when he urges that developing and strengthening these 'two crucial ingredients of personhood' should be seen as a central task of education in schools.

Pierre Bourdieu and cultural capital

While the work of Vygotsky and Bruner has been concerned with challenging theories of mind and mental functioning which take no account of the impact of culture on human development, the work of the sociologist Pierre Bourdieu has been concerned with exposing the part that culture plays in the production of success and failure in schools. In Chapter 2, we discussed his disturbing but persuasive suggestion that success in school depends primarily not on what is taught in school but on the way teachers differentially recognize and reward the cultural skills, understandings and habits which children from dominant social classes bring with them, while ignoring or denying the cultural learning of children from other social classes. We related this thesis to the research findings of Shirley Brice Heath. Unlike Bourdieu, whose account can seem very pessimistic, she was encouragingly able to show teachers' ability to learn to recognize, and to take account of, the cultural achievements of children from a culture different from that of the school. How does our model relate to these ideas?

Simply asking that question brings home to us that our model is one of classroom teaching and learning. Even in so far as the teachers recognize individual children as coming from distinctive cultural backgrounds, their response is an interpersonal one within the classroom. The model emphasizes caring for and working together with all individuals so that they are helped to be safe and confident, so that their contributions are recognized, and so that their learning capacity is enhanced.

We are confident that the model of classroom teaching and learning that we have developed is one that, effectively implemented, can greatly enhance the learning capacity of all students. For some students, the effects will be long-lasting and will transform their lives. But such major and long-lasting benefits can be expected for all students only if their experience of classrooms is generally of this kind. Even then, however, we would be left with the question of whether individual teachers, acting within their individual classrooms, can overcome the massive disadvantages that our present system of schooling imposes on children from working-class and other cultural backgrounds to which schools are not well attuned. That is a question to which we do not know the answer. It is clear, however, that extending and extrapolating our model from the individual classroom to the whole school would be as valuable as it is challenging. A whole school committed to enhancing the learning capacity of all its students might need to reinvent itself so that co-agency was extended to the wider community and, especially at primary school level, to the parents of working-class children.

There is encouraging evidence that such an approach is indeed possible in the influential work of the Pen Green Centre for under fives and their families, a multifunctional service staffed by a multidisciplinary team and managed jointly by health, social services and the local education authority. Over the past 20 years, the staff team have developed a ground-breaking collaborative approach to their work with parents and families, founded on the principle of affirming and supporting parents as their children's prime educators (Whalley 2001). While the Pen Green approach remains distinctive, and finely tuned to local political and cultural contexts, it is worth noting that it also owes much to other significant international developments in early childhood education, notably the work of Margaret Carr and her colleagues in New Zealand (Carr 2001) and the educators in Reggio Emilia (Edwards *et al.* 1998), whose philosophy and practice are described briefly below (p.257).

Cooperative and interactive learning and Success for All

Robert Slavin's efforts to provide an alternative to ability labelling, or what he calls 'the sorting paradigm', have produced some of the the most impressive research-based claims for success in the reform of schooling in the USA in recent years. This paradigm, he writes, 'depends in large part on a belief that children have relatively unchangeable intellectual capabilities and that the best that schools can do is provide instruction to each child's innate talents ... an alternative to the sorting paradigm is practices based on the belief that all children can learn to high levels' (Slavin 1996: 1). He suggests that the urgency of the problem stems from the facts that 'the students who are sorted into the lowest categories are disproportionately those from poor and minority families' and that 'in every advanced democracy ... the persistent correlation between social class and educational performance indicates a chasm between national ideals and daily reality' (*ibid:* 1–2).

At the core of Slavin's work has been the development, evaluation and reviewing over several decades of classroom strategies of cooperative learning, involving small heterogeneous teams of students working together in classrooms to ensure that they all master ideas or skills initially presented by the teacher. One element of the rationale for cooperative learning is motivational, with students encouraging each other to succeed and the development of peer-group norms of working for the success of all. The other element is cognitive, building on Vygotsky's ideas of social learning and scaffolding and also on the evident value of peer tutoring, not only for those being tutored but also for the tutors. Evidence from around a hundred studies consistently suggests that cooperative learning leads to substantially improved achievements for all participants, that its effectiveness generally depends on the team being rewarded for the successful learning of each individual member and that its effectiveness can be further enhanced if the team members are taught strategies for supporting each other's learning. Slavin summarizes what he sees as the factors involved in the model shown in Figure 17.2.

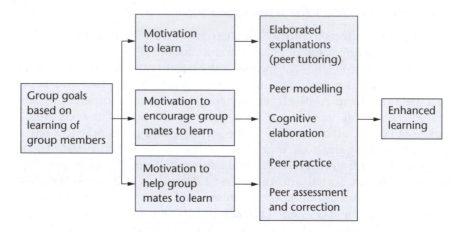

Figure 17.2 Model of factors influencing learning gains in cooperative learning (from Slavin 1996)

There is clearly common ground between the emphasis in our model on collaboration among students in their classroom learning and Slavin's model. Indeed, the very extensive research and development work in the United States that underpins Slavin's model provides a rich source of ideas on which teachers pursuing our model could fruitfully draw. The same is true of Slavin's more recent work, directed 'toward the idea of building a high floor under the achievement of all students' (*ibid:* 83). In the Success for All programme, cooperative learning is combined with other research-based ideas, including collaboration with families, to inform the teaching of reading from the earliest stages. 'The most important idea' informing this programme 'is that the school must relentlessly stick with every child until that child is successful' (*ibid:* 86); and the programme has achieved very impressive results on a wide scale, especially in schools serving disadvantaged populations.

Slavin's approach suffers from many of the problems that we noted in relation to Bloom's mastery learning, in that he has a similar concern to exercise tight control over classroom teaching and learning. This is again reflected in a narrowness and a rigidity with regard to what is valued in teachers' and students' activities and achievements, and in the lack of replication in other contexts of the impressive findings achieved when the tight controls are in place. From our perspective, while many of the ideas incorporated into Success for All are valuable, the approach as a whole is too prescriptive and does not sufficiently trust teachers, students and parents to take necessary intelligent initiatives suited to their situations. None the less, it does give some indication of the potential effectiveness of initiatives directed towards 'success for all'.

The Reggio Emilia approach

The northern Italian town of Reggio Emilia has become recognized, world-wide, for the extraordinary qualities of its municipal services for young children: infant schools for children from three to six years and infant toddler centres for children from three months to three years. They are character-ized by 'a distinctive and innovative set of philosophical assumptions, cur-riculum and pedagogy, method of school organisation, and design of environments' (Edwards *et al.* 1993: 3), which, taken as a whole, has become known as the Reggio Emilia approach. At the heart of the approach is a particular construction of children as powerful and articulate learners, and of the pre-eminent place of the expressive arts in their learning. Just as distinctive is a view of the child–educator relationship, conceived in terms of reciprocity. The third distinguishing feature of the approach is the strength of the relationship between school, family and community.

First, and most fundamental, is the Reggio approach to children. Carlina Rinaldi, until recently Director of Services for young children in the region, summarizes their position:

> The cornerstone of our experience, based on practice, theory and research, is the image of children as rich, strong and powerful ... They have potential, plasticity, the desire to grow, curiosity, the ability to be amazed and the desire to relate to other people and to communicate ... [they are] eager to express themselves within the context of a plurality of symbolic languages, and ... are open to exchanges and reciprocity as deeds and acts of love which they not only want to receive but also want to offer.
>
> (Edwards *et al.* 1993: 101–2)

This view of young children unequivocally excludes the possibility that because of their age and biological immaturity they are in any sense weak, needy, ignorant or lacking in ability. The approach focuses on children's powers, not their weaknesses, their capacity, not their inadequacy, their potential for growth in the future, not their incapacity in the present. Rinaldi continues:

> These potentials are expressed and achieved first and foremost within a group learning context. This fact has involved us in a con-tinuous search for an educational approach that breaks ranks with traditional education ... The emphasis of our approach is ... on each child in relation to other children, teachers, parents, his or her own history and the societal and cultural surroundings ... The teacher must establish a personal relationship with each child and ground this relationship in the social system of the school. Children, in turn,

do not just passively endure their experience, but also become active agents in their socialisation, co-constructed with their peers.

(*ibid:* 103)

The key theme here is the pedagogy of relationships, between child and child, between educators and children. Equally important are the relationships between educators, who always work together, in pairs, with classes of children, and who see their own growth and professional development as an absolute necessity for the educational well-being of the children. Years of working together in this way have given them exceptional professional strength, confidence and security in their capacity to undertake the complex tasks of the Reggio educator, in which the key idea of the reciprocity of teaching and learning, of adult and child, is constantly emphasized. The much revered pioneer and philosopher of the Reggio approach, Loris Malaguzzi, formulates this relationship in these terms:

Learning is the key factor on which a new way of teaching should be based, becoming a complementary resource to the child, and offering multiple options, suggestive ideas and sources of support. Learning and teaching should not stand on opposite banks and just watch the river flow by; instead they should embark together on a journey down the water. Through an active reciprocal exchange, teaching can strengthen learning how to learn.

(Edwards *et al.* 1993: 79)

The pedagogy of relationships extends beyond the walls of the early childhood settings in Reggio; the educators have established a particularly strong relationship between school, family and community. The idea of participation, a cultural and political characteristic of this part of Italy, is a defining characteristic of the relationship between parents, families and the educators in the settings. Rinaldi emphasizes its importance in existential terms:

participation is an educational strategy that characterizes our way of being and teaching. Participation of the children, the teachers and the families, not only by *taking part* in something, but by *being* part of it, its essence, part of a common identity, a 'we' that we give life to through participation.

(Rinaldi, quoted in Valentine 1999: 9)

The Reggio approach, it is apparent, suggests a number of connections with elements of our model. Among the most striking is the principle of trust, expressed in their unassailable belief in the 'rich, strong and powerful' child. This position explicitly rejects, as we do, the use of the categories of relative or fixed ability as an appropriate basis for education. We may also note the Reggio emphasis on relationships and their significance for pedagogy: their conception of a community of learners, engaged in reciprocal and cooperative acts of meaning-making, mirrors our principles of co-agency and the ethic of everybody. And, finally, we share with the Reggio educators an optimistic vision of the future, and our capacity to transform it. Malaguzzi himself expresses something of the same commitment to transformation: 'The continuing motivation for our work has been an attempt ... to liberate hopes for a new human culture of childhood. It is a motive that finds its origin in a powerful nostalgia for the future and for mankind' (Edwards *et al.* 1993: 88).

Arthur Pearl and 'Democratic education as an alternative to deficit thinking'

Arthur Pearl's (1997) chapter in Valencia's edited collection of essays exploring the phenomenon of deficit thinking, an act of mind closely related to ability labelling, presents his own version of a transformative agenda, which he defines as democratic education. Pearl contends that there are four requirements of democratic education: knowledge; rights; participation; encouragement. It is the last of these that has most relevance for our model of transformative pedagogy.

In his discussion of encouragement, Pearl explains how unequal encouragements contribute to lasting social inequity, the enduring hierarchy of privilege and wealth and the important inequalities that are created and maintained in classrooms. The alternative is to recognize the desires that are universal to all human beings, and to reconstruct classrooms so that these desires are equally fulfilled, for all students. Equal encouragement in nine specific areas of desire will, argues Pearl, drive out the injustice caused by deficit thinking and all its works. These nine areas are:

- *Security*: 'in school, security, in addition to providing a safe environment, means willingness to take risks ... a democratic classroom encourages all students equally to take chances.'
- *Comfort*: (relief from unnecessary pain) 'in school, unnecessary pain takes the form of humiliation, boredom and loneliness ... A democratic classroom strives to eliminate unnecessary pain.'
- *Competence*: 'competence in school is measured by evaluated performance – that is, grades ... But grades are far less a measure of competence than a means to encourage and discourage ... Competence will be universally attained when all students are encouraged equally to be competent.'

- *Belonging*: 'in school, belonging is active participation ... in a democratic classroom, all students are made equally welcome and effort is made to make the classroom an inclusive community.'
- *Meaning*: 'for there to be meaning in school, there must be demystification, discussion and negotiation. A democratic class explains and demystifies equally to all students' (so that they all understand what is happening to them and why).
- *Usefulness*: 'for those saddled with alleged deficits school offers little in the way of usefulness. In a democratic classroom, all students are given equal opportunities to be useful.'
- *Hope*: 'students who have been designated with deficits have little to be hopeful about. In a democratic classroom all students are provided reasons to be hopeful.'
- *Excitement*: 'classrooms can be exciting if students are encouraged to participate in activities where they generate knowledge and make important discoveries. The opportunity for such excitement needs to be extended to those now denied – those with deficits.'
- *Creativity*: 'creativity exists for all: it is not a province of the gifted ... In a democratic class, all students are encouraged to be constructively creative and to use creativity in community building, that is to make the classroom a far more exciting place than is currently the case' (Pearl 1997: 229–34).

Pearl's nine universal desires, which are to be equally fulfilled in the democratic classroom, constitute an interesting representation of the ideas that we have expressed as the practical purposes of teaching for transformability, and that we summarized earlier in this chapter. Like us, Pearl identifies cognitive, affective and social elements of the democratic classroom (the transformative classroom, in our terms). With equal encouragement for all, Pearl argues, in line with our principle of everybody, a comprehensive democratic education becomes possible: in its wake come 'freedom and justice for all', a truly transformative ideal.

Brian Simon and comprehensive education

Echoes of our model of pedagogy are certainly vivid in the writings of Brian Simon, perhaps the most powerful and persuasive of twentieth-century campaigners against ability labelling, and a man who understood the practical realities of classrooms. Writing fifty years ago, Simon drew much of his theoretical inspiration from the classical Pavlovian psychology of the Soviet Union (the academic tradition to which Vygotsky belonged). He quoted

Pavlov's account of 'the extraordinary plasticity of [human higher nervous] activity and its immense potentialities; nothing is immobile or intractable, and everything may always be achieved, changed for the better, provided only that the proper conditions are created' (I. P. Pavlov, *A Physiologist's Reply to Psychologists*, in Simon 1953: 104); and he gave accounts of Soviet psychologists' highly successful efforts, through building on what learners did understand, to teach children who had seemed incapable of learning things. Simon's account of the approach used by teachers who start out from the conviction that all the children under their care are educable is strikingly in tune with key features of our model:

> The teacher who sets out to educate the children under his care, meets them as human beings. He first searches for ways of welding his class together as a group, knowing that learning is not a purely individual affair which takes place in a vacuum, but rather a social activity; and that the progress of each child will be conditioned largely by the progress of the group as a whole. He begins, then, by concentrating on the interests children have in common, rather than by underlining their individual differences. As the work of the class takes shape, however, individual children make varying contributions; some may draw well, others may be good readers, others may be quick with figures. The teacher's task is not, of course, to see that the children who are good at some particular activity shine to the detriment of their companions, but rather to see that each child contributes to and enlivens the work of the class as a whole, and that all encompass the necessary basic skills. There is no better means of ensuring this than the stimulus given by other children within a cohesive group.
>
> (Simon 1953: 103)

Teachers committed to the educability of all students do not, he says, shut their eyes to obvious differences in attainment. But, as with the nine project teachers, they refuse to be blinded by the assumption that degrees of attainment reflect degrees of intelligence. What are decisive, he argues, are

> the opportunities for engaging in different activities and the help that the child is given to master them, to develop new abilities and make new achievements. The teacher is specifically skilled in this complex and important task. He sets about it in a systematic manner. To do precisely this is the essence of education.
>
> (*ibid:* 105)

Through this examination of other published work by educators whose values, theories and pedagogical ideas have close links with our own, we have been able to sharpen our own and, we hope, our readers' awareness both of the distinctive concerns and assumptions implicit in our model and of the continuities between our model and other historical and current pedagogical thinking. We are in no doubt that further comparison and synthesis with other theoretical writings could be very fruitful for advancing our own thinking and that of others. Here we have simply made a modest start at exploring how our model relates to the community of ideas of which our project forms a part.

An alternative improvement agenda

Our primary purpose in this project has certainly not been a theoretical one, concerned only with enriching our understanding. Our purpose was instead to contribute directly to realizing a vision of schooling that 'allows everyone to enjoy a full education' (Chitty 2001a: 20). In particular, our aim was to contribute to the construction of an alternative improvement agenda for English schooling today. We shall not therefore have succeeded at all unless our work is used in the construction of such an alternative agenda.

Specifically, our purpose was to articulate one or more models of teaching, showing how the ideas and values that lead to a rejection of ability labelling could be translated into a coherent, principled and practicable pedagogy. The starting point of the project was an awareness of the severely negative effects of ability labelling and a commitment therefore to working against the limits it imposed on learning. At that stage, we were only able to envision a model of pedagogy in terms of what it was against, not what it was for. Now, as a result of analysing the thinking underlying the nine teachers' practice, we are able to formulate the teaching task not primarily in terms of opposition to something negative, but as one of commitment to something positive: transforming the capacity to learn.

Implications for teachers

We believe that this positive reformulation of the teaching task and the model of teaching we have constructed send a number of messages of encouragement and hope to teachers. First, we have demonstrated that the possibility of developing learning without limits, learning of the second kind described at the start of this book, is not a naive fantasy but something that these nine teachers – and no doubt many others – are already deeply committed to, and indeed are working to achieve in their own classrooms.

Second, we hope that the contrast we have drawn between ability-based and transformability-based pedagogy will encourage teachers to question official discourses of good practice, including the assumed benefits of ability grouping for both teachers and young people, and the more recently established idea that differentiation according to ability is the hallmark of good teaching. We hope that it will help to strengthen the resolve of teachers who are familiar with all the arguments we presented in Chapter 2 to express their concerns and influence policy in their schools, as well as remain stead-fast to their values and conceptions of good practice, in developing their own classroom work.

Third, we hope that the nine accounts of teachers' work will provide reassurance that teaching for learning without limits is not something esoteric and mysterious, but includes many of the good practices that are part of the established repertoires of most experienced teachers. We are confident that every experienced teacher who reads this book will find a great deal in it that is reminiscent of their own practice and classroom experience. There are good reasons for this. On the one hand, as argued earlier, teachers strive to use their power as educators to have a positive impact upon young people's lives; they build up a wealth of knowledge and expertise to help them to do this. It is to be expected, then, that experienced teachers will in many cases have come to similar conclusions about the kinds of approaches and practices that best facilitate and those that limit learning. On the other hand, teaching in classrooms imposes its own distinctive disciplines and all classroom teachers are faced with the same challenging task of establishing conditions in which young people can learn. Therefore, the nine teachers with whom we worked, deeply committed, hard-working and highly skilled as they are, are not a breed apart. Just like the hundreds of thousands of other teachers in English schools, they vary considerably among themselves; much of what these nine have in common, they also have in common with other teachers.

The key difference is that, in teaching for transformability, 'good practice' is not just about what teachers *do*, but also what they do *not* do. As we saw in Chapter 14, the practices included in these teachers' repertoires have been sifted very carefully. They select those practices that seem most likely to increase young people's capacity to learn, and reject anything that might limit or impede the achievement of the core purposes for everybody. The practices they reject include sorting pupils (in their mind or in practice) into ability groups, and differentiating teaching (expectations, tasks, content, questions, interactions, feedback on work) on the basis of such judgements. These processes are so familiar and commonplace that, at first, it seems impossible that teachers can accomplish all the essential tasks of teaching and manage a class of thirty without recourse to such judgements and practices. Yet the nine accounts of practice in Part 2 provide nine uniquely different examples of how teachers do achieve this, and the model that we have developed in Part 3 explains the core ideas, purposes and principles that enable them to do so.

Fourth, then, we hope that our alternative model of pedagogy will provide a stimulus for teachers to review their values and reconsider their choices – what they do and do not do – as they try to realize these values in practice. We hope that we have provided enough detail for teachers to do this, simply by reflecting on their work, although it can be much more stimulating and informative to examine teaching with a group of supportive colleagues in a spirit of collaboration and shared learning.

Fifth, and perhaps most importantly, we hope and expect that the main message our model conveys will be an empowering one for teachers; we trust that the model will help them to clarify, optimistically yet realistically, the extent of their power to make a difference to young people's capacity to learn, if the ability template is set aside and their task formulated instead in terms of intervening to strengthen and enhance learning capacity. We recognize, however, that to pursue this other way of thinking and teaching, in the current context, is not an easy course of action. Teachers have for most of the past century been under pressure, both from official policies and from the common sense of dominant social groups, to construct their practices in terms of ability. But that is not all. Faced with the ever-increasing complexity of classroom teaching as public expectations of schooling have risen, teachers themselves have found it necessary to simplify that complexity and have found the officially approved way of construing their pupils in ability terms a helpful kind of simplification.

We recognize that, under present circumstances, adopting our alternative model is undoubtedly challenging. Teachers will be persuaded to adopt it, we believe, if we have offered persuasive answers to the following questions:

1   Is this alternative approach clear and coherent in its principles and purposes?
2   Is it based on sound educational values with which teachers agree, and is the change of approach necessary for the realization of these values?
3   Is adopting this approach in each teacher's own working context practically possible and worth the costs involved?

We hope that the evidence and argument of this book will go some way towards providing positive answers to these questions. Beyond that, we would ask teachers primarily to reflect on their experience. We would ask them to trust their experience that young people can constantly surprise them by their understanding, their skills and their seriousness of purpose.

We would ask them to trust their experience that, given the right conditions, all young people can with time be enlisted as co-agents in their own learning. Most of all, we would ask teachers to believe in the rightness and relevance of their own commitment to young people, and join with us in campaigning for national policies of this more educational kind. Words written nearly 100 years ago by the inspirational thinker, writer and former Chief Inspector of Schools, Edmond Holmes, still have powerful resonance today: 'The day is coming, if I do not misread the signs of the times, when the teachers of our elementary schools will have to choose between making a bolder use of their freedom and having it ruthlessly abridged' (Holmes 1914: 227–8).

Implications for government

We are bold enough to hope that the alternative model of pedagogy we have articulated in this book also carries a message of hope and encouragement for government. It shows that school improvement may not, after all, be dependent on schools being put under continuous surveillance and constant pressure, bombarded by a succession of externally imposed initiatives and external accountability measures. The implication of the arguments reviewed in Chapter 2 is that it is the ability–predictability template that is responsible for inertia in the system, because it induces in teachers a sense of powerlessness and acceptance of limited achievement. In contrast, our model represents practice as being in a continual state of development. The drive to improve things, to keep looking for ways to increase and enhance everybody's capacity for learning, is inscribed in the nature of teaching. It does not have to be imposed on teachers and superimposed on existing practice, by managers or inspectors, because the driving force comes from teachers' commitment as educators, their desire to make a difference in whatever way they can to young people's future lives.

As we indicated in Chapter 1, we do not doubt the seriousness of the present British government's commitment to education and to raising educational standards in England. Yet that same government has seemed especially keen to espouse the outdated twentieth-century ideological view that there is a limited 'pool of ability', that the ability range as currently conceived is part of the natural order of things. In doing so, it is unwittingly tying one hand behind its back in its efforts to do what it claims to be its most important task. Quite apart from the destructive effects of ability labelling on millions of individuals' lives, no twenty-first-century country is going to be able to afford to view a third or more of its population as educational failures instead of capitalizing on their potential as intelligent citizens and workers. So we suggest that the biggest contribution that the government could make to raising educational standards is to untie its other hand and recognize the enormous scope that exists for enhancing the learning capacity of all its citizens, and especially of all school students.

What might that mean in practice? Most obviously, it would mean abandoning the pressure on schools to group students in terms of 'ability'. It would mean an end to tiered GCSE examinations. It would also mean an end to differentiated 'targets' for students according to their 'abilities' and for schools according to their populations, and therefore to accountability in terms of 'value-added' calculations. It would certainly not mean an end to holding teachers and schools accountable for their work, but it would mean holding them accountable in broad terms that make sense to teachers themselves, to their students and to their students' parents. An excellent starting point for thinking about a more constructive accountability framework would be the ten kinds of practical purposes that we have identified within our model of transformability-based teaching (see Table 17.3).

As we saw in Chapter 13, these are not just hopes and aspirations, but the criteria that the teachers rigorously use to check on the quality of their teaching. Such purposes are relevant both to day-by-day classroom practice and to the longer-term purposes and achievements of schools. Any valid accountability framework, however, would necessarily take much more account than current procedures of the complexity of the tasks facing teachers and schools, and would have to be based on combining observation of what happens in classrooms with listening to teachers' own accounts of their purposes and of the strategies they use to achieve them.

What our research shows more than anything is that teachers committed to developing the learning capacity of all their students do so by having confidence in all their students as active partners in the educational process. Any significant raising of standards will necessarily be based on working with students as active agents rather than putting them through predetermined processes. But responsiveness to students as trusted and respected partners can only be expected only from teachers who are themselves trusted and respected partners in the educational process. Reform is certainly necessary in English schools, and indeed much more radical reform than that which has been imposed in recent decades; but effective reform will be possible only when it is both conceived and implemented in dialogue with teachers.

Our model offers a map to guide the early exploration of how transformative classroom teaching can be effectively implemented. Given supportive policies and official encouragement, many teachers will be eager to develop that map further, examining more fully the classroom conditions that need to be created and maintained, providing many more examples of how this can be done, probably articulating additional practical pedagogical principles and certainly demonstrating the different implications of the model for different contexts, content and phases of schooling. A government

Table 17.3 Teachers' purposes

Building confidence and emotional security	Do all students feel emotionally safe, comfortable and positive about their participation in learning activities?
Strengthening feelings of competence and control	Do their classroom experiences strengthen or restore all students' feelings of competence and control?
Increasing enjoyment and purposefulness	Are classroom activities experienced by all students as interesting, enjoyable and purposeful?
Enhancing young people's identities as learners	Do all students experience sustained success and achievement in their learning, and recognition of that achievement?
Increasing hope and confidence in the future	Do all students recognize their own power to make a difference to their own future development? Do they develop constantly expanding conceptions of what is possible? Are they hopeful and confident for the future?
Increasing young people's sense of acceptance and belonging	Do all students feel that they are looked upon by others as an equal member of the classroom community? Do they feel that their contributions are recognized and valued by their peers, as well as by their teacher?
Increasing young people's capacity to work as a learning community	Have all students developed the skills needed to work together constructively as a team? Do they accept responsibility for working effectively as a learning community?
Providing successful access for all young people to whatever knowledge, understanding and skills are intended to be the focus of a lesson	Have all students understood and engaged with the content and learning intentions of the lesson? Have they engaged in worthwhile learning in relation to these intentions?
Increasing relevance, enhancing meaning	Have all students found the content and tasks of the lesson relevant to their lives and concerns? Has it created intellectual connections for them? Has it opened up new horizons and led to recognition of new meanings and relevances?
Enhancing thinking, reasoning, explaining	Have all the students been helped to think, to talk about their thinking, to reflect on their learning and what helps them to learn?

committed to raising standards and to the transformation of learning capacity for all will provide such support and encouragement.

Furthermore, as we noted in Chapter 1, the present government has shown a strong commitment to challenging assumptions about the educational achievements to be expected of young people from disadvantaged social backgrounds and to reducing class-based discrepancies in achievement. That is an agenda to which our model can certainly make a substantial contribution; but there is much work to be done on how schools and teachers can more fully collaborate with parents and local communities in countering low expectations and, more positively, in enabling children to make effective use of schools to sustain the development of their learning capacity.

Implications for school managers

Concerned though they were with wider issues, it was generally beyond the power of the nine teachers (and beyond the remit that they and we had accepted for this research) to try to develop whole-school policies or structures that would contribute to the transformation of learning capacity. Yet as Slavin (1996) found in the United States, any reform of classroom teaching approaches without corresponding reform in whole-school and wider practices is likely to be fragile. The responsibility falls to school managers to decide whether or not to give active support and encouragement to the development of teaching for learning without limits as a general policy direction in their schools.

Since there were, among the members of the team, teachers who held or were subsequently promoted to senior management positions, we asked for their thoughts in order to draw out some of the implications of the project's findings for school managers. Even if school managers are committed to this particular approach for their schools, just how realistic is it to attempt to make progress in the current context? If they do, what strategies are most likely to be effective in encouraging and empowering everyone to become involved? Four key issues were identified.

First, colleagues acknowledged the enormous pressures created for school managers by central policy initiatives and externally defined models of good practice that make it difficult and risky for schools to take up approaches other than those that are officially 'approved' and sponsored. These pressures are not just created by managers' interpretations of the expectations and requirements of initiatives such as the National Literacy and Numeracy Strategies. They also come from LEA advisors, who have clear expectations of the models of good practice that they expect to see in operation in their schools. Managers have to feel very confident, very sure of themselves and their staff, to resist these expectations and pressures and commit themselves to an alternative approach. This is especially the case for schools regarded as having serious weaknesses or that, following an Ofsted inspection, have found themselves in Special Measures.

There is a second problem, too, in that having been inundated with different directives and increasingly prescriptive external initiatives over a number of years, teachers have started to become conditioned to accepting and following externally delivered guidelines. There has been precious little time or encouragement for teachers to exercise their creative and critical faculties with respect to what they are being asked to do. Widespread complaints about work overload, plus feelings of demoralization especially amongst teachers in schools designated 'failing', mean that staff may not be immediately receptive to new ideas, no matter how sound or potentially appealing to teachers' fundamental values and commitments as educators.

Third, while acknowledging these very real constraints, colleagues in managerial positions were nevertheless persuaded that, just as in any classroom, there is always the potential for progress to be made in any school, whatever the external conditions. In translating externally imposed initiatives into practice, there is always scope for creative interpretation. Managers, through the ways in which they organize and structure INSET sessions, for example, can actively encourage their staff to adopt a mind-set in which they do not simply receive and follow external prescriptions as they stand, but subject them to careful critical scrutiny in the light of their own understandings, values and conceptions of good practice.

Fourth, and perhaps most importantly, colleagues claimed that the same core ideas, purposes and principles apply just as much to adults' learning as to young people's learning. Rather than imposing their own ideas and vision of the future, managers must find ways to enlist the willing engagement of staff in what can only be a joint enterprise; it is essential to build a sense of community and encourage teamwork, since people accomplish so much more together than they do operating in isolation; they become more committed to developments that they have actively helped to create and shape themselves. Creating the conditions in which a whole school staff, pupils and parents move towards the ideal of learning without limits is a long-term task. It clearly cannot happen overnight, but it is unlikely to happen at all unless everyone feels supported and valued, feels safe enough to take risks and try new things, knowing that their efforts will be supported and endorsed by the whole community.

Implications for academics

We hope that most teacher educators, working in university faculties of education, will want to examine with their students the ideas put forward in this book. In England, these educators have in recent years found themselves severely constrained in what they do, especially in initial teacher education, but also increasingly in continuing teacher education. First, there is the requirement to work in close partnership with schools, which means both that the agenda must be practical and relevant and that students have relatively little of their time to spend in university-based studies. Second, government specifications of what must be covered and what must be achieved by students have become very demanding. Just like creative and committed teachers, however, teacher educators can find ways of fulfilling their role as critical, questioning educators while also meeting external specifications. Furthermore, since school-based teacher educators have proved that they are entirely capable of inducting student teachers effectively into the adoption of schools' existing practices (Furlong *et al.* 2000), there is little point in universities being involved in teacher education if they do not see their primary role to be that of questioning existing practices and helping their students to examine alternative ideas that are educationally principled and important, theoretically coherent, evidence-based and practically realistic. Since we believe that our model of the transformability of learning capacity meets all these criteria, we hope that it will be considered a prime candidate for inclusion in both initial teacher education and continuing professional development curricula.

This book has been all about the damaging effects of, and realistic alternatives to, the use of crude, oversimplifying and debilitating constructs of ability in teaching. As educational researchers, we should give a little space to the comparable use and damaging effects of similar constructs in educational research. A great deal of research – for example, in the field of school effectiveness – makes use of 'general ability' variables in its analyses of the impact of different factors on student achievements and attitudes. Analysis in terms of such variables has, of course, a major impact on the ways in which the processes of schooling, teaching and learning are understood. If most of the variance in students' achievements can be accounted for by extracting the 'effects' of general ability, then the problematic variance that needs to be explained is not only much smaller but also very different in kind. If 'general ability' variables were not used, we would have to ask more serious questions about the processes underlying all the variation in achievement.

There will, of course, be many researchers, like many teachers, who will claim that they interpret general ability not as a fixed underlying entity that has a causal effect on achievement, but as a conveniently simple way of summarizing evident realities. Our response is that by using this conveniently simple device they give it a spurious theoretical legitimacy that does enormous damage. By using it, they are avoiding the possibility of confronting the real issue and their real responsibility. Their job, our job, is not to find convenient ways of simplifying things, but to explain the complex realities of things in ways that can help in the construction of a better education system.

Finally, what further research projects are implied by the model that we have constructed? As we noted in the context of implications for government, there is a need for a variety of work with teachers: to test and to elaborate the model, to explore what it might imply for whole schools and to develop ways in which schools can work in partnership with parents and with local communities to enhance young people's learning capacity. With or without the support of government, there is an important task for researchers there. Perhaps even more immediately, there are questions that government itself will want answered before investing in this alternative to ability labelling. Most immediately they will ask: is this an effective alternative approach? That is a good question, one that we have not attempted to answer. We would want to answer it in four stages. First, is it an approach that other teachers can learn to use? What will they find difficult? What kinds of support will be helpful for them? How much work will they need to do in order to use this approach fluently? Second, when teachers are using this approach fluently, how successful are they, in the short term and the longer term, in achieving the ten purposes that we have identified? Answering this question will involve very useful work in elaborating the concepts involved and in collaborating with teachers to identify the kinds of evidence that they can use in order to make confident judgements in relation to these diverse criteria. Third, when teachers are effectively achieving the distinctive purposes that they set themselves when using this model, how does their work compare with other teachers' effectiveness in relation to the current commonly used criteria: examination results, Ofsted ratings, students' satisfaction, parental satisfaction and teachers' own job satisfaction? Fourth, although we are very confident that in general the findings of this third question will show clearly the strengths of our model, it will also make clear that this model, like any other, can be used more or less well. So researchers will need to ask: what is involved in using this model well ?

Conclusion

Although the structure and sequence of the book have led us to conclude with a consideration of implications for our academic colleagues, we hope it has been clear from the opening stages that we have written this book for a very much wider audience: for all who work closely with young people, and for all who work with teachers and other educators. We hope that the book provides convincing arguments and evidence to demonstrate that there *is* a more promising, just and constructive alternative improvement strategy that we could pursue. We believe it is one worth fighting for. What will be lost, if we do not recognize the importance of making this our priority, is movingly illustrated by one of the teacher members of the project team in the following account.

Postscript

I first came to know Claudia when she was 7 years old. Claudia was born with paraplegia and cerebral palsy. Doctors believed that she would never be able to walk or talk. She was fostered and adopted by an amazing woman called Sue Salmons. Sue supported Claudia from the earliest days in her belief that nothing was impossible. She gave Claudia every opportunity to learn from others and to develop her independence. Sue believed that Claudia would learn best by watching her peers and by interacting with them. She was adamant that the best school for her daughter would be the local mainstream church school and refused all suggestions of special school education.

When Claudia started school, she was permanently in a wheelchair. She communicated through gesture and had begun to learn Makaton sign language. She had a statement of special educational needs and was provided with one-to-one classroom assistant support from Juliet.

Juliet and Claudia developed a close friendship and tried as best they could to be included in everything that went on in the classroom. However, staff found that it was easy to forget Claudia because she was silent and very easily pleased. The children began to make firm friends with her and loved her company. However, by the age of 7, Claudia had still not learnt to read and for the first time she was allocated teaching hours as part of her statemented provision. The headteacher knew me as a parent at the school and asked whether I could spare several hours a week to teach Claudia how to read. I had no preconceived notions of what Claudia could achieve and so we began our learning journey together.

Claudia had a tremendous sense of fun. She was inquisitive, full of determination and extremely courageous. Her only vocal sounds were her laughter and the words 'Why?' and 'Yeah'. Together, we began to explore early reading books. As Claudia recognized words in print, she signed their meaning. With Juliet's help, I began to learn Makaton and Claudia began to read.

Claudia was advised by the consultant surgeon that, as she had curvature of the spine, she should not put weight on her legs. However, no one was going to stop this girl from achieving what she wanted. As her reading ability increased, so did her confidence. The reading scheme materials were stored at the end of the corridor. Each time we finished a book, Claudia wanted to choose the next title. We began by using the wheelchair, gradu-ated to a walking frame and then, one very memorable day, Claudia motioned that she wanted to leave the frame behind and walk unaided. She managed to walk the entire length of the corridor without help and as she passed each classroom door, the children stood up and applauded her until it seemed the whole school was celebrating her success with her.

Claudia went from strength to strength. She became computer literate and, in Year 7, transferred to the local mainstream secondary school. The latest photograph I have of her is as a netball player in the school team. She knew what she was capable of doing, but needed to break free from the limits imposed on her by others. She has been my greatest inspiration in so many ways. I certainly owe my belief in learning without limits to this wonderful young woman. Thank you, Claudia.

Bibliography

Alexander, R. (1984) *Primary Teaching*. Eastbourne: Holt, Reinhart and Winston.

Alexander, R. (2000) *Culture and Pedagogy. International Comparisons in Primary Education*. Oxford: Blackwell.

Ball, S. (1981) *Beachside Comprehensive. A Case Study of Secondary Schooling*. Cambridge: Cambridge University Press.

Ball, S. (1986) The sociology of the school: streaming and mixed ability and social class, in R. Rogers (ed.) *Education and Social Class*. Lewes: Falmer.

Bannister, D. and Fransella, F. (1986) *Inquiring Man: The Theory of Personal Constructs*, 3rd edn. London: Croom Helm.

Bennett, A. and Williams, H. (1992) What would happen if … ? An active approach to mathematics teaching, in T. Booth, P. Potts and W. Swann (eds) *Curricula for Diversity in Education*. London: Routledge.

Bettelheim, B. (1950) *Love Is Not Enough*. New York: The Free Press.

Bloom, B. (1976) *Human Characteristics and School Learning*. New York: McGraw-Hill.

Bloom, B. S. (1984) The 2-sigma problem: the search for methods of instruction as effective as one-to-one tutoring, *Educational Researcher*, 13(6): 4–16.

Boaler, J. (1997a) Setting, social class and survival of the quickest, *British Educational Research Journal*, 23(5): 575–95.

Boaler, J. (1997b) When even the winners are losers: evaluating the experiences of 'top set' students, *Journal of Curriculum Studies*, 29(2): 165–82.

Boaler, J., William, D. and Brown, M. (2000) Students' experiences of ability grouping – disaffection, polarisation and the construction of failure, *British Educational Research Journal*, 26(5): 631–48.

Board of Education (1938) *Report of the Consultative Committee on Secondary Education* (The Spens Report). London: HMSO.

Bourdieu, P. (1976) The school as a conservative force: scholastic and cultural inequalities, in R. Dale, G. Esland and M. MacDonald (eds) *Schooling and Capitalism*. London: Routledge and Kegan Paul.

Bourne, J. and Moon, B. (1995) A question of ability?, in B. Moon and A. Shelton Mayes (eds) *Teaching and Learning in the Secondary School*. London: Routledge.

Brown, S. and McIntyre, D. (1993) *Making Sense of Teaching*. Buckingham: Open University Press.

Bruner, J. (1996) *The Culture of Education*. Cambridge, MA: Harvard University Press.

Carr, M. (2001) *Assessment in Early Childhood Settings*. London: Paul Chapman Publishing.

Central Advisory Council for Education (1967) *Children and Their Primary Schools* (The Plowden Report). London: HMSO.

Chamberlain, V. (1996) *Starting out on MI Way. A Guide to Multiple Intelligences in the Primary School*. Bolton: Centre for the Promotion of Holistic Education.

Chitty, C. (2001a) Selection by specialisation, in C. Chitty and B. Simon (eds) *Promoting Comprehensive Education in the 21st Century*. Stoke-on-Trent: Trentham Books.

Chitty, C. (2001b) IQ, racism and the eugenics movement, *Forum*, 43(3): 115–20.

Coe, J. (1966) The junior school: approaches to non-streaming, *Forum*, 8(3): 76–9.

Coleman, J. (1966) *Equality of Educational Opportunity*. Washington, DC: US Government Printing Office.

Cooper, P. and McIntyre, D. (1996) *Effective Teaching and Learning. Teachers' and Students' Perspectives*. Buckingham: Open University Press.

Croll, P. and Moses, D. (1985) *One in Five. The Assessment and Incidence of Special Educational Needs*. London: Routledge and Kegan Paul.

Cummins, J. (1996) *Negotiating Identities. Education for Empowerment in a Diverse Society*. Ontario, CA: California Association for Bilingual Education.

Cummins, J. (2000) *Language, Power and Pedagogy. Bilingual Children in the Crossfire*. Clevedon: Multilingual Matters.

Daniels, H. (2001) *Vygotsky and Pedagogy*. London: Routledge.

Daunt, P. E. (1975) *Comprehensive Values*. London: Heinemann.

Department for Education and Employment (1997) *Excellence in Schools*. London: HMSO.

Department for Education and Employment (2000) *Research into Teacher Effectiveness. A Model of Teacher Effectiveness*. Report by Hay McBer to the DfEE.

Dewey, J. (1899) *The School and Society*. Chicago: University of Chicago Press.

Dewey, J. (1902) *The Child and the Curriculum*. Chicago: University of Chicago Press.

Dixon, A. (1989) Deliver us from eagles, in G. Barrett (ed.) *Disaffection from School*. London: Routledge.

Douglas, J. W. B. (1964) *The Home and the School. A Study of Ability and Attainment in the Primary School*. London: MacGibbon & Kee.

Drummond, M. J. (1993) *Assessing Children's Learning*. London: David Fulton.

Dweck, C. S. (2000) *Self Theories: Their Role in Motivation, Personality and Development*. Philadelphia: Taylor and Francis.

Edwards, C., Gandini, L. and Forman, G. (eds) (1993) *The Reggio Emilia Approach to Early Childhood Education*. Norwood, NJ: Ablex.

Edwards, C., Gandini, L. and Forman, G. (eds) (1998) *The Hundred Languages of Children: The Reggio Emilia Approach – Advanced Reflections*. Norwood, NJ: Ablex.

Edwards, D. and Mercer, N. (1987) *Common Knowledge. The Development of Understanding in the Classroom*. London: Routledge.

Engestrom, Y. (1996) Non scolae sed vitae decimus: toward overcoming the encapsulation of school learning, in H. Daniels (ed.) *An Introduction to Vygotsky*. London: Routledge.

Entwhistle, H. (1979) *Antonio Gramsci: Conservative Schooling for Radical Politics*. London: Routledge and Kegan Paul.

Fielding, M. (2001) Beyond the rhetoric of student voice: new departures or new constraints in the transformation of 21st century schooling?, *Forum*, 43(2): 100–9.

Floud, J. (1963) Further Memorandum to *Higher Education* (The Robbins Report): Evidence Part II (documentary evidence). London: HMSO.

Ford, J. (1969) *Social Class and the Comprehensive School*. London: Routledge and Kegan Paul.

Frederiksen, J. R. and White, B. J. (1997) Reflective assessment of students' research within an inquiry-based middle school science curriculum. Paper presented at the Annual Meeting of the AERA, Chicago.

Furlong, J., Barton, L., Miles, S., Whiting, C. and Whitty, G. (2000) *Teacher Education in Transition: Reforming Professionalism?* Buckingham: Open University Press.

Galton, M., Simon, B. and Croll, P. (1980) *Inside the Primary Classroom*. London: Routledge and Kegan Paul.

Gardner, H. (1983) *Frames of Mind: The Theory of Multiple Intelligences*. New York: Basic Books.

Gardner, H. (1999) *Intelligence Reframed: Multiple Intelligences for the 21st Century*. New York: Basic Books.

Gillborn, D. and Youdell, D. (2000) *Rationing Education. Policy, Practice, Reform and Equity*. Buckingham: Open University Press.

Giroux, H. (1997) *Pedagogy and the Politics of Hope: Theory, Culture and Schooling*. Boulder, CO: Westview Press.

Goldstein, H. and Noss, R. (1990) Against the stream, *Forum*, 33(1): 4–6.

Gould, S. J. (1981) *The Mismeasure of Man*. New York: Norton.

Hacker, R. G., Rowe, M. J. and Evans, R. D. (1991) The influences of ability groupings for secondary science lessons upon classroom processes. Part 1: homogeneous groupings (science education notes), *School Science Review*, 73(262): 125–9.

Hargreaves, D. H. (1967) *Social Relations in a Secondary School*. London: Routledge and Kegan Paul.

Hargreaves, D. H. (1980) Social class, the curriculum and the low achiever, in E. C. Raybould, B. Roberts and K. Wedell (eds) *Helping the Low Achiever in the Secondary School*. Birmingham: University of Birmingham.

Hargreaves, D. H. (1982) *The Challenge for the Comprehensive School*. London: Routledge and Kegan Paul.

Hart, S. (1996a) Differentiation and equal opportunities, in S. Hart (ed.) *Differentiation and the Secondary Curriculum: Debates and Dilemmas*. London: Routledge.

Hart, S. (1996b) *Beyond Special Needs. Enhancing Children's Learning through Innovative Thinking*. London: Paul Chapman Publishers.

Hart, S. (1998) A sorry tale: ability, pedagogy and educational reform, *British Journal of Educational Studies*, 46(2): 153–68.

Hart, S. (2000) *Thinking through Teaching*. London: David Fulton Publishers.

Hart, S. (2003) Learning without limits, in M. Nind, K. Sheehy and K. Simmons (eds) *Inclusive Education: Learners and Learning Contexts*. London: David Fulton.

Hartley, R. (1985) Imagine you're clever, *Child Psychology and Psychiatry*, 27(1): 383–98.

Heath, S. B. (1983) *Ways with Words. Language, Life and Work in Communities and Classrooms*. Cambridge: Cambridge University Press.

Heim, A. (1954) *The Appraisal of Intelligence*. London: Methuen.

Holmes, E. (1914) *In Defence of What Might Be*. London: Constable.

Holt, J. (1990) *How Children Fail*, rev. edn. London: Penguin.

Hull, R. (1985) *The Language Gap. How Classroom Dialogue Fails*. London: Methuen.

Isaacs, S. (1932) *The Children We Teach: Seven to Eleven Years*. London: London University Press.

Jack, B. (1996) *Moving on MI Way. A Guide to Multiple Intelligences in the Secondary School*. Bolton: Centre for the Promotion of Holistic Education.

Jackson, B. (1964) *Streaming: An Education System in Miniature*. London: Routledge and Kegan Paul.

Jackson, P. (1968) *Life in Classrooms*. New York: Holt, Rinehart and Winston.

Jencks, C., Smith, M., Acland, C., Bane, M. J., Cohen, D., Gintis, H., Heyns, B. and Michelson, S. (1972) *Inequality: A Reassessment of the Effects of Family and Schooling in America*. New York: Basic Books.

Keddie, N. (1971) Classroom knowledge, in M. F. D. Young (ed.) *Knowledge and Control: New Directions for the Sociology of Education*. London: Collier Macmillan.

Kelly, G. A. (1955) *The Psychology of Personal Constructs*. New York: Norton.

Kelly, G. A. (1970) A brief introduction to personal construct theory, in D. Bannister (ed.) *Perspectives in Personal Construct Theory*. London: Academic Press.

Lacey, C. (1970) *Hightown Grammar: The School as a Social System*. Manchester: Manchester University Press.

McDermott, R. P. (1996) The acquisition of a child by a learning disability, in S. Chaiklin and J. Lave (eds) *Understanding Practice: Perspectives on Activity and Context*. Cambridge: Cambridge University Press.

Morrison, A. and McIntyre, D. (1969) *Teachers and Teaching*. Harmondsworth: Penguin.

Muckle, J. (1988) *A Guide to the Soviet Curriculum: What the Russian Child Is Taught in School*. London: Croom Helm.

Nash, R. (1973) *Classrooms Observed. The Teacher's Perception and the Pupil's Performance*. London: Routledge and Kegan Paul.

Oakes, J. (1982) The reproduction of inequity: the content of secondary school tracking, *The Urban Review*, 14(2): 107–20.

Oakes, J. (1985) *Keeping Track: How Schools Structure Inequality*. New Haven, CT: Yale University Press.

Opie, I. (1993) *The People in the Playground*. Oxford: Oxford University Press.

Pearl, A. (1997) Democratic education as an alternative to deficit thinking. In R. Valencia (ed.) *The Evolution of Deficit Thinking: Educational Thought and Practice*. London: Falmer Press.

Quicke, J. and Winter, C. (1996) Autonomy, relevance and the National Curriculum: a contextualised account of teachers' reactions to an intervention, *Research Papers in Education*, 11(2): 151–72.

Richardson, R. (2002) Expectations great and small – the mental maps of teachers and systems, *Race Equality Teaching*, 21(1): 15–20.

Rose, H. and Rose, S. (1979) The IQ myth, in D. Rubinstein (ed.) *Education and Equality*. Harmondsworth: Penguin.

Rosenthal, R. and Jacobson, J. (1968) *Pygmalion in the Classroom*. New York: Holt, Rinehart and Winston.

Salmon, P. (1988) *Psychology for Teachers. An Alternative Approach*. London: Hutchinson.

Salmon, P. (1995) *Psychology in the Classroom. Reconstructing Teachers and Learners*. London: Cassell.

Simon, B. (1953) Intelligence testing and the comprehensive school, in B. Simon (1978) *Intelligence, Psychology and Education*, rev. edn. London: Lawrence and Wishart.

Simon, B. (1955) *The Common Secondary School*. London: Lawrence and Wishart.

Simon, B. (1998) *A Life in Education*. London: Lawrence and Wishart.

Slavin, R. (1996) *Education for All*. Abingdon: Swets and Zeitlinger.

Sternberg, R. (1998) Abilities are forms of developing expertise, *Educational Researcher*, 27(3): 11–20.

Stevenson, H. W. and Stigler, J. W. (1992) *The Learning Gap: Why Our Schools Are Failing and What We Can Learn from Japanese and Chinese Education*. New York: Simon and Schuster.

Stredder, K. (1999) Cultural bridging and children's learning, in P. Murphy (ed.) *Learners, Learning and Assessment*. London: Paul Chapman Publishing.

Suknandan, L. and Lee, B. (1998) *Streaming, Setting and Grouping by Ability. A Review of the Literature*. Slough: NFER.

Taylor, N. (1993) Ability grouping and its effect on pupil behaviour: a case study of a Midlands comprehensive school, *Education Today*, 43(2): 14–17.

Thomson, L. and Thomson, A. (1996) A constructivist view of education, *Forum*, 38(1): 29–31.

Tizard, B. and Hughes, M. (1984) *Young Children Learning. Talking and Thinking at Home and at School*. London: Fontana.

Valencia, R. R. and Solorzano, G. (1997) Contemporary deficit thinking, in R. R.Valencia (ed.) *The Evolution of Deficit Thinking. Educational Thought and Practice*. London: Falmer Press.

Valentine, M. (1999) *The Reggio Emilia Approach to Early Childhood Education*. Dundee: Scottish Consultative Council on the Curriculum.

Vygotsky, L. S. (1962) *Thought and Language* (ed. and trans. E. Hanfmann and G. Vakar). Cambridge, MA: MIT Press.

Vygotsky, L. S. (1978) *Mind in Society: The Development of Higher Psychological Processes* (ed. and trans. M. Cole, V. John-Steiner, S. Scribner and E. Soukerman). Cambridge, MA: MIT Press.

Watson, J. (1983) *Talking in Whispers*. London: Gollancz.

Whalley, M. (2001) *Involving Parents in Their Children's Learning*. London: Paul Chapman Publishing.

White, B. Y. and Frederiksen, J. R. (1998) Inquiry, modeling and metacognition: making science accessible to all students, *Cognition and Instruction*, 16(1): 3–118.

Whitehead, A. N. (1932) *The Aims of Education*. London: Williams & Norgate.

Willes, M. J. (1983) *Children into Pupils. A Study of Language in Early Schooling*. London: Routledge and Kegan Paul.

Willis, P. (1977) *Learning to Labour*. London: Saxon House.

Index